Global United Methodism

Methodism

*Telling the Stories, Living
into the Realities*

Elaine A. Robinson & Amos Nascimento

GENERAL EDITORS

Global United Methodism: Telling the Stories, Living into the Realities

The General Board of Higher Education and Ministry leads and serves The United Methodist Church in the recruitment, preparation, nurture, education, and support of Christian leaders—lay and clergy—for the work of making disciples of Jesus Christ for the transformation of the world. The General Board of Higher Education and Ministry of The United Methodist Church serves as an advocate for the intellectual life of the church. The Board's mission embodies the Wesleyan tradition of commitment to the education of laypersons and ordained persons by providing access to higher education for all persons.

The Wesley's Foundery Books is an imprint of the General Board of Higher Education and Ministry, The United Methodist Church, and named for the abandoned foundery that early followers of John Wesley transformed, which became the cradle of London's Methodist movement.

Global United Methodism: Telling the Stories, Living into the Realities

GBHEM Publishing is an affiliate member of the Association of University Presses.

All web addresses were correct and operational at the time of publication.

ISBN 978-1-945935-45-9

Manufactured in the United States of America

Contents

Acknowledgments

We wish to thank the authors for their willingness to share an indigenous understanding of the origins of Methodism in their respective countries. Although many United Methodist annual conferences are not included here, our hope is to begin telling the story of global United Methodism and to initiate a dialogue about what it means to be a global denomination.

Funding for this project was provided by the following agencies and foundations: "The World Is My Parish" grant from the General Commission on Archives and History of The United Methodist Church; the Office of the General Secretary, Director of Mission Theology, of the General Board of Global Ministries of The United Methodist Church; and the Woodworth Foundation of the Oklahoma Annual Conference. Their willingness to partner on this important project is deeply appreciated.

Finally, Kathy Armistead, publisher at GBHEM, whose dedication to publishing works in United Methodist Studies enabled this volume to become a reality.

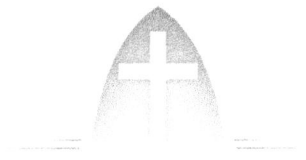

Contributors

Pablo R. Andiñach (Argentina) is Doctor in Theology and Professor of Old Testament and Ancient History at the Argentina Catholic University (UCA) and Professor of Biblical Hebrew and Exegesis at Saint Thomas Aquinas University (UNSTA) in Buenos Aires.

Daniel Bruno (Argentina) is the Coordinator of the Methodist Center for Wesleyan Studies of the Argentine Methodist Protestant Church (Iglesia Evangélica Metodista Argentina), Director of the Historical Archive for the Church, and Editor of *Revista Evangélica de Historia*.

Chan-Hie Kim (Korea) is Emeritus Professor at Claremont School of Theology.

M. Fulgence Nyengele (Congo) is Professor of Pastoral Care and Counseling in the Chryst Chair in Pastoral Theology and Director, Master of Arts in Counseling Ministries Program at Methodist Theological School in Ohio.

Amos Nascimento (Brazil) is Associate General Secretary, Global Education at the General Board of Higher Education and Ministry of The United Methodist Church.

Sergei V. Nikolaev (Russia) is the E. Stanley Jones Professor of Evangelism in the Ruediger and Gerlinde Minor Chair and President, Moscow Theological Seminary of The United Methodist Church.

Luther J. Oconer (Philippines) is Assistant Professor of United Methodist Studies and Director of the Center for EUB Heritage at United Theological Seminary.

Elaine A. Robinson (United States) is Professor of Methodist Studies and Christian Theology at Saint Paul School of Theology. She is the co-pastor of Village United Methodist Church, a multiethnic church in Oklahoma City.

Ulrike Schuler (Germany and Western Europe) is Professor of Church History, Methodism, and Ecumenism at Reutlingen School of Theology.

Júlio André Vilanculos (Mozambique) is Director of the Cambine Theological Seminary in Mozambique and President of the African Association of United Methodist–Related Theological Institutions (AAUMTI).

Introduction

Global United Methodism:
Setting the Conversation

Amos Nascimento and Elaine A. Robinson

Why Global United Methodism?

Over the past decade, United Methodism has sought to reimagine itself as a global denomination. Once (and arguably, still) controlled by the United States, the denomination has begun to wrestle with what it means to be global, beyond simply the connectional structure of local churches spread across the globe. General Conferences have considered proposals for restructuring and initiated a "General Book of Discipline" that allows for adaptation in different regional contexts. General Agencies have established centers in central conferences as the church seeks to live into its global nature. Such changes are necessary and prudent. Yet, a genuinely global denomination requires not only thoughtful polity and structural adaptations, but also widespread global sensibilities among the clergy and laity alike. Developing awareness and appreciation for our global nature can be aided by hearing the stories of United Methodist origins in countries other than the United States. In this volume, we intend to let scholars tell the stories of the origins and development of United Methodism in their own contexts.

To lay the groundwork for these histories, we begin by addressing a linguistic tension between "Global Methodism" and "World Methodism" in which "global" points to forces of globalization and homogeneity, while "world" attempts—not entirely successfully—to move toward multiple perspectives and contextualization. Our aim is to clarify why we choose the language of "Global Methodism." We then briefly review some of the literature related to this discussion as the framework for the chapters to follow. Finally, we introduce the specific histories in this volume by placing their stories into the larger regional context.

The selected indigenous authors bring different lenses to this work, reflecting their unique contexts as well as transcending those contexts through critical analysis. While embracing multiplicity, they nevertheless share basic premises of the Wesleyan movement and Methodist theology. Their contributions allow us to see the emergence of a new project that can be defined as the task of understanding United Methodism as a global force expressed in a plurality of ways, informed by various contexts, open to multiple perspectives, and expressed through specific histories. Together, these voices point toward a more accurate, nuanced, and comprehensive understanding of United Methodism, of what it means to be a global denomination in the twenty-first century. This conversation is much needed and long overdue.

Making Sense of the Global

A focus on multivocal histories can expose both the perils and possibilities found in the linguistic and conceptual tension between Global Methodism and World Methodism. The global role of Wesleyan and Methodist traditions in the twenty-first century in various parts of the world remains under-researched and eclipsed by discussions that focus on structural issues, polity controversies, church statistics, and financial concerns.[1] Oftentimes, important doctrinal questions, theological values, missionary actions, and

---

1 R. Richey, "The United Methodist Church at 40: Where Have We Come From?" *Methodist Review* 1 (2009): 30.

evangelistic witness lack careful reflection and are reduced to immediate needs or fall prey to the latest fads. Moreover, narrow discussions premised on defending particular perspectives tend to occlude the variety of voices and viewpoints that express wider concerns, concrete experiences, and unique contributions of different strands and contexts of Wesleyanism and Methodism that have shaped today's United Methodism. There are multiple perspectives and histories that, together, reflect the fullness of what it means to be a global denomination.

As we explore multiple historical perspectives, new and positive outlooks emerge. While acknowledging plural and decentralized expressions of United Methodism, commonalities or points of unity are clear. The Wesleyan tradition emerged as part of a globalizing movement at the margins of the British Empire and Western colonialism,[2] but it was also contextualized in such a way that basic theological tenets, liturgical practices, educational initiatives, a polity rooted in democratic and participatory structures, and the commitment to mission, evangelization, health care, and education took on different shapes in different places. The differentiated developments of Methodism bring us hope for the future when viewed as incarnational reflections of the particularity, as well as universality, in which God has created the world and its peoples. Beyond the always-present threat of a denomination dominated by one or two histories, there exist alternative and autochthonous worldviews that can open us to understand the church in new ways.

At present, there is no widely accessible textbook that addresses the histories and developments of United Methodism from the perspective of indigenous authors. The history of The United Methodist Church continues to focus on "American" (i.e., United States) Methodism. While this history is important and necessary, it also perpetuates a US-centric identity and self-understanding. This volume thus presents some alternative voices—though far from exhaustive—to share historical developments in

---

2   Elaine Robinson, *Restructuring The United Methodist Church in an Age of Empire* (Nashville: General Board of Higher Education and Ministry, 2007).

other nations and help the church enter into deeper discussions about who we are as a global denomination. Each author in this collection offers a particular, specific perspective on the development and future of United Methodism. They pursue a common goal: to reflect on how the Methodist movement became a worldwide force incarnate in particular contexts, while together "making disciples of Jesus Christ for the transformation of the world"—the mission of The United Methodist Church as it reflects the Great Commission.[3]

An Analysis of Globalization

We are living in a new historical moment, characterized as globalization, which presents a series of challenges and fears, as well as opportunities and possibilities. On the one hand, globalization is considered dangerous and requires appeals to immediate and simplistic answers that can manifest as racism, populism, xenophobia, and other forms of prejudice. Such responses attempt to salvage what is considered authentic in particular cultures and contexts while rejecting whatever is deemed foreign or "other." On the other hand, if globalization is viewed as utterly positive, it runs the risk of becoming a vehicle for exploiting the many in favor of gains and advantages of the few, without recognizing that globalization can project imperialistic desires, enable neocolonial and exilic practices, and generate inequalities.[4] To better understand globalization as an intercultural phenomenon and to consider its theological grounds, impact on Christianity, and role in Methodism, it is important to examine the multiple challenges, complex processes, and differentiated ways in which globalization affects us.[5]

---

3 *The Book of Discipline of The United Methodist Church 2016* (Nashville: The United Methodist Publishing House), ¶120. See also Elaine Robinson and W. Stephen Gunter, eds., *Considering the Great Commission: Evangelism and Mission in the Wesleyan Spirit* (Nashville: Abingdon, 2005); Mitzi Smith and Jayachitra Lalitha, eds., *Teaching All Nations: Interrogating the Matthean Great Commission* (Minneapolis: Fortress Press, 2014).

4 Elaine Robinson, *Restructuring The United Methodist Church in an Age of Empire* (Nashville: General Board of Higher Education and Ministry, 2007), 1, 3–5.

5 Janice Love, "United Methodism in a World Context: Navigating the Local and the Global," *GBHEM Occasional Papers 100*, December 2006 (Nashville: General Board of Higher Education and Ministry, 2006).

First, there is a seemingly irreversible movement toward a *globalization of the economy*. This term refers to the expansion of a global market economy, increasingly integrated through technology, generating what Latin American economist Celso Furtado defines as "one of those times when the insufficiency of the conceptual framework fails to apprehend a rapidly changing reality."[6] Many argue that this globalization of economic power can be traced back to the era of Portuguese and Spanish "discoveries"—considered conquests in Latin America—whose negative effects still motivate anti-globalization movements in the Global South. Others see globalization as generating a new and uncontrollable migration of goods, finances, cultures, and peoples in processes that are deplored by anti-globalization movements in the Global North. The nature of this economic globalization is, however, much more complex. There are now technological means to establish connections in more instantaneous ways, enabling the transfer of resources, monetization of knowledge and information, the rapid flow of finances, and multifaceted human interactions that defy scrutiny. There are automated processes that affect human labor. These conditions affect Methodism as well, and many theologians have attempted to develop a critique of economic globalization based on Wesleyan theology.[7]

Second, the rapid economic changes have affected the livelihood of millions of people in different parts of the world, leading to a *globalization of peoples*. For instance, the rise of multinational corporations has resulted in the trans-nationalization of resources. As a result, the shape of migratory flows has changed and new global migration patterns are present. While at the beginning of the twentieth century, migration was marked by the movement of people toward central locations for corporate activities, now businesses have better technology and mobility to exploit natural and human

---

6 Celso Furtado, *O Capitalismo Global* (Rio de Janeiro: Paz e Terra, 1998), 21.

7 Theodore W. Jennings Jr., *Good News to the Poor: John Wesley's Evangelical Economics* (Nashville: Abingdon, 1990); M. Douglas Meeks, ed., *The Portion of the Poor in the Wesleyan Tradition* (Nashville: Kingswood, 1995); and Richard P. Heitzenrater, *The Poor and the People Called Methodists* (Nashville: Kingswood, 2002).

resources, causing the exclusion of populations, establishing new classes of workers, creating alternative products, and generating a growing inequality that does not respect geographic boundaries. This process, together with the growth of intranational forces and secessionist ethnic groups, along-side the weakening of nation-states, has led to a new postnational era in which the flow of people—including through trade and tourism—questions borders and generates large-scale dislocations. Christian activists, including Methodist theologians, have attempted to address these issues.[8]

Third, a *globalization of culture* exists.[9] The dissolution of firm barriers and national borders allows for the rapid exchange of ideas, artistic expressions, and cultural traditions. Communities now experience pluralistic values and perspectives, often accompanied by pressure from local movements that feel long-held traditions are threatened and, in response, seek to enforce local, regional, and national cultural identities, ethnic distinctiveness, and languages. The globalization of culture thus generates multiculturalism but also stimulates forces of resistance that, at times, can lead to violence. Methodists in various contexts have expressed their concerns for the way globalization can engender uncritical cultural retrenchment.

Fourth, in response to situations of conflict and violence, the globalization of human rights as the defense of universal human dignity has become a central concern. Many authors are careful to utilize the term *universalization* instead of *globalization* when referring to rights and duties, though some argue that universalism can be characterized as the flip side of imperialism. At other times, concern for human rights is viewed as the projection of Western values at the expense of national sovereignty. Even so, the intercultural consensus seems to consider human rights as both the norm promulgated in the 1948 *Universal Declaration of Human Rights* and a consensus found

---

8 Hugo Assman, *Crítica à Lógica da Exclusão: Ensaios sobre Economia e Teologia* (São Paulo: Paulus, 1994), 5.

9 Nestor G. Canclini, *Consumidores y Ciudadanos. Conflictos Multiculturales de la Globalización* (México, DF: Grijalbo, 1995).

in the core values of many religions.[10] This interreligious theological dimension is present in United Methodism. For instance, through the *Social Creed* and the *Social Principles*, United Methodists have insisted that human rights are compatible with, even necessitated by, ecumenical ideals.

Fifth, there is the *globalization of environmental awareness*. According to this view, both natural and constructed environments require care in keeping with the stewardship of God's creation so as to ensure resources for future generations. In response, activism and initiatives related to curbing pollution and greenhouse gas emissions, the critique of pesticides and genetic engineering in relation to food supplies, and the opposition to global anthropogenic climate change have arisen. While these concerns initially seemed of interest only to experts, many others now recognize that they are of concern to indigenous African groups, victims of natural disasters in Asia, displaced farmworkers in the Americas, and citizens who argue for sustainable practices in Europe. Here, again, theological responses to this form of globalization have been offered. Pope Francis has issued an encyclical, and various Methodists have also addressed the challenges of environmental globalization.

Finally, the *globalization of education* is also a factor in the expansion and democratization of the knowledge and skills necessary for life and work, the promotion of human rights and universal responsibilities, and the formation of the character and virtues needed for the exercise of participatory citizenship. As the globalization of education unfolds and is intertwined with the economic and political issues already mentioned, some national governments are dismantling or denying public education, such that education falls to the private sector and raises concerns about access. At the same time, with the growing number of students and the demands for information, education can become a commodity that aims at financial outcomes and lucrative jobs. United Methodist education plays an important, albeit ambiguous, role as it

---

10 Johannes Morsink, *Universal Declaration of Human Rights: Origins, Drafting, and Intent* (Philadelphia: University of Pennsylvania Press, 1999); Matthias Lutz-Bachmann and Amos Nascimento, eds., *Human Rights, Human Dignity, and Cosmopolitan Ideals* (London: Routledge, 2014).

affirms the value of universal education long associated with the Methodist tradition in different contexts, while also discouraging the mere economic motives. It is worth noting that theological education has also been globalized. Theological reflection and writing occurs in various centers found in the Global South and is no longer limited to the North Atlantic region.[11] As educational opportunities spread, new perspectives open conversations and reshape communities.

Viewed together, the processes of globalization suggest a growing multiplicity and contextualization, as well as the rise of what Lamin Sanneh, inspired by Tertullian, has called "cosmopolitan characteristics of classical Christianity."[12] The plurality of Christian and United Methodist expressions are international, transnational, and multinational. Globalization is not univocal, but it brings tensions, resistance, and differences, depending on the specific context in which it has developed. Globalization, the interconnection of the world for good and for ill, characterizes the twenty-first century. Being a global denomination means that United Methodism is subject to, but not defined by, the forces of globalization. Voices from across United Methodism can help us negotiate the forces of globalization in light of the mission of God in the world and the church's mission.

Global Methodism or World Methodism?

Whenever we speak of "globalization," we must recognize the tension it evokes between generalization and contextualization, between worldwide connections and specific contexts in which practices emerge. As Mark Noll states, "The magnitude, the multiplicity, the material conditions, the political implications and the theological challenges of Christianity's current

---

11 Dietrich Werner, David Esterline, Namsoon Kang, Joshva Raja, eds., *Handbook of Theological Education in World Christianity: Theological Perspectives—Regional Surveys—Ecumenical Trends* (Oxford: Regnum, 2010). See particularly the chapter by Patrick Streiff, Robert Kohler, and Robert Solomon on "Theological Education in Methodist Churches," 676–85.

12 Lamin Sanneh, *Disciples of All Nations: Pillars of World Christianity* (New York: Oxford University Press, 2008), x, 29–32. On this cosmopolitan dimension see Amos Nascimento, *Building Cosmopolitan Communities* (New York: Palgrave-MacMillan, 2013).

situation open a new epoch in religious history."[13] In an attempt to address the global character of twenty-first-century Christianity, new concepts and practices have emerged that seek to address perceived concerns related to Global Christianity and Methodism. To this end, some suggest that the language of "Global" should be replaced by "World" Christianity and "World" Methodism as more appropriate to and less problematic in the current situation. Rather than ignoring this ongoing conversation, we wish to provide a brief consideration of what seems to be at stake.

Global Christianity is the result of the confluence of traditional Christian practices, long-standing missiological approaches, more recent ecumenical initiatives, and even newer globalizing tendencies within Christian churches. These factors emerged as a result of the wider communication and interactions among peoples and cultures since the sixteenth century.[14] Global Christianity has antecedents in at least two important practices and experiences that are relevant to this volume. First, the global nature can be traced to the missionary efforts of the Catholic Church in the sixteenth century, when religious orders, especially the Jesuits, were active in evangelizing the native peoples of various cultures in Africa, the Americas, and Asia.[15] Second, it can be argued that Methodism emerged at the margins of the British Empire, where members of the Wesleyan movement mirrored the pietistic practices of the Society for Promoting Christian Knowledge and then expanded its vision by establishing, under the leadership of Thomas Coke in 1813, the Wesleyan Methodist Missionary Society, intended for foreign missions. The missionary impetus of promoting the spread of the gospel in areas where Britain had established trade connections motivated

---

13 Mark Noll, *The New Shape of World Christianity: How American Experience Reflects Global Faith* (Westmont, IL: InterVarsity Press, 2009), 37.

14 Jens Holger, Norman A. Hjelm Schjørring, and Kevin Ward, eds., *History of Global Christianity*, 3 vols. (Leiden: Brill, 2007–2018). See also Lamin Sanneh and Michael J. McClymond, eds., *The Wiley Blackwell Companion to World Christianity* (Oxford: Wiley-Blackwell, 2016); Joerg Rieger, *Christ and Empire: From Paul to Postcolonial Times* (Minneapolis: Fortress, 2007).

15 Thomas Banchoff and José Casanova, eds., *The Jesuits and Globalization: Historical Legacies and Contemporary Challenges* (Washington, DC: Georgetown University Press, 2016).

early Methodists such as John Wesley, George Whitefield, Thomas Coke, Francis Asbury, and others to go to British America and elsewhere in their attempt to evangelize the peoples.[16] The history of missions does not provide us with a full understanding of Global Christianity or Global United Methodism.

Global Christianity has also been defined in terms of statistics, indicating the number of Christians in various parts of the world, calculating their impact, and offering formulas for their strategic positioning. Research conducted by the Pew Center shows that in 1910, about two-thirds of the world's Christians lived in Europe. By 2010, they estimated the distribution of Christians as follows: in Europe (26 percent), in the Americas (37 percent), in sub-Saharan Africa (24 percent), and in Asia Pacific (13 percent).[17] Moreover, in 1910 the total number of Christians was 611,810, and in 2010 the total was 2,260,440,000. During this same period, the world population grew from 1.8 to 6.9 billion. Therefore, throughout the past century, roughly 30 percent of the world's population identified as Christians.[18] Numbers, while significant, also do not fully account for the global nature of Christianity or United Methodism.

The approach traditionally taken in studying Global Christianity often succumbs to many of the challenges of globalization mentioned above and tends to project a certain homogeneity across the globe. In some ways, it presses toward "sameness" and shared characteristics. Yet, those who tell the history and publish the studies generally can shape the narrative to confirm to their own perspectives and cultural norms. As an alternative, some scholars have proposed the use of "World" to highlight the diversity and multiplicity

---

16 Mark Noll, *The Rise of Evangelicalism: The Age of Edwards, Whitefield and the Wesleys* (Downers Grove, IL: InterVarsity Press, 2003); D. Hempton, *Methodism: Empire of the Spirit* (New Haven: Yale University, 2005).

17 Pew Research Center, *Global Christianity: A Report on the Size and Distribution of the World's Christian Population* (Washington, DC: The Pew Forum on Religion and Public Life, 2011), 9.

18 Todd M. Johnson and Brian J. Grim, eds., *World Religion Database* (Leiden and Boston: Brill, 2018), accessed at www.worldreligiondatabase.org/ on July 6, 2018, indicate that Christians corresponded to 34.8 percent of the world population in 1910 and 32.8 percent in 2010. See also the reflections on this report by Todd M. Johnson, "Globalization and Identity: Globalization, Christian Identity, and Frontier Missions," in *International Journal of Frontier Missiology* 27, no.4 (Winter 2010), 165–69.

of Christian expressions worldwide.[19] A growing body of research has contributed to defining the meaning of World Christianity.[20] Scholars from many
countries have added anthropological and historiographic details, as well as
raised philosophical and theological challenges to this emphasis of "World"
Christianity: in Africa, new studies have emerged about Angola, Kenya, Mozambique, Nigeria, Sierra Leone, South Africa, and Zimbabwe; in Asia and
the Pacific, studies and practices in China, India, Philippines, and South Korea
have shown the vitality of Christianity in the region; in the Americas, authors
from Argentina, Brazil, Chile, Mexico, and Peru have expanded studies in liberation theory and Pentecostalism to characterize the realities in their context;
in Europe, there are new developments in Germany, Romania, Russia, and
the British context; the United States has been a fertile ground for research
on this subject as well. Moving beyond the framework of traditional theology, some evangelical theologians have attempted to reconsider the theory
and practice of Christianity in light of these worldwide developments.[21] The
same is true for Pentecostal theology, which has offered important insights
in this discussion about Global Christianity and World Christianity.[22]

Wesleyans and Methodists have likewise entered into the discussion

---

19 Sebastian C. H. Kim and Kirsteen Kim, *Christianity as a World Religion* (London and New York: Continuum, 2008); Dana Lee Robert, *Christian Mission: How Christianity Became a World Religion* (Chichester,
UK, and Malden, MA: Wiley-Blackwell, 2009).

20 See, for instance, the work of David Martin, *Tongues of Fire: The Explosion of Protestantism in Latin
America* (Oxford: Blackwell, 1993); Andrew Walls, *The Missionary Movement in Christian History: Studies in Transmission of Faith* (Maryknoll, NY: Orbis, 1996); Lamin Sanneh, *Disciples of All Nations: Pillars
of World Christianity* (New York: Oxford University Press, 2008); Dana L. Robert, "Shifting Southward:
Global Christianity Since 1945," in *International Bulletin of Missionary Research* 24, no. 2 (April 2000):
50–58; and Dana L. Robert, *Christian Mission: How Christianity Became a Global Religion* (Chichester, UK:
Wiley-Blackwell, 2009); Philip Jenkins, *The Next Christendom: The Coming of Global Christianity* (Oxford:
Oxford University Press, 2002); and *The New Faces of Christianity: Believing the Bible in the Global South*
(New York: Oxford University Press, 2006), among many others.

21 Some examples are Craig Ott and Harold A. Netland, eds., *Globalizing Theology: Belief and Practice in
an Era of World Christianity* (Grand Rapids: Baker Academic, 2006), and Timothy C. Tennent, *Theology
in the Context of World Christianity: How the Global Church Is Influencing the Way We Think About and
Discuss Theology* (Grand Rapids: Zondervan, 2007); Donald Lewis, ed., *Christianity Reborn: The Global
Expansion of Evangelicalism in the Twentieth Century* (Grand Rapids: Eerdmans, 2004).

22 See Allan Anderson, Michael Bergunder, Andre F. Droogers, and Cornelis van der Laan, eds., *Studying
Global Pentecostalism: Theories and Methods* (Berkeley: University of California Press, 2010); Amos Yong,
"The Emerging Field of World Christianity: A Renewal Reading of the Cambridge Dictionary of Christian-
ity," in *Journal of World Christianity* 4, no. 1 (2011): 27–43; Amos Yong, *Renewing Christian Theology:
Systematics for a Global Christianity* (Waco, TX: Baylor University Press, 2014).

about Global Christianity and the alternative, World Christianity.[23] From a global perspective focused on statistics, the Wesleyan and Methodist movement involves nearly eighty countries and 133 church bodies, bringing together a community of roughly eighty million people connected to the World Methodist Council. Global United Methodism naturally emerges as an important and specific component of Global Christianity and Global Methodism, not only due to its sheer size amid the various Methodist traditions, but also due to its historical importance as the tradition from which many other denominations have emerged. United Methodism's institutional structures and intellectual impact should likewise be noted. Structurally, The United Methodist Church is present in Africa, Asia, Europe, Latin America, and North America. Of course, annual conferences outside the United States are grouped into "central conferences" (the equivalent of US jurisdictions). In terms of membership, United Methodism numbers nearly twelve million members worldwide, served by almost fifty thousand clergy. The United Methodist educational system in the United States alone represents nearly 13 percent of all church-related institutions and some 5 percent of institutions of higher education; and Methodists have established schools, colleges, universities, and theological seminaries in many other countries as well.[24]

From a "world" perspective, however, one of the biggest challenges for churches and institutions within Methodism is the need to affirm and justify their global relevance in the twenty-first century in light of a changing environment and multicultural societies. This context requires a more plural, decentralized, adaptable, and connectional approach to being United Methodists.

23 Dana L. Robert, "Shifting Southward: Global Christianity Since 1945," *International Bulletin of Missionary Research* 24, no. 2 (April 2000): 50–58; Philip Jenkins, *The Next Christendom: The Coming of Global Christianity* (Oxford: Oxford University Press, 2002); Todd M. Johnson and Kenneth R. Ross, eds., *Atlas of Global Christianity* (Edinburgh: Edinburgh University Press, 2009); Dana L. Robert, *Joy to the World: Mission in the Age of Global Christianity* (New York: Women's Division, GBGM, The United Methodist Church, 2010).

24 See the IAMSCU Directory (Nashville: General Board of Higher Education and Ministry, 2016) for more details. D. Jacobsen and R. Jacobsen, "The Ideals and Diversity of Church-Related Higher Education," in D. Jacobsen and R. Jacobsen, eds., *The American University in a Postsecular Age* (Oxford: Oxford University Press, 2008), 71–75.

As the focus shifts from the work of traditional missionaries to indigenous perspectives and their role in establishing Methodist communities in various parts of the world, new understandings of United Methodism will emerge.

Whether utilizing the terminology of "Global" or "World," we conclude that the self-understanding, identity, and polity of United Methodism is interdisciplinary by nature and requires the contributions of various methods of study. We must be conscious of the ways we promote structures and practices that may be detrimental to living out our worldwide connection in a manner reflective of the gospel of Jesus Christ, embracing each part of the body of Christ expressed through our global connection. As the subsequent chapters illustrate, the ambiguities of global perspectives and diverse worldviews complicate what it means to be United Methodist and, at the same time, bring us closer to living into and expressing more fully our global nature.

Literature on Global/World Methodism

One of the contributions of the present volume is to address the challenges, opportunities, and tensions discussed above by proposing a decentralized approach to telling the story of Methodism and allowing different voices within United Methodism to speak. The chapters collected here are exemplary and explore some of the key traditions among groups that are directly and indirectly, as well as historically or currently, related to United Methodism.

Global United Methodism retains loose connectional ties to other Methodist denominations known officially as Autonomous Methodist Churches and Affiliated Autonomous Methodist Churches. An Autonomous Methodist Church is "self-governing" and, while in relationship to United Methodism, cannot send delegates to General Conference.[25] In this volume, we include the history of the autonomous Korean Methodist Church as a significant part of our global connection. More significant, perhaps, are the Affiliated Autonomous churches that United Methodism or one of its predecessor denominations had a role in establishing but have since left the denomination.

---

25 *Book of Discipline 2016*, ¶570.1.

The Commission on the Structure of Methodism Overseas (COSMOS) in the 1960s and early 1970s worked through a process of allowing central conferences to choose autonomy or to remain under the existing connection. Many chose to become affiliated autonomous churches, such as the Methodist Church in Argentina. We include a chapter on Argentina to highlight the connection of United Methodism to these churches that are entitled to one clergy and one lay delegate at General Conference with all rights and privileges except to vote.[26] Today, central conferences retain the right to become autonomous, as specified in ¶1572 of *The Book of Discipline*. How have and do these global churches contribute to United Methodist history and the need to develop more pronounced global sensibilities? While this volume cannot begin to address the complexities, the histories of Korean and Argentine Methodism are illuminating.

Those interested in learning more about histories within the global context can turn to publications focused on particular countries or churches. For instance, in Africa local research is available on the Democratic Republic of Congo, Mozambique, South Africa, and Zimbabwe.[27] Similar resources are available for learning about Asia, though not all of these are written by indigenous voices.[28] In Europe, there is a steady production of historical materials about local Methodism, especially in Britain and Germany.[29] Latin America

---

26 *Book of Discipline 2016*, ¶570.2.

27 L. C. Ferreira, *Igreja Ministerial em Moçambique: Caminhos de Hoje e de Amanhã* (Maputo: Imprimi Potest, 1987); J. W. Kurewa, *The Church in Mission: A Short History of The United Methodist Church in Zimbabwe 1897–1997* (Nashville: Abingdon Press, 1994).

28 For a more general approach, see David W. Scott, *Mission as Globalization: Methodists in Southeast Asia at the Turn of the Twentieth Century* (Lanham, MD: Lexington Books, 2016). For Korea, see Charles D. Stokes, *History of Methodist Missions in Korea: 1885–1930* (New Haven, CT: Yale University Press, 1947); Ken Kroehler, "A Century After: The Legacy of the Appenzeller, Pioneer Missionaries to Korea," in *Journal of the Historical Society of the EPA Conference* 2 (2005): 15–34.

29 For an overview of Methodism in the European context, see the corresponding chapters in Wade Crawford Barclay and J. Tremayne Copplestone, *History of Methodist Missions*, 4 vols. (New York: Board of Missions, 1949–1973); Peter Stephens, *Methodism in Europe* (Peterborough, UK: Methodist Publishing House, 1998); Marc Lüthi, *Aux sources historiques des Églises Évangéliques: L'évolution de leurs ministères et de leurs ecclésiologies en Suisse Romande* (Bevaix, Suisse : Éditions Je Sème [Dossier Vivre, Hors Série], 2003); Patrick Ph. Streiff, *Der Methodismus in Europa im 19. Und 20. Jahrhundert* (Stuttgart: EmKGM 50, 2003) [in Engliilsh: *Methodism in Europe: 19th and 20th Century* (Tallinn: Baltic Methodist Theological Seminary, 2003)] and (ed.), *Der europäische Methodismus um die Wende vom 19. zum 20. Jahrhundert* (Stuttgart: EmKGM 52, 2005); Friedrich Hecker, Vilém Schneeberger, and Karl Zehrer, *Methodismus in*

has a rich bibliography in Spanish and Portuguese. However, there remains the need for a better overview of these many and varied contexts to provide the reader with a map of the terrain.

Recent literature on Global Methodism or World Methodism aims precisely at offering this overview, as well as the framework for studying these countries and regions. For example, the *Ashgate Companion to World Methodism* is a comprehensive and well-researched collection, which seems to avoid the problematic dimensions of the "global," though it utilizes the same structures and centralized approaches that have been criticized in relation to processes of globalization.[30] The *Companion* emphasizes the British and American history of Methodism, relying heavily on authors from England and the United States. Moreover, it focuses on more generic concepts—on important topics such as ecumenism, holiness, women, liberation, and globalization—without giving much expression to the diversity that characterizes the Wesleyan and Methodist movement currently.

Kenneth Cracknell and Susan White produced *Introduction to World Methodism*, presenting a dynamic historical narrative that is attentive to international varieties of Methodism, offshoots from larger bodies, and their connections to the Holiness and Pentecostal movements.[31] Using an historical approach, they start with John Wesley and Thomas Coke, then expand to British Methodism and North American Methodism, showing how their respective conference and episcopal structures gave birth to other church bodies in other parts of the world. They apply a "participant observation"

Osteuropa: Polen—Tschechoslowakei—Ungarn (Stuttgart: EmKGM 51, 2004); Ulrike Schuler, *Die Evangelische Gemeinschaft: Missionarische Aufbrüche in gesellschaftspolitischen Umbrüchen* (Stuttgart: emk studien 1, 1998), as well as "Methodism in Northern and Continental Europe," in Charles Yrigoyen Jr., ed., *T & T Clark Companion to Methodism* (London: T & T Clark, 2010), 166–87, "Crisis, Collapse, and Hope: Methodism in 1945 Europe," in *Methodist History* LI/1-2 (2012): 5–27, and (ed.) *Glaubenswege–Bildungswege. 150 Jahre theologische Ausbildung im deutschsprachigen Methodismus Europas* (Reutlingen, 2008 [EmKG 29/2008, 1–2]). See also Paul W. Chilcote and Ulrike Schuler, "Methodist Bible Women in Bulgaria and Italy," in *Methodist History* LV/1–2 (October 2016 and January 2017): 108–27; and "Methodist Women Missionaries in Bulgaria and Italy," in *Methodist History* LV/3 (April 2017): 180–95.

30 William Gibson, Peter Forsaith, and Martin Wellings, eds., *The Ashgate Research Companion to World Methodism* (Surrey: Ashgate, 2013).

31 Kenneth Cracknell and Susan White, *An Introduction to World Methodism* (Cambridge: Cambridge University Press, 2003).

methodology, avoid triumphalism, and do not shy away from the contradictions they observe. Nevertheless, it is their voices, not indigenous ones, telling the history.

Walter Klaiber's edited collection, *Methodistische Kirchen*, addresses this concern.[32] The title is indicative as the book includes a variety of authors who provide contextual perspectives on the development of Methodism. This collection allows the reader to hear firsthand from other voices that know the culture, language, and history of the Wesleyan and Methodist tradition in their particular setting. Moreover, it helpfully frames World Methodism in terms of regions—Africa, Asia and Oceania, Europe and Eurasia, and the Americas (North, Central, and South). However, Klaiber's book is published in German and, thus, is not widely accessible, nor does it focus on United Methodism.[33]

These and similar initiatives have helped to define a broader understanding of Global Methodism. However, in view of the limitations mentioned above, there is a need to complement these publications, learn from the experiences of studies on the North American context and the church in the United States, and consider contributions from other parts of the world more systematically. This process can help us appreciate different perspectives, hear alternative stories, and paint a more complex picture that acknowledges the various contextual contributions to United Methodism. The essays brought together in this collection contribute to this task, albeit in a partial and incomplete manner.

Placing United Methodist Histories in the Larger Christian Context

We utilize decentralized geographic and cultural markers represented by five continental regions—Africa, Asia and Pacific, Europe and Eurasia, Latin America and the Caribbean, and North America—in order to better characterize

---

32 Walter Klaiber (Hrsg.), *Methodistische Kirchen*, edition Ruprecht (Göttingen: Bensheimer Hefte, 2001).

33 The irony here does not escape the editors. While we urge United Methodism to develop global sensibilities, we also recognize the predominance of English in United Methodism (and the monolinguistic nature of the United States compared to many other nations).

the peoples, their cultures and languages, specific structures, and autochthonous contributions to United Methodism. People on the ground know
best their needs, have direct involvement in the building of infrastructures,
share a common history, and have cultural affinities that are better articulated by this decentralized approach. However, these regions are not isolated
and self-enclosed; rather, each region is interconnected with the others, promoting interactions that lead to a richer form of connectionalism definitive
of United Methodist identity. The intercultural interactions among diverse
local contexts enables United Methodism's structural connection to flourish.
We become the incarnate body of Christ, not through structural conformity,
but through the relational diversity and contextualization that exists across
the global connection.

Africa is an important context for a particular expression of Christianity
that can be traced to early communities in Nubia and Ethiopia, to the Patris-
tic Era, and to theologians such as Tertullian and Augustine, who were originally from Northern Africa and played a key role in defining the Christian
tradition.[34] After many centuries of change, Christianity remains side by side
with traditional African religions as well as Islam, which has had an impact
especially in Northern Africa.[35] United Methodism is part of this rich tapestry.
Although maintaining a small presence in northeastern areas such as South
Sudan, it is primarily present in Sub-Saharan Africa in West, East, and Southern Africa. Methodism arrived in Africa at the end of the nineteenth century,
first in Liberia, and then expanded in the western part of the continent. It
then included missions in the southern part of the continent, in places such as
South Africa, Angola, Zimbabwe, and Mozambique, eventually creating missions and schools in the Congo, which are active to this day. After centuries
of European colonialism, the last four decades of the twentieth century set

---

34 See Sanneh, *Disciples of All Nations: Pillars of World Christianity*, 59.

35 See Bengt Sundkler and Christopher Steed, *A History of the Church in Africa* (Cambridge: Cambridge Uni-
versity Press, 2004); John Mbiti, *African Religions and Philosophy* (Portsmouth, NH: Heinemann, 1969);
Ogbu Kalu, ed., *African Christianity: An African Story* (Pretoria: University of Pretoria Department of Church
History, 2005).

the stage for a series of dynamic events all over Africa, especially revolution-ary and independence movements that gave power to the indigenous peo-ples. This process also involved major civil wars in countries such as Angola, Burundi, Ethiopia, Côte d'Ivoire, Ghana, Liberia, Mozambique, Rwanda, Si-erra Leone, South Africa, Sudan, the Democratic Republic of Congo, Uganda, and Zimbabwe, as well as profound transformations in Nigeria, Libya, Sudan, and South Africa. The continent has also witnessed natural disasters such as drought and floods, and pandemics of AIDS, malaria, and Ebola, which have led to famine, starvation, widespread devastation, and impoverishment. Among all these complex issues, those countries that were able to promote peace have not only gained stability, but also contributed to the develop-ment of both the continent and Christianity.

As a result, Christianity has experienced significant growth on the African continent. In 1900, there were less than 10,000,000 Christians in the conti-nent. The number of Christians in Africa is projected to reach 634,000,000 by the year 2025. Similar growth is occurring in United Methodism.[36] With a chapter dedicated to the history and current developments of United Method-ism in the Democratic Republic of Congo, written by M. Fulgence Nyengele, and another chapter by Júlio André Vilanculos on Mozambique, this book provides information that is often available only in French and Portuguese and offers insights into Methodist histories in Africa.

Asia and the Pacific is the broader context for traditional civilizations, cul-tures, philosophies, and religions. For millennia, religious groups have been in conflict with each other, so the pursuit of peace has been an important

---

36 For Methodism in Africa, see the corresponding chapters in Barclay and Copplestone, *History of Method-ist Missions*; Francis L. Bartels, *The Roots of Ghana Methodism* (Cambridge: Cambridge University Press, 1965); Peter Marubitoba Dong, *The History of The United Methodist Church in Nigeria* (Nashville: Abing-don Press, 2000); Eva Coates Hartzler, *Brief History of Methodist Missionary Work in the Southern Congo during the First Fifty Years* (Elisabethville: Methodist Church of Southern Congo, 1960); Alf Helgesson, *Church, State, and People in Mozambique: An Historical Study with Special Emphasis on Methodist De-velopments in the Inhambane Region* (Uppsala: Uppsala University, Swedish Institute of Missionary Re-search, 1994); John Wesley Z. Kurewa, *The Church in Mission: A Short History of The United Methodist Church in Zimbabwe: 1897–1997* (Nashville: Abingdon Press, 1997); Beauty Maenzanise, "The Church and Zimbabwe's Liberation Struggle," in *Methodist History* 46 (January 2008): 68–86; and Dana L. Rob-ert and David W. Scott, "World Growth of The United Methodist Church in Comparative Perspective: A Brief Statistical Analysis," in *Methodist Review* 3 (2011): 37–54.

theme in the region. Many countries in Asia have been influenced by impe-rialism, colonialism, and political revolutions. Thus, although forms of natu-ralist religions such as Shamanism and Shintoism remain strong, Buddhism spread eastward from India through China and Korea to Japan, Confucian-ism has had a great influence in East Asia as well as Southeast Asia, and the region was later influenced by Islam. European forms of Christianity ar-rived in China and the Philippines in the sixteenth century, mainly through the influence of Portuguese, Spanish, and Italian missionaries of the Cath-olic Church, while trade with the British Empire opened the way to Protes-tantism in Asia, as in the case of Thomas Coke and the British Missionary Society's involvement in India and Ceylon, now Sri Lanka. Toward the end of the nineteenth century, American Methodism began to have a stronger presence in Japan, Korea, China, and India, reaching out to many countries such as Singapore, Malaysia, and the Philippines. As a result of this mission-ary effort, Methodist schools were established, often before a church was constructed. The Asian context is represented by Luther Oconer's chapter on United Methodism in the Philippines and Chan-Hie Kim's chapter on Korean Methodism.

European Methodism is marked by plurality as well. Although Britain is the original context in which the Wesleyan and Methodist movement emerged, churches in other countries are pursuing Methodism in diverse ways.[37] The

---

37 For an overview of Methodism in the European context, see the corresponding chapters in Barclay and Copplestone, *History of Methodist Missions*; Peter Stephens, *Methodism in Europe* (Peterborough, UK: Methodist Publishing House, 1998); Lüthi, *Aux sources historiques des Églises Évangéliques*; Patrick Ph. Streiff, *Der Methodismus in Europa* im 19. Und 20. Jahrhundert (Stuttgart: EmKGM 50, 2003) [in English: *Methodism in Europe: 19th and 20th Century* (Tallinn: Baltic Methodist Theological Seminary, 2003)], and (ed.), *Der europäische Methodismus um die Wende vom 19. zum 20.* Jahrhundert (Stuttgart: EmKM 52, 2005); Friedrich Hecker, Vilém Schneeberger, and Karl Zehrer, *Methodismus in Osteuropa: Polen—Tschechoslowakei—Ungarn* (Stuttgart: EmKGM 51, 2004); Ulrike Schuler, *Die Evangelische Gemeinschaft: Missionarische Aufbrüche in gesellschaftspolitischen Umbrüchen* (Stuttgart: emk studien 1, 1998), as well as "Methodism in Northern and Continental Europe," in *Companion to Methodism*, ed. Charles Yrigoyen Jr. (London: T & T Clark, 2010), 166–87; "Crisis, Collapse, and Hope: Methodism in 1945 Europe," in *Meth-odist History* 51, nos. 1–2 (2012): 5–27; and (ed.) *Glaubenswege–Bildungswege. 150 Jahre theologische Ausbildung im deutschsprachigen Methodismus Europas* (Reutlingen, 2008 [EmKG 29/2008, 1–2]). See also Paul W. Chilcote and Ulrike Schuler, "Methodist Bible Women in Bulgaria and Italy," in *Methodist History* 55, nos. 1–2 (October 2016 and January 2017): 108–27; and "Methodist Women Missionaries in Bulgaria and Italy," in *Methodist History* 55, no. 3 (April 2017): 180–95.

Methodist Church in Britain is the largest European Methodist church, but in most cases, Methodist churches are a minority in their countries. The United Methodist Church is represented by its central conferences in southern, central, and northern Europe, but there are autonomous Methodist churches in Italy and Portugal, among others. Some of these churches have a long history and well-established structures, while others are newer or have been reestablished after the collapse of the Soviet Union in Eurasia. They evolved in the shadow of historically dominant Christian churches, some of which have an official relationship with the state. United Methodist churches have experienced a steady growth in some countries, remained stable in others, and shown decline in a few. A common feature in many countries is the development of congregations among historically minoritized ethnic communities such as Valdensians, Roma, and others, as well as new minorities created by immigration from Africa, Asia, and Latin America. In this volume, there is a chapter on Continental Europe, with particular attention to Germany, by Ulrike Schuler and a chapter on Eurasia, as Sergei Nikolaev tells the history of Russian Methodism.

Latin America is not so much a geographic concept as a cultural marker, pointing to localities, countries, and regions in North America, Central America, and South America that were colonized by the Portuguese and Spanish Empires. Latin America now includes Latinx and Hispanic groups within the United States and groups in the Caribbean, and it stretches down to Patagonia in Chile and Argentina. Marked by a history of colonialism between 1500 and 1800, Latin America was inhabited by indigenous peoples, received European immigrants, and was influenced by slaves brought from Africa, generating complex multicultural societies strongly influenced by Christianity.[38]

While Catholicism was the most important influence during the colonial period, Protestantism in general and Methodism in particular emerged as a

---

38 Enrique Dussel, *Historia de la iglesia en América Latina: Coloniaje y liberación* (Barcelona: Nova Terra, 1974).

modern force in relation to a series of independent and liberal movements after 1810.[39] During this period, Methodism was influential, especially in South America, due to a long tradition of missionary work by the Methodist Episcopal Church and the Methodist Episcopal Church, South, which established churches and schools in Argentina, Brazil, Bolivia, Chile, Peru, and Uruguay.[40] Methodism was similarly influential in Mexico. After the 1960s, Latin America witnessed difficult historical processes that included military dictatorships, revolutionary movements and civil wars, and the establishment of more stable democratic institutions. Liberation theology emerged alongside these processes, inviting Christian churches to choose the "preferential option for the poor."[41] Due to nationalism and ideological differences, many Methodist churches became affiliated autonomous or autonomous churches in the twentieth century, but they still maintain historical ties and official links with The United Methodist Church. In this collection, Latin America is represented with a chapter by Pablo Andiñach and Daniel Bruno, who analyze this complex relationship to United Methodism in the Southern Cone, with a focus on Argentina.

Of course, North America was the first context outside Europe in which Methodism developed, starting within the British colonies and gaining more traction as a revival movement and fledgling church after the founding of the United States. Although John Wesley himself initiated a missionary endeavor in the colony of Georgia in 1736, and Welsh, Irish,

---

39 José Miguez Bonino, Carmelo Alvarez, and Robert Craig, et al., *Protestantismo y liberalismo en América Latina* (San José, Costa Rica. DEI, 1983); José Duque, *La Tradición Protestante en la Teología Latinoamericana—Primer intento: Lectura de la tradición metodista* (San José, Costa Rica: DEI, 1983); José Carlos Barbosa, *Salvar e educar: O Metodismo no Brasil do século XIX* (Piracicaba, SP: CEPEME, 2005).

40 On Protestantism and Methodism in Latin America, see James Kennedy, *Cincoenta annos de Methodismo no Brasil* (São Paulo, SP: Imprensa Metodista, 1926); Henry K. Carroll, *Around and Across South America: Viewing the Mission of the Methodist Episcopal Church* (New York: Missionary Society of the Methodist Episcopal Church, Open Door Emergency Commission, 1905); Justo González, *The Development of Christianity in the Latin Caribbean* (Grand Rapids, MI: Wm. B. Eerdmans, 1969); David Martin, *Tongues of Fire: The Explosion of Protestantism in Latin America* (Oxford, UK: B. Blackwell, 1990).

41 José Miguez Bonino, *Metodismo: Uma releitura latino-americana* (Piracicaba: Editora UNIMEP, 1983); José Miguez Bonino, *Doing Theology in a Revolutionary Situation* (Philadelphia: Fortress Press, 1975).

and African families helped to establish the first Methodist societies, as well as the first church, in the city of New York, in 1766,[42] it was not until 1784 that the Methodist Episcopal Church was formally established and held its first conference led by Francis Asbury. The development of Methodism in North America during colonial times, its growth through great revivals in the nineteenth century, and its role as the largest church body in the United States is well documented. However, the tensions within the various branches of Methodism in the United States, due especially to differing views on issues such as slavery, workers' rights, interpretation of doctrines, emphases on opposing social and political views or questions of gender and sexuality need to be acknowledged and put into dialogue with other global issues.[43] However, those questions are beyond the scope of the present volume.

Conclusion

United Methodism is a global connection that has long been centered in and driven by US concerns. The story of "American" Methodism has often been told by British and US voices, though *The Methodist Experience in America*, recently authored by Russell Richey, Kenneth Rowe, and Jean Miller Schmidt, does include material about the development of Methodism beyond the borders of the United States. A deeper understanding of our global nature requires that we learn the histories of United Methodists around the world, told in their own voices, as well as wrestle with the ongoing differences and perspectives that exist among these histories. This volume is far from exhaustive, for such an endeavor would require decades

---

42 David C. Jones, *Glorious Work in the World: Welsh Methodist and the International Evangelical Revival: 1735–1750* (Chicago: University of Chicago Press, 2004); Dee E. Andrews, *The Methodists and Revolutionary America, 1760–1800: The Shaping of an Evangelical Culture* (Princeton: Princeton University Press, 2000); James Haskins, *The Methodists* (Ann Arbor: The University of Michigan Press, 1992); David Hempton, *Methodism: Empire of the Spirit* (New Haven: Yale University Press, 2005); Russell Richey, Kenneth E. Rowe, and Jean Miller Schmidt, *The Methodist Experience in America: A History*, vol. 1 (Nashville: Abingdon Press, 2010); Rodney Stark and Roger Finke, *The Churching of America, 1776–2005: Winners and Losers in Our Religious Economy* (New Brunswick: Rutgers University Press, 2005).

43 See General Board of Higher Education and Ministry, *Unity of the Church and Human Sexuality: Toward a Faithful United Methodist Witness* (Nashville: General Board of Higher Education and Ministry, 2017).

of research, multilayered discussions, and practical initiatives to bring to fruition. It is, however, a step toward increasing our global understanding and identity as a denomination. Our hope is that this book might be used widely in United Methodist history classes as one modest step toward living into our global nature. Perhaps in doing so, we might also live more fully as "united" Methodists.

AFRICA

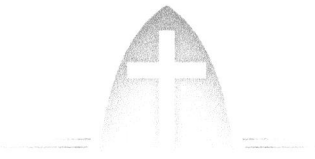

The Development and Spread of United Methodism in the Democratic Republic of Congo

M. Fulgence Nyengele

We need to say this more forcefully: If we want to be an adult and mature Congolese Church, we must cease to depend totally on others. A Church of this stature is supposed to have its own financial means independent of external sources. . . . The most important resource for taking responsibility for the church is its own members.[1]

—Bishop Katembo Kainda, Retired, South Congo Conference

Preliminary Comments

United Methodism in DR Congo has multiple origins. These include the work of William Taylor in the Lower Congo; the pioneering work of John M. Springer in Southern Congo; and the initiative of Walter Russell Lambuth

---

1 Katembo Kainda, "La Prise en Charge de l'Eglise Méthodiste-Unie au Sud-Congo par Ses Fid les: Stratégies et Perspectives d'Avenir," in *L'Eglise Méthodiste-Unie au Katanga à 100 Ans: Hier, Aujourd'hui, Demain*, ed. J. Jeffrey Hoover, Leonard Kabwita Kayombo, and Jean-Marie Nkonge (Mulungwishi, Congo: Presses de l'Université Méthodiste au Katanga, 2010), 227; my translation.

in Central Congo. Taylor and Springer were missionaries of the Methodist Episcopal Church (MEC). Lambuth was a bishop of the Methodist Episcopal Church, South (MECS). Although generally not recognized as missionaries, Congolese freed slaves from Angola were also instrumental in the work of evangelizing and starting churches in the Congo. Of note are people like Kayeka Changand and Kalwashi in Southern Congo and North Katanga, respectively, and Charles Kimbulu in the Central Congo area.[2] As they returned home, the Congolese freed slaves established relationships with missionaries in their eagerness to help with evangelizing and starting churches.[3] The former slaves brought with them skills in masonry, carpentry, agriculture, farming, and evangelism that were very helpful in the advancement of mission work.[4]

However, they were to work under the leadership of the missionaries of the MEC and MECS—two American Methodist denominations that originated from the split over the issue of slavery in 1844 but reunited with the Methodist Protestant Church in 1939 to form The Methodist Church and later merged with the Evangelical United Brethren to form The United Methodist Church (UMC) in 1968. Congolese Methodism has maintained a close relationship with American Methodism and, even though the church has grown significantly, has developed a strong indigenous leadership, and is now organized as a separate central conference, with fourteen annual conferences, it has remained an integral part of the UMC, which some arguably suggest is still largely an American Church with constituents in Africa, Asia, and Europe.[5]

---

2   See John M. Springer, *I Love the Trail: A Sketch of the Life of Helen Emily Springer* (Nashville and Elisabethville: Congo Book Concern, 1952), 73–74; and John Springer, *Christian Conquest in the Congo* (New York: Methodist Book Concern, 1927), 23–24; Charles Kimbulu was captured as a slave in an Arab raid when he was a child. He was liberated after many years and then came to Wembo Nyama to work in the carpentry shop.

3   David Maxwell, "Freed Slaves, Missionaries, and Respectability: The Expansion of the Christian Frontier from Angola to Belgian Congo," in *Journal of African History* 54 (2013): 79–102.

4   On the economic exploitation of slaves in the 1800s in Luba and Lunda territories see David Gordon, "Wearing Cloth, Wielding Guns: Consumption, Trade, and Politics in the South Central African Interior during the Nineteenth Century," in *The Objects of Life in Central Africa*, ed. Robert Ross et al. (Boston: Brill, 2013), 22–24.

5   Janice Love, "Is United Methodism a World Church?" in *Questions for the Twenty-First-Century Church*, ed. Russell Richey, William B. Lawrence, Dennis M. Campbell (Nashville: Abingdon Press, 1999), 260–65.

Lower Congo/Western Congo

Methodist presence in Lower Congo was a result of the vision and missionary effort of William Taylor, an energetic evangelist who traveled all over the world between 1857 and 1884 to preach the gospel. His work in South Africa, from 1866 to 1868, got him more interested in presenting to the MEC the need for an African mission. In 1884 the general conference elected him as a missionary bishop with the charge to supervise missionary work in Liberia, as well as to establish missions in various parts of Africa.[6] He served in this capacity until his retirement in 1896 at age seventy-five. Taylor's aim was to plant a chain of self-supporting mission stations across Africa based on the model he had used successfully in India and South America. Missionaries were expected to have some other kind of occupation, such as teaching, in order to financially support themselves and, at the same time, evangelize in relationship with their work or in their free time.[7]

In 1885 Bishop Taylor arrived in Luanda, Angola, with thirty missionaries plus sixteen children, and they chose five sites for mission work.[8] In 1886 another group of missionaries came up the Congo River and selected several sites on either side of the river near Matadi. They founded eight stations, with the oldest and best known at Vivi, which was then the capital of the *Etat Indépendent du Congo*; other stations were created at Isangila near Matadi and at Kimpoko near Leopoldville,[9] which later became the capital of Belgian Congo. A medical doctor from the Angola group, Dr. William Summers, was so committed to Bishop Taylor's vision that he was bothered by the slowness of their progress and thus decided to leave the last station in Angola to go into the heart of the Congolese territory. He arrived at Luluabourg (now Kananga) the same year the other missionaries

---

6   Charles Yrigoyen Jr., ed., *T&T Clark Companion to Methodism* (New York: T&T Clark International, 2011), 494.

7   Eva Coates Hartzler, "The Methodist Church in the Congo," in *Congo Profile 1965*, ed. Joseph M. Davis and L. Earl Griswold (World Division of the Board of Missions: The Methodist Church, 1965), 122.

8   Coates Hartzler, "The Methodist Church," 122.

9   Eva Coates Hartzler, *Brief History of Methodist Missionary Work in the Southern Congo during the First Fifty Years* (Elisabethville: Methodist Church of Southern Congo, 1960), 6.

arrived near Matadi. He started practicing medicine but unfortunately died within a few months "as a result of caring for others while he himself was ill with malaria."[10]

The climate in Lower Congo was not hospitable to many missionaries, and several succumbed to the rigors of climate and illness.[11] In 1898, a little more than ten years after the arrival of missionaries near Matadi, "the missionary staff in the Matadi area had been so decimated that newly elected Bishop Joseph Hartzel closed the Congo work."[12] One female missionary was transferred to Luanda, Angola, and she took with her four young Congolese, including John and Miriam Webba who later married and together contributed so much to mission work in Angola.[13] Even though mission work was discontinued in the Lower Congo, Taylor had set the patterns for Methodist expansion in Angola, the Congo, and beyond. For example, the mission station Dr. Summers established at Luluabourg, which was named the "Lunda District" because of the intent to reach the Lunda, remained in missionary records with the note, "[missionary] to be named." It was this Lunda District initiative that later inspired John Springer to (re)establish Methodist work in Southern Congo.[14]

Perhaps it is also helpful to note that William Taylor has been described not only as one of the greatest missionary thinkers produced by American Methodism, but also as someone who had a positive view of African culture and Africans. Some have pointed out that "his African experiences in the 1860s had led him to believe that African culture was comparable to his own culture and that he made no effort to reformulate it, trusting Africans

---

10 Coates Hartzler, *Brief History*, 6.

11 Contrast this with Springer's description of the climate in Southern Congo and Southern Rhodesia: "[The elevation in] much of the two Rhodesias and the Southern Congo is 4,000 feet or more above sea level. It is thus a happy circumstance that our missionaries in these regions, as well as in the interior of Angola, live and labor in one of the most salubrious climates of the world." Springer, *I Love the Trail*, 32.

12 Coates Hartzler, "The Methodist Church," 122.

13 John Springer, *The Heart of Central Africa* (New York: Methodist Book Concern, 1909), 214.

14 Jeffrey Hoover, "Les Origines de l'Eglise Méthodiste-Unie au Congo, 1886–1944," in *L'Eglise Methodiste-Unie au Katanga*, ed. Hoover, 4, 6, 9.

to be able to express the Christian faith in their own way."[15] This quality distinguishes him from many missionaries of his time who dismissed African culture as heathen, backward, and lacking anything good and that it was an expression of "uncivilized" beliefs and practices that needed to be completely destroyed and eradicated. Taylor's view of African culture is a challenge even to some Africans who have internalized Western prejudice against African cultures and traditions and rejected them as incompatible with Christian values and teaching.[16]

Southern Congo

The presence of Methodism in Southern Congo is a result of the vision and effort of John Springer (1873–1963), Helen Emily Springer (1868–1949), and a group of Congolese freed slaves from Angola. John Springer was appointed to missionary service in Southern Rhodesia in 1901. Prior to being appointed to Southern Rhodesia in 1901, Helen went to Matadi in 1891 as one of the self-supporting missionaries of William Taylor. She married William Rusmussen, a fellow Matadi missionary from Denmark, who died in 1895. She herself became very ill and a grave was even dug in anticipation of what seemed to be her certain death.[17] When she recovered she returned to the United States with her little son in 1896, after staying with her mother-in-law for about a year in Denmark. Her son died in 1900 and shortly after that she was recruited again and appointed to Southern Rhodesia.[18] She and Springer married in 1905. The Springers believed that they had a divine vision to start

---

15 Kenneth Cracknell and Susan J. White, *An Introduction to World Methodism* (New York: Cambridge University Press, 2005), 73–74.

16 I have argued in some of my work that for Christianity to be deeply rooted on the African continent, there is a need to pay greater pastoral and theological attention to the significance of African Traditional Religion (ATR) in its diverse cultural expressions as a force that continues to influence the spirituality, values, and worldview of African peoples. Identifying central themes in ATR and exploring their affinity with Christianity can be one way to deepen Christian witness and hone pastoral skills in effectively working with Africans in their various contexts. See M. Fulgence Nyengele, "African Spirituality and the Wesleyan Spirit: Implications for Spiritual Formation in a Multicultural Church and Culturally Pluralistic World," at https://oimts.files.wordpress.com/2013/10/2013-4-nyengele.pdf.

17 Springer, *I Love the Trail*, 28–29.

18 Springer, *I Love the Trail*, 31.

mission work among the Arund or Lunda in Southern Congo. Thus, at the occasion of their furlough, they set out toward Angola in November 1906 to explore Southern Congo on their way to America. They visited the mining towns of Kambove, Ruwe (Kolwezi), and Musonoi, where they realized that the mining regions would provide great opportunities for the evangelization of large numbers of people.[19]

John and Helen Springer returned to the Congo in 1910, after spending two years in America, with plans to start mission work in Southern Congo. Herman Heinkel, who had worked with them in Southern Rhodesia, joined them at Broken Hill, Northern Rhodesia, where they selected twelve Christian young men to go with them. They arrived at Kalulua, Southern Congo, and found an abandoned Belgian work camp where they settled for the rainy season.[20] They resumed contact with colonial Belgian authorities to renew their request to begin mission work in the country.[21] After the rainy season ended they moved to Lukoshi, a village ruled by a Lunda chief, and started conducting training for the young men they brought with them; they also started to learn the Lunda language in anticipation of the evangelization of the Lunda.[22] This was the beginning of the Fox Bible Institute, which would later become the Congo Institute, Springer Institute, and several years later l'Institut Kitabataba (a high school), a theological school at a university level, and later l'Université Méthodiste au Katanga, with various faculties.[23] Some observers suggest that it was the establishment of this school at Lukoshi in

---

19 For more details, see Springer, *The Heart of Central Africa*.

20 Coates Hartzler, "The Methodist Church," 125.

21 While the Springers were on furlough, the country changed its name from *Etat Independent du Congo* to *Congo Belge* and became a Belgian colony. This change was largely due to international pressure denouncing the atrocities committed by King Leopold's colonial administration. For details on the atrocities and their collective traumatizing effects on the Congolese people, see M. Fulgence Nyengele, "Healing Postcolonial Trauma in the African Experience: The Case of DR Congo," in *Pastoral Care, Health, Healing, and Wholeness in African Contexts*, ed. Tapiwa Mucherera and Emmanuel Lartey (Eugene, OR: Wipf & Stock, 2017), 76–98.

22 Coates Hartzler, "The Methodist Church," 125.

23 Kongolo Chijika, "Education Théologique," in *L'Eglise Méthodiste-Unie au Katanga*, ed. Hoover et al., 129–50.

1910 that justified the celebration of one hundred years of Methodism in Southern Congo and Zambia in 2010.[24]

It is also at Lukoshi that the Springers met Kayeka Changand, a former slave from Angola who made an important contribution to mission work in Southern Congo. Kayeka told the Springers that he had been praying for twelve years for a missionary to go to his people. So he saw their presence as an answer to his prayers. Kayeka went back to Angola to bring his family so he could join the Springers in evangelization and other mission work.

In 1912 the Springers went to see Mwant Yav, the emperor of the Lunda people, at Kapanga (Musumba). John Springer asked him what kind of missionary he wanted first: a preacher, a medical doctor, or a teacher. Mwant Yav chose a medical doctor. Dr. A. L. Piper arrived in 1914. In 1913 the Springers moved to Kambove, a mining and administrative center, to establish a station there. They believed that this location, being situated on the railway line, had great potential for reaching more people.

Meanwhile, Kayeka, his family, and six other people came from Angola and joined Herman Heinkel and three of the young people who had studied with the Springers at Lukoshi (including James Lubona and Jacob Mawene) to go to Kapanga to start the work. In 1914, when Dr. A. L. Piper and his family arrived at Kapanga, a house was ready for them. Some parts of the Bible had also been translated in Lunda, and the church had been established. During that same year, forty more freed slaves arrived from Angola and settled at Kapanga.[25] The church grew rapidly at Kapanga, and a good number of students enrolled in the primary school.[26]

When Kayeka came back to the Congo with his family, a Luba by the name of Kalwashi also came along to check if it was safe for the Luba

---

24 Hoover, "Les Origines de l'Eglise Méthodiste-Unie," 12.

25 Coates Hartzler, "The Methodist Church," 125.

26 Abraham Katwebe Mwenze Mutumbe, "La Mission Méthodiste au Shaba: Facteur d'Emancipation Religieuse et Socio-Culturelle," PhD thesis, Faculté Universitaire de Théologie Protestante, Bruxelles, 1986, 109; cited in Hoover, "Les Origines de l'Eglise Méthodiste-Unie," 14.

ex-slaves to return home. Kalwashi also seized the opportunity to preach. People were so eager to hear the good news that Kalwashi preached until he lost his voice.[27] After meeting the Springers, Kalwashi, like Kayeka, went back to Angola to bring his family, anticipating that when he returned Springer would also have a missionary for his people.

The mission station at Elisabeth (now Lubumbashi) was established in 1917, based on a group the Springers had organized in 1914 to support the Nyasalanders (now Malawians) who had requested the backing of the Methodists so their prayer meetings would receive official approval by the colonial administration and by their employers. Springer saw the strategic importance of Lubumbashi as the new capital of Katanga and the fact that the city was attracting a variety of ethnic groups and nationalities. He writes: "We reached Elisabethville on February 20, 1917. It did not take Mrs. Springer long to see how greatly she as a missionary woman was needed in this young, lively, budding metropolis. In the nearly seven years since the rails were laid into the site for this capital town, no Protestant missionary had been in residence here."[28]

That same year (1917) Kalwashi, after returning from Angola, helped the Springers establish a station at Kabongo, north of Lubumbashi, in the capital of Chief Kabongo's kingdom. Just as they had started a station at Kapanga, the capital of the Lunda, now they were making another strategic move by establishing another station at Kabongo.[29] Freed slaves from Angola also helped the missionaries establish the church at Kabongo just as they did at Kapanga.

Unfortunately, the Methodists decided in 1933 to hand over the Kabongo station to the Congo Evangelistic Mission (CEM) because of several difficulties, including the lack of personnel and funds due to the global financial crisis at that time.

---

27 Coates Hartzler, "The Methodist Church," 125. For more details, see also Coates Hartzler, *Brief History*, 20–26.
28 Springer, *I Love the Trail*, 95.
29 Coates Hartzler, "The Methodist Church," 127.

In 1918, the Fox Bible Training School moved to Mulungwishi; but they moved it to Kabongo in 1919 because they were not able to secure a concession from the government. Kabongo turned out to be too far from the other major stations that needed to send students for training as teacher-pastors. So the Fox Bible Training School was transferred to Kanene in 1924, halfway between Kabongo and Kapanga, and sixty-five kilometers southwest of Kamina.[30] It became the Congo Institute. Other stations were established at Sandoa and Mwajinga (1922), with the help of Kayeka and others; Likasi (1924);[31] Mulungwishi (1936), since the government finally approved the establishment of a station and school there; and Kolwezi (1939). The church has expanded its outreach in most of southern Congo and established congregations in neighboring Zambia. Today, the South Congo episcopal area is organized into five annual conferences: Lukoshi, Northwest Katanga, Southwest Katanga, South Congo, and Zambia.

Before discussing developments in other regions of the Congo, it is important to note that one of the major challenges early Methodist and other Protestant missionaries encountered was the Belgian colonial suspicion that Protestant missionaries were agents of Anglo-Saxon interests in the Congo. Even though Protestant missionaries enjoyed the freedom to evangelize and provide social services such as health care and education, the colonial administration favored Catholic missions and provided subsidies to support their mission projects such as building schools, health clinics, and even churches. The Catholic Church was considered a national church and the Protestant churches as *foreign* churches.[32] Indeed, Catholic mission projects were subsidized handsomely by the colonial government from the very beginning of the Belgian colonial occupation, and the subsidies became formalized in

---

30 Hoover, "Les Origines de l'Eglise Méthodiste-Unie," 21–22; see also Omar Hartzler, *Sold for a Dollar: The Story of Coleman Clark Hartzler and Lucinda Lee Padrick*, vols. 1 and 2 (unpublished; Claremont, 1993), chapter 13, 8. Available at the Methodist Archives at Drew University.

31 With mining activities at Kambove being transferred to Panda (Likasi), the Springers followed the people and established a station in Likasi. See Coates Hartzler, *Brief History*, 27–30.

32 From the very beginning of the colonial enterprise in the Congo, King Leopold actively sought to have a Belgian majority among the various Catholic religious congregations who served in the country.

1906 through a concordat signed with the Vatican. Protestant missions did not receive any subsidies for their schools until 1948. In many places "the Catholic missionary was the only representative of the State in that area, and his presence and authority became synonymous with that of the state."[33] Because of this alliance, it has been said the Congo was ruled by a trinity of powers: the Belgian government, the major corporations, and the Catholic Church.[34] Given this privileged position of the Catholic Church, as well as the suspicion and fear of the Protestants during the colonial era, Methodist missions under Springer and his successors always sought to show Belgian authorities their willingness to establish respectful collaboration with the colonial government.[35] However, it is interesting to note that this strategy of relating to the colonial government has resulted in Congolese Methodists, in independent Congo, becoming less prophetic in their attitude toward public issues affecting ordinary Congolese, while the Catholics, who held a close relationship with the colonial government, have ironically developed a more liberationist perspective and thus have played a prominent role in denouncing gross violations of human rights and abuses of power by the Congolese government.[36]

North Katanga

The Methodist Church returned to the North Katanga in 1962. Rev. David Kumwimba Ilunga, one of those who went with the Congo Institute from Kabongo to Kanene, was the principal agent in reviving Methodist work in the whole of North Katanga after 1960. The work started at Kalemie on April 2, 1962.[37] In August 1962, the South Congo Annual Conference meet-

---

33 Richard M. Kendall, "The Development of the Roman Catholic Church in the Congo," in *Congo Profile*, 101.

34 Kendall, "The Development of the Roman Catholic Church," 95, 107.

35 Hoover, "Les Origines de l'Eglise Méthodiste-Unie," 32.

36 For a larger context for understanding the irony of these dynamics, see Hoover, "Les Origines de l'Eglise Méthodiste-Unie," 31–33.

37 David Kumwimba Ilunga, "Outline History of The United Methodist Church in the North Shaba, 1917–1970" (unpublished speech translated from Swahili by Omar Lee Hartzler), 1.

ing at Kapanga approved the church in North Katanga as a seventh district within the South Congo Conference. Ilunga states that it was an act of faith for Bishop Newell Booth to appoint people to this work. He describes Bishop Booth as "a man of faith who placed his confidence in people and had the [habit] of always saying 'people will do it!'"[38]

However, the Annual Conference meeting at Kapanga was doubtful that beginning work without a budget and with insufficient personnel would yield good results. But Bishop Booth said, "Let us begin with the few people we already have."[39] Thus the conference agreed to assign three pastors and four school principals to join Rev. David Ilunga to carry forward the work of developing North Katanga. The following people were appointed: Rev. Joel Bulaya Ngoi-a-Sanza as pastor at Manono and Malemba, with Jason Mukanya and Pierre Mwamba as school principals for Manono and Malemba, respectively. Rev. André Mundele was appointed pastor at Kabongo, with Paison Mpoyo as school principal. Rev. Kazembe Albert Mukumbi was appointed to Albertville (now Kalemie), with Gaspar Bondo as school principal. Esaie Kabange Yenda was appointed school inspector for all the schools, and Rev. David Ilunga was appointed district superintendent.[40] David Ilunga viewed these places as "sub-districts," in the sense that he expected all these locations would become districts in their own right.

The first missionary to visit North Katanga and penetrate that area since the early evacuation in 1933 was Rev. Dr. Omar L. Hartzler, who at some point had served as assistant to Bishop Booth, in addition to his teaching at Mulungwishi.[41] Hartzler arrived at Kalemie on May 3, 1963, and traveled

---

38 Ilunga, "Outline History," 1.

39 Ilunga, "Outline History," 1.

40 Ilunga, "Outline History," 2.

41 Omar L. Hartzler was born in the Congo. He was present with his parents in the early mission work at Kabongo and Kanene from 1918 to 1933, before going to the United States for college. Like his parents, he was in continuous correspondence with many Congolese pastors till his return to the Congo in 1953. In 1993, while studying at Claremont School of Theology in California, I translated for him from Kiluba into English many letters from Congolese pastors relating important aspects of church work and life in the Congo, as his grasp of Kiluba, "[his] second language as a child, had been becoming weaker and weaker." Recognizing the treasure they represented, Hartzler used these and other letters to write a book on the story of his parents' missionary and pastoral career in the Congo. See Hartzler, *Sold for a Dollar*, chapter 17, 711.

with Rev. David Ilunga to visit all four stations: Kalemie, Manono, Malemba, and Kabongo in order to confer with him on their needs. Bishop Newell Booth also visited Kalemie, Manono, Kabongo, and Kamina.[42] Four other South Congo missionaries also visited Kalemie and Manono to see the work.[43] Their presence was significant because it brought visibility to the work and highlighted the needs in North Katanga. In 1964, Omar Hartzler visited Kamina and Kanene, and in the summer of 1970 he spent three or four days each at Kamina, Kanene, Kabongo, Kabalo, Mwanza, and Manono. Seeing the missional vitality and needs of the church, Hartzler recommended that "a few strategically placed missionaries undergirded by adequate budget would provide great returns."[44] Several years later, Hartzler was invited out of his retirement by Bishop Ngoy Kimba Wakadilo, in 1986–1987, to serve as the first principal of the then newly created Teachers' College in Kamina, the first institution of higher education in North Katanga and a great contribution to higher education by The United Methodist Church.[45]

The work in North Katanga grew rapidly. In 1964 the number of districts increased from one to three, just in a couple of years. That same year, John Wesley Shungu was elected as the first Congolese bishop for the two Congo conferences. David Ilunga describes him as "someone of astonishing capacity who reminded us of an elephant." In a path where an elephant has passed, "he opens the way without difficulty."[46] During the first four years of Bishop Shungu's episcopacy, the number of districts grew to six. In 1968 the six districts comprising the North Katanga were authorized by

42 It appears that the work at Kamina was established after 1962.

43 Rev. Douglas Moore, Rev. Richard Kendall, Rev. George Thomas, and Rev. Everett Woodcock visited Kalemie.

44 Omar L. Hartzler, "Memorandum on the North Katanga Annual Conference of The United Methodist Church" (1970): 3.

45 He and his spouse, Eva Coates Hartzler, spent sixteen months in 1986–87 in Kamina helping to establish the *Institut Superieur Pedagogique de Kamina*.

46 Ilunga, "Outline History," 2.

the General Conference to constitute a Provisional Conference. And then in 1970 the special session of the General Conference authorized the transformation of the Provisional Conference, which now had seven districts, into a full Annual Conference.[47] Ilunga credits most of this work to Bishop Shungu, saying, "This is how our Elephant has worked."[48] In 1970, at the first session of the North Katanga Annual Conference, Superintendent Ilunga expressed North Katanga's appreciation of Bishop Shungu for his hard work and encouragement, and shared that North Katanga had given him a new name: *Mukamba Fikile Ulu*,[49] which means a pillar that reliably holds things together, and someone without whom the whole structure collapses. It should be observed, however, that even though David Ilunga seemed deferential to Bishop Shungu, many of his clergy colleagues and laypeople during those years and beyond viewed him as a tower of strength, hard worker, and visionary who, indeed, was the principal agent in reviving Methodist work in the whole of North Katanga. For many people, to say *North Katanga* was to say *David Ilunga*. Indeed, David Ilunga, in his role as general superintendent representing the bishop, was not only the champion of North Katanga. He was North Katanga.[50]

Today, the North Katanga area has significantly expanded and is now divided into three annual conferences: North Katanga, Tanganyika, and Tanzania. The Tanzania mission project started in 1989 with a focus on evangelistic ministry and planting of churches in Tanzania. Bishop Ngoy Kimba Wakadilo was the principal initiator of that project. In the beginning, the bishop appointed Rev. Muyombi Kapanda Makozo as the first Congolese missionary to Tanzania. In 1989 Muyombi started a church at Kigoma, a lake port on

---

47 Hartzler, "Memorandum," 1.

48 Ilunga, "Outline History," 2.

49 Ilunga, "Outline History," 3.

50 This point was also reiterated by this author's father, Rev. André Ngoy Nyengele, retired, who had just completed seminary in 1970 and was poised to continue his pastoral ministry in the new North Katanga Conference. Of course, the names of Joel Bulaya, André Mundele, Albert Mukumbi, Kalonda Loshita, and others should always be viewed alongside that of David Ilunga in terms of their significance and impact on the North Katanga Conference. A. Nyengele, Personal Communication, 2018.

Lake Tanganyika. In 1990 Bishop Ngoy appointed Rev. Kasweka Tshifunga and Rev. Numbi Ilunga, a clergy couple, to join Muyombi. They arrived at Dodoma with their two children and started a church in that town. In 1992, Rev. Mutwale Ntambo Wa Mushidi was appointed to join the team. He and his spouse, Kabaka Ndala, and their four children went inland to Tabora. That same year Rev. Umba Ilunga Kalangwa was also appointed to Tanzania. He and his spouse, Ngoy, and their four children went to Morogoro, a city west of Dar es Salaam, the capital city, and started a church there. Rev. Kazadi Umba and his spouse and their four children went to Kigoma.

These Congolese missionaries encountered several difficulties. First, the lack of sufficient funds to underwrite mission work was a major problem. Second, the Congo Swahili they spoke was different from the Swahili spoken in Tanzania, which is described as Swahili Bora (perfect Swahili). This required significant effort to master Tanzanian Swahili in order to communicate effectively the gospel and to carry out meaningful pastoral work. Third, the challenge of adjusting to the new environment and learning to function effectively in a different national context. Fourth, the challenge of establishing churches in a context where Islam is popular. Fifth, difficulty with children's education because of lack of adequate financial resources, as well as the difficulty with language. Some decided to send their children back to the Congo to avoid the complications related to language and a different educational system.[51] Bishop Ngoy died in 1994 and Bishop Katembo Kainda of South Congo was assigned by the Council of Bishops to be the interim bishop for North Katanga. In 1995 the conference decided to recall most of the pastors back to the Congo; only two pastors remained in Tanzania. Bishop Katembo appointed Rev. Mutwale to Kigoma and also gave him the responsibility to supervise the work in the whole country, including the existing eleven churches.

Beginning in 2001, Mutwale and some of his colleagues were employed

---

51 Mutwale, personal email communication, 2018.

as missionaries of the General Board of Global Ministries (GBGM). This development provided great stability and considerably helped advance the work in Tanzania. In 2016 the General Conference authorized the UMC in Tanzania to become a full Annual Conference. It has ten districts, more than one hundred churches, fifty-nine ordained elders, and fifteen deacons. The peace and calm in the country makes it possible to continue the church's witness and to grow.[52]

Central Congo

Mission work in Central Congo was primarily started by Bishop Walter Russell Lambuth (1854–1921) of the MECS in the United States.[53] Lambuth was elected bishop in 1910 and appointed to Brazil and Africa. Congolese historian Michael Kasongo points out two factors that seem to have awakened Lambuth's interest in doing a mission in Africa. The first factor is a one-hour conversation he had with Henry M. Stanley during one of his visits in Nashville. Having explored the interior of the Congo, Stanley insisted on the need "to pour the western civilization into the barbarism of Africa," and that without such an effort "Africa would be Mohammedan if Christian missionaries failed to win the whole continent for Christ."[54] After his interview with Stanley, Lambuth wrote that he was confirmed in his purpose to start a Methodist mission in Africa.[55] Another factor is the repeated urging of the Southern Presbyterians who had planted a mission at Luebo in the Province of Kasai in 1891, focusing on reaching out to the Baluba Kasai, Lulua, Basonge, and Bakuba ethnic groups. They wanted the Southern Methodists to establish mission work among the Atetetla in Sankuru.

From the very beginning, the Board of Missions of the Southern Presbyterian Church established an interracial effort for the work of evangelization

---

52 Mutwale, personal email communication, 2018.

53 Yirigoyen Jr., *T & T Clark Companion to Methodism*, 438; see also Michel Kasongo, *History of the Methodist Church in the Central Congo* (Lanham, MD: University Press of America, 1998), 6–7.

54 Kasongo, *History of the Methodist Church*, 7.

55 Kasongo, *History of the Methodist Church*, 7.

in Africa. White mission boards were particularly eager to send black American missionaries to Africa "because certain areas were seen as 'white man's grave' and it was believed [wrongly] that blacks had an immunity to the diseases of tropical Africa."[56] Thus, African Americans were recruited to accompany almost every white missionary pioneer. For example, William Sheppard, a black minister from Virginia, and Samuel N. Lapsley, a white minister, were appointed to serve as missionaries in the Kasai.[57]

Lambuth followed the Southern Presbyterians' interracial approach and wanted the Southern Methodist mission in Central Congo to be a joint project of the black churches and white churches. He reached out to the Colored Methodist Church and chose Dr. John Wesley Gilbert, a professor at Paine College in Augusta, Georgia, to go with him on the exploration trip. In October 1911, Lambuth and Gilbert traveled from Antwerp, Belgium, to Matadi and then to Luebo where they stayed for fifteen days. On December 22, 1911, they left on foot for Ewangu, the village of Chief Wembo Nyama, which they reached on February 1, 1912. They received a warm welcome and Chief Wembo Nyama made a declaration that his entire kingdom was open to the Methodist mission.[58] Six missionaries arrived at Wembo Nyama on February 2, 1914, to start the work. Among them were Daniel L. Mumpower (a medical doctor) and his spouse (a trained nurse); Charles C. Bush (a preacher) and his wife (a teacher); and John Stockwell and his spouse (name not provided).[59] There were also two Congolese evangelists and thirteen church members from Luebo who decided to go back to their people at Wembo Nyama. But there were no black American missionaries in the group. The mission at Wembo Nyama was officially inaugurated by Bishop Lambuth on February 12, 1914. But Lambuth never came back after this. The main

---

56 Sylvia Jacobs, *Black Americans and the Missionary Movement in Africa* (Westport, CT: Greenwood Press, 1982), xi.

57 Robert Benedeto, ed., *Presbyterian Reformers in Central Africa: A Documentary Account of the American Presbyterian Mission and the Human Rights Struggle in the Congo, 1890–1918* (Leiden: Brill, 2016), 56–91.

58 Coates Hartzler, "The Methodist Church," 126.

59 Coates Hartzler, "The Methodist Church," 126; see also Kasongo, *History of the Methodist Church*, 11–12.

focus of mission work initially involved putting the Atetela language into writing and organizing the primary school and an Evangelistic Training School.[60]

Other stations were established in 1921 at Lubefu and Kabengele; then they were moved to Minga in 1922; Tunda (1921);[61] Kombe (1922); Lomela (1933); and Kandolo (1935). More stations were created in the 1930s and 1940s, including work in the Katako-Kombe territory (1943) and Kindu (1954).[62] By the mid-1950s and beyond there was a significant increase in the number of churches, church members, and the Atetela preachers.[63] The Methodist Church established a strong foundation with many primary schools, some medical clinics, and strong evangelistic programs that included revivals and preaching in villages by native evangelists such as Moise Ngandjolo, who was nicknamed the Tetela Billy Graham.[64]

The Methodist Church in Central Congo has expanded its work in most of the Kasai Provinces and extended into the South Kivu, North Kivu, and Equateur Provinces and beyond.[65] They have also established churches in the Central African Republic, the Republic of Congo, and Gabon. In 2012 the General Conference authorized the creation of the East Congo Conference, as the fourth episcopal area in the Congo. But the church in these provinces experienced significant setback through years of war (1997–2003) and the ongoing armed conflicts in most of East Congo. However, the new East Congo Episcopal area is one of the most vibrant conferences in the Congo, and the church there is deeply committed to its expanding ministry as it continues to make a difference in the lives of persons and communities affected

---

60 Coates Hartzler, "The Methodist Church," 127.

61 Chief Tunda saw what was happening at Wembo Nyama and wanted the church to send missionaries at Tunda specially to establish a hospital.

62 Coates Hartzler, "The Methodist Church," 131.

63 For more on the impact of Methodist mission in Central Congo, see Paul-Amy Djundu Lunge, "Analyse Socio-Culturelle et Spirituelle de l'Oeuvre Missionaire de l'Eglise Méthodiste-Unie Parmi les Tetela du Zaire Central," unpublished PhD thesis, Université Laval, Canada, 1991.

64 Coates Hartzler, "The Methodist Church," 131. See also Kasongo, History of the Methodist Church, 64, for a more critical appraisal of the work of Ngandjolo.

65 Bill Lovell, 100th Anniversary of The United Methodist Church in Central Congo, 1912–2014: A Pictorial Resource, accessed on February 15, 2018, https://www.scribd.com/doc/155215510/100th -Anniversary-of-the-Methodist-Church-in-Central-Congo-1912-present.

by violence. Bishop Gabriel Y. Unda, who was elected in 2012, has put together an ambitious plan for rebuilding the church in an area deeply devas-
tated by an unjust war. He has called all United Methodists in East Congo
to rise up and rebuild.[66]

Episcopal Leadership

In the beginning, Methodism in the Congo was closely connected with MEC
work in Liberia, Angola, Rhodesia, and Mozambique by way of a common
episcopal supervision provided by a succession of American missionary bishops from 1886 to 1964. Bishop Taylor served from 1884 to 1896. Bishop
Joseph Hartzell served from 1896 to 1916. Bishop Eben Samuel Johnson
served from 1916 to 1936. Methodist work in Central Congo, from 1912 to
1939, was under the supervision of missionary bishops of the MECS: Walter Lambuth, James Cannon, and Arthur Moore. After the MEC and MECS
merged in 1939, their Congo missions became part of the Methodist Church
under the leadership of Bishop John Springer, who was elected in 1936 as
bishop for Africa, and served until his retirement in 1944. Newell S. Booth
was elected bishop in 1944 and he served until 1964, when Rev. John Wesley Shungu was elected as the first Congolese bishop for the entire Congo.
Bishop Booth was then appointed bishop of the Harrisburg area, Pennsylvania,
in the United States, and he served in that conference until his death in 1968.

Bishop Shungu was known as a charismatic leader and great organizer
who wanted to see results when he visited districts and various church programs, including those led by missionaries. But his confrontational leadership
style led to his demise. He was ahead of his time in terms of his attempts
to confront missionaries who still had a lot of power in the African annual
conferences in those years. Shungu's discontent and power struggles with
missionaries may have started in 1952 when he traveled to the United States
as the first Congolese delegate to General Conference from Central Congo.

---

66 Gabriel Yemba Unda, "The United Methodist Mission in Eastern Congo," *New World Outlook* (Novem-
ber/December): 2014, 6–9.

While in the United States, Shungu attended a special talk by a Southern Congo missionary who was showing slides on "African people and their needs." Before the meeting ended, "Shungu walked out, protesting that missionaries had always shown unflattering pictures [of Africans] in order to raise money in the United States."[67]

In 1972 Rev. Onema Fama was elected bishop to replace Shungu. Bishop Onema was credited with introducing a bold vision for training new *cadres* or leaders for the critical areas of church work: theological education, medicine, aviation, and other areas. Onema was also instrumental in initiating the petition in 1992, reclaiming the creation of a francophone central conference. The 1992 General Conference approved the request, and the first session of the Congo Central Conference took place in 1996 at Wembo Nyama.[68] In 1976, the South Congo episcopal area was created, and Rev. Ngoy Kimba Wakadilo was elected bishop for this conference. Onema remained bishop for the Central Congo area until his retirement in 2005.

In 1980, the South Congo area was divided into two episcopal areas, with Rev. Kainda Katembo being elected bishop for the South Congo and Rev. Ngoy Kimba Wakadilo becoming the first bishop for the North Katanga. A leader with a deep sense of humility, Bishop Ngoy was widely appreciated in Congolese Methodism as a truly Christian leader, a pastor, and *mulami wa bantu* (literally, a caring people keeper). Ngoy initiated several projects in medical and higher education, evangelism, and construction. He also spearheaded women's access to ordained ministry, when he ordained the first woman elder in Congolese Methodism in 1979. When Bishop Ngoy died in 1994, Bishop Katembo served as interim bishop of North Katanga for two years. A deeply self-reflective leader, Katembo is known for his innovations in liturgy and worship, as well as for his initiative to teach the southern Congo area to be financially self-sufficient, as

---

67 Kasongo, *History of the Methodist Church*, 91.
68 Edouard Ndua, "De La Mission à l'Eglise Méthodiste-Unie," in *L'Eglise Méthodiste-Unie au Katanga à 100 Ans*, 84.

reflected in the quote at the beginning of this chapter. Katembo's initiative has resulted in the building of large UMC temples in Kolwezi, Likasi, and Lubumbashi with funds raised entirely within the Congo. He retired in 2016. In 1996 Rev. Ntambo Nkulu Ntanda was elected bishop for the North Katanga area. Bishop Ntambo was known for his efforts in establishing an orphanage, attending to the needs of people displaced by the 1997–2003 war, and creating Kamina Methodist University, as well as other similar programs. He retired in 2016.

In 2005 Rev. David Yemba was elected bishop for the Central Congo area to replace Onema Fama. Bishop Yemba is a veteran theological educator, a scholar, and an ecumenist. In 2012 the Central Congo area was divided into two episcopal areas. Yemba remained bishop for the Central Congo episcopal area, and Gabriel Y. Unda was elected bishop for the newest episcopal area: the East Congo Conference.[69] Yemba retired in 2016.

The 2016 Congo Central Conference elected the following new bishops: Rev. Mande Muyombo (North Katanga area); Rev. Kasap Owan (South Congo area); Rev. Daniel Onashuyaka Lunge (Central Congo); and Rev. Gabriel Y. Unda (East Congo area, was reelected for life). Today, the Congo Central Conference, authorized in 1992 by General Conference, is now organized into four episcopal areas, with fourteen annual conferences, and with mission work extending into the nine neighboring countries. In 2015 United Methodism in the Congo enjoyed a total membership of 3,081,590.[70] The new episcopal leaders, the clergy and laity, are poised to take Congolese United Methodism to a new phase.

Concluding Observations

The following can be said about United Methodist work in the Congo. First, early Methodist missionaries and their progeny used a *holistic approach* to

---

69 Perhaps before too long, Congo will elect a female bishop since there is now a significant presence of very capable Congolese clergy women serving as district superintendents and in other leadership roles in all episcopal areas.

70 "State of the Church 2017," *United Methodist Interpreter* (May–June 2017): 26.

mission. They preached the gospel not only in word but also in deeds through educational, medical, agricultural, and evangelistic work.[71]

Second, Methodist mission in the Congo played a significant role in education from the very beginning. Even though many Congolese did not have access to higher education until five or so years before independence in 1960, Methodist missions were among a few mission groups that provided most of the primary and secondary education in the Congo and, therefore, played an important role in the training not only of religious leaders, but also of future political and civic leaders who fought for independence. Third, the ecumenical spirit characterized early Methodist work, and this is true to this day. Methodists worked in collaboration with other Protestant groups in order to strengthen their collective witness and service in a colonial setting that was hostile to Protestant efforts and more favorable to Catholic initiatives in the various religious and social endeavors.[72]

Fourth, even though early Methodist missionaries taught a holistic gospel of love, one need not search hard for racist language in some of their writings. Many missionaries equated African culture with heathenism and "darkness."[73] Early missionaries were children of their own cultures and times. The blatant racism, white supremacy, and Western superiority reflected in their work should not be overlooked or be sugarcoated because of the great achievements of their mission endeavors. These issues are reminders, or perhaps even revelations, of the human brokenness and sin that continue to afflict our contemporary race relations in the global church and in the larger world even today. These issues point to the need for redemption and reform for our religious and social institutions, our relationships across cultures, as well as a call for our personal transformation by the gospel of Jesus Christ who calls us to truly love our neighbor. We should not underestimate the

---

71 Newell S. Booth, *The Cross Over Africa* (New York: Friendship Press, 1945), 124–40.

72 For an example of collaborative work, see Munayi Muntu-Monji, *Les Vingt-Cinq Ans de la Faculté de Théologie Protestante au Zaire 1959–1984* (Kinshasa: Faculté de Théologie Protestante, 1984).

73 John Wesley Kurewa, *The Church in Mission: A Short History of The United Methodist Church in Zimbabwe, 1897–1997* (Nashville: Abingdon Press, 1997), 9, 38–39.

ongoing impact on race relations of what Congolese philosopher V. Y. Mudimbe has called the "colonial library" and the *invented Africa* it represents. Mudimbe calls for a deconstruction of such a benighted picture of Africa in order to create more empowering narratives.[74] Indeed, contemporary missions should not continue to feed or nurture the hunger for the exotic found in some missionary writings and in certain circles of Western society, but rather equip people with intercultural sensibilities and competencies that empower our churches to practice dignity-promoting missions that advance human well-being and the flourishing of all in an interconnected world.

Fifth, the church needs to be able to adjust to the constantly changing nature of mission in order to understand God's calling in a changing world. John Wesley Kurewa suggests that "God's mission, which is to be understood in the historical context, can never be perceived in the same way through all the ages. Because history is constantly changing, our perception of God's mission must change too."[75] Indeed, even though the UMC in the Congo is a socially engaged church, it has not kept up with the changes happening in the country, and thus it has not yet developed a clear and consistent prophetic voice to address public issues of significance such as the gross violation of human rights, destruction of the environment, mismanagement of the country's resources, and political violence by those in power that have continued to afflict the country even since its independence in 1960. The Wesleyan tradition has great resources to inform United Methodism's thinking and action to fully engage the struggles of ordinary Congolese and to provide a prophetic and truly transformative presence and witness that calls forth a new consciousness and a new socially just society into existence.

---

74 V. Y. Mudimbe, *The Invention of Africa: Gnosis, Philosophy, and the Order of Knowledge* (Indianapolis: Indiana University Press, 1988), especially chaps. 1–3.

75 Kurewa, *The Church in Mission*, 15.

Historical Growth of The United Methodist Church in Mozambique

Problems and Possibilities in the Present and Future

Júlio André Vilanculos

The church in Mozambique started with the Roman Catholic Church, following the arrival of Vasco da Gama in 1498 on his way to India; more than three hundred years later, the Protestant churches emerged in Mozambique. One of these Protestant churches was the Methodist Episcopal Church, now known as The United Methodist Church. The United Methodist Church in Mozambique was established in 1890 through missionaries from the United States and is now entering its second century. Since the introduction of this Christian denomination, the church has experienced both successes and challenges. This chapter discusses the historical growth of The United Methodist Church in Mozambique and analyzes the problems and possibilities in the past, present, and future.

Introduction

The United Methodist Church in Mozambique is part and parcel of the Methodist Episcopal Church in Africa, which was started by lay preacher Daniel

Coker (an African American immigrant). He came to Africa in response to the needs of the Methodist Episcopal Church on the continent. In 1822, he first started the church in Liberia, and in 1885 his ministry expanded to Angola and Zaire (now the Democratic Republic of Congo) in the same year. Subsequently, in 1890 the Methodist Episcopal Church came to Mozambique and in 1897 to Rhodesia, which is now the Republic of Zimbabwe. On March 8, 1833, Melville Cox came to Africa as the first American missionary and settled in Liberia. In 1884 William Taylor came to Africa as the first missionary bishop.[1]

The Establishment of the Methodist Episcopal Church in Southern Mozambique

In the nineteenth century, following the Berlin conference (1884–1885), the partition of Africa took place. Protestant churches were allowed to establish and spread their missions in Africa.[2] It was in this context that the first missionaries sent by the American Board of Commissioners for Foreign Missions (today known as the United Congregational Church) come to Mozambique in order to establish their mission fields, especially in the Inhambane region. According to Rev. João Guezi Gujamo, these missionaries came on July 18, 1884, and the team was composed of seven missionaries under the leadership of Rev. Dr. Erwin Richards.[3] They started their mission in Mongue before moving to Cambine, Phembe, Phanga, Mocodoene, and Chicuque. The missionaries were successful in building churches in Cambine, Mocodoene, and Chicuque. (These churches still exist, and Christians still worship in them except in Cambine, which is no longer in use because it needs to be rebuilt.)

However, these initial missionary efforts did not take root because of two major problems. First, malaria struck the missionaries, and so Inhambane was

---

1   J. W. Kurewa, *The Church in Mission: A Short History of The United Methodist Church in Zimbabwe 1897–1997* (Nashville: Abingdon Press, 1997), 19.

2   A. Helgesson, *Church, State and People in Mozambique: A Historical Study with Special Emphasis on the Methodist Developments in the Inhambane Region* (Uppsala: Tryck AB Press, 1994), 53.

3   Rev. João Guezi Gujamo, personal communication.

regarded as an unhealthy place. As a result, the majority of the congregational missionaries left Mozambique and went to Natal, where they established the Umzila mission in South Africa. Second, Rev. Richards went through a serious personal crisis. Miss Dalila Isaacs, a prominent black woman in the region, was his concubine, which was morally wrong and violated church rules.[4] This painful experience closed his missionary career in Mozambique, and the home board secretary in Boston called Rev. Richards back to America, where he was dismissed from the American Board of Missions.

Despite the unfortunate situation with the Rev. Dr. Richards, he remained interested in returning to Africa to continue his missionary work. For this reason, soon after his dismissal from the American Board of Missions, he began investigating other possibilities for missionary work in Africa. Toward the end of 1890, Richards approached the Methodist Episcopal Church and in particular, Bishop William Taylor. Helgesson records that "on the eve of Christmas, 1890, Richards received permission from the Bishop William Taylor to raise funds to proceed to Africa."[5] It is clear that Richard's request to return to Africa as a Methodist Episcopal missionary was well received by Bishop Taylor because at that time the "Bishop had a plan of planting chains of mission stations across Africa from the West to the Southwest."[6] He was sent to East Africa and settled in the Inhambane area, which is considered the beginning of the Methodist Episcopal Church in Mozambique.

The Expansion of the Methodist Episcopal Church in Southern Mozambique

Immediately after his arrival in Inhambane, Rev. Richards started negotiating with the owners of the former missions at Cambine and Mocodoene, which were sold by the American Board's missionaries when they left Mozambique; these two missions were recovered by Richards as his new mission stations.[7]

---

4 A. Helgesson, *Church, State, and People in Mozambique*, 59.

5 A. Helgesson, *Church, State, and People in Mozambique*, 90.

6 J. W. Kurewa, *The Church in Mission*, 19.

7 A. Helgesson, *Church, State, and People in Mozambique*, 104.

Richards started a school for girls in Chicuque that gained a good reputation in the area. He kept close contact with two local people—namely, Tizora Navesse and Muti Sikobele who first worked with the Congregationalists. The former had occupied the house in Mocodoene, and the latter was in Cambine. These two people are considered by Bishop Carvalho as the pillars of Methodism in Mozambique because of their courage and zeal.[8] Moreover, another local leader by the name Neli Kuambani was sent by Richards to Mongue to start another school and to teach young people how to sing, sew, read, and study the Bible. At this time, four missions were operated by the Methodist Episcopal Church: Cambine, Mocodoene, Mongue, and Chicuque.[9]

As a way of responding to the situation of ensuring the missions were self-supporting, self-governing, and self-propagating, as stressed by Bishop Taylor, the two indigenous people, Navesse and Sikobele, assisted in a practical manner by helping Richards obtain animal skins, bows, arrows, and shields for local sale and export. Richards also explored the potential market for his photographic skill and equipment, and the money received from this business was used to run the activities of the new Methodist Episcopal Church.

Richards and the first Mozambican lay leaders were involved in the process of evangelization. As a result, people were converted to Methodism, and later some of these new converts became prominent leaders. Kurewa suggests that Farangwane, Matew, Angilazi, Kalije, Jossiah Hayes, Xinzabani Hayes, and Gigalamugyo were key leaders in church planting.[10] As these leaders were preaching the gospel, an important event occurred in the history of Methodism in Africa. "On November 16, 1901 the East Central Africa Mission Conference was organized in Umtali-Rhodesia, by Bishop J. C. Hartzell."[11] A delegation of the Methodist Episcopal Church in Inhambane (Mozambique) attended that conference. Consequently, Bishop Hartzell made the

---

8 E. J. M de Carvalho, *A Igreja Africana no Centro da sua História* (Luanda: Centro de Publicações Cristãs, 1995), 97.

9 A. Helgesson, *Church, State, and People in Mozambique*, 105.

10 J. W. Kurewa, *The Church in Mission*, 51.

11 *Report of East Central Africa Mission Conference* (1901), 1.

first official appointments for the Inhambane district. First, in Chicuque he appointed Rev. Erwin Richards, Mrs. E. H. Richards, and (two local teachers) Farangwane and Matew. Second, in Cambine he appointed Frank D. Wolf, Mrs. F. D. Wolf, and (three local teachers) Muti Sikobele, Angilazi, and Kaliji. Lastly, in Mocodoene three local teachers were appointed: Tizora Navesse, Josiah Hayes, and Xinzabani Hayes.[12] With these appointments the Methodist Episcopal Church started to spread in all areas of Inhambane, as well as in other areas of the southern part of Mozambique.

The process of evangelism was also accelerated when miners, converted in South Africa, returned home with the gospel. Rev. Richards declared: "We are constantly astonished at the numbness of all symptoms of church wisdom, from those who are converted at the Rand [i.e., in South Africa] and have no life but the Rand life. However, some of these men and women are doing splendid work. They only need a second training in the country. They are all trustworthy as church leaders among us."[13]

In 1919 Johannesburg was considered as a branch of the Methodist mission in order to accommodate the miners working in the area. By this time, there was a notable growth of the church among the Chopi people in the south of Inhambane. From this growth two young people emerged, Jorge Makupulane and Filipe Gwambe, who were converted in South Africa.[14] Through the Chopi people, Methodism spread up to the Gaza area and to Lourenço Marques, currently known as Maputo.

The growth of the church during this time was a result of many factors, such as the use of indigenous African converts for evangelism and the establishment of schools in villages. Missionaries trained people who were converted in South Africa so that they could join in the process of evangelism and the production of booklets in the local language (Xitshwa). On a positive note, these booklets also spread Methodism to the miners in South Africa.

---

12 *Report of East Central Africa Mission Conference* (1901), 134.

13 A. Helgesson, *Church, State, and People in Mozambique*, 133.

14 A. Helgesson, *Church, State, and People in Mozambique*, 134.

In addition the most important factor was the translation of the New Testament into Xitshwa in 1905. In the same year, the first pastor of the Methodist Episcopal Church, Tizora Navesse, was ordained.[15]

The spread of the Methodist Episcopal Church in South Inhambane was under the supervision of Tizora Navesse. Most significantly, Muti Sikobele, having completed studies in Natal Province, South Africa, was heavily involved in the translation of the entire Bible from English into Xitshwa, which was published in 1917. This Bible in Xitshwa is still used by various churches who utilize the indigenous language in their services, including the Roman Catholic Church. Sikobele also traveled to different areas of Inhambane, such as Macaringue, Bembe, Massinga, and Vilanculo, just to mention a few. During his travels, Sikobele preached and taught in-depth Bible studies. It is also worth noting that in 1909, in order to make the work easier and better organized during the East Central Mission conference, the church established the first three ecclesiastic districts: Inhambane District with two circuits (Inharrime and Usakeni); Morrumbene District with four circuits (Mocodoene, Massinga, Panda, and Morrumbene); and lastly, Lipompo District with three circuits (Zavala, Bilene, and Chibuto).[16]

As the church was spreading in the south of Mozambique, the missionaries also planned to enhance education and health care. Consequently, in 1910 in the Cambine area a school was built for boys, which was called "Keys School" because the funds used to establish the school were donated by an American named Keys. At the same time, two training centers for teachers and nurses were established in the Chicuque area, and the girls' school started by Richards remained effective. A school for preachers was also started in Cambine,[17] which later became a theological school. In 1923, the first group of students and their wives studied not only theology but also agriculture and carpentry so they could become self-supporting, self-governing, and

---

15 *Mahlahle: Boletim Informativo da Igreja Metodista unida em Moçambique,* vol. 6 (2006), 2.

16 Report, *East Central Africa Mission Conference* (1909), 28.

17 A. Helgesson, *Church, State, and People in Mozambique,* 177.

self-sustaining in order to fulfil the stated goal of Bishop Taylor.[18] By 1913 the first medical doctor missionary, C. Stauffacher, came to Mozambique, thereby improving health care in the country. As a result a hospital was built in Chicuque, which today is the second largest in Inhambane Province.[19]

It is significant to note that the dedication of local leaders and missionaries culminated in the creation of the Portuguese[20] East Africa Mission Conference, which became the conference in Mozambique on February 8, 1915. The first provisional conference of this area was held in Chicuque in 1916, with Bishop W. Taylor presiding. The secretary was missionary P. W. Keys, and the conference roll included four members.[21] With this division, the Methodist Episcopal Church grew significantly.

Another important event in the history of the Mozambican church happened when Bishop Escrivão Anglaze Zunguze, a Mozambican pastor, was elected in 1964 as one of the first two African bishops of the Methodist Church. As the first African bishop in Mozambique, his episcopacy was characterized by expansion and starting new churches in areas where the missionary pastors had not been able to reach. Bishop Zunguze is described as a person who placed emphasis on pastoral visitation. He was a leader who visited all pastors in their circuits in order to talk to them about the pastoral life of their church.

Bishop Zunguze was succeeded by the Bishop Almeida Penicela Nhambio, who was elected in 1976. Penicela's term as the bishop was characterized by further development of the church in Mozambique. It was during his time that pastors started to have scholarships to go overseas for training. According to Rev. Cesar Seventine Pongo, despite the disabling condition he suffered from a car accident while traveling from Maputo to Inhambane for his episcopal consecration, Bishop Penicela was a dedicated person and

---

18 A. Helgesson, *Church, State, and People in Mozambique*, 201.

19 A. Chamusso, *50 Wa Malembe na hi Muthlangano wa Lembe* (2005), 3.

20 It was called by this name because it happened before the independence of Mozambique and was still under Portuguese domination.

21 A. Chamusso, *50 Wa Malembe na hi Muthlangano wa Lembe* (2005), 2.

was good at communicating events of the church through writing and re-plying to letters.[22] It was during his episcopacy that, in 1979, women were first ordained in Mozambique: Rev. Amina Isaias Valoi and Rev. Lea Jotamo Mapsanganhe. Rev. Mapsanganhe later became the first female district su-perintendent in Mozambique.

After Penicela's retirement in 1988, he was replaced by Bishop João So-mane Machado. His episcopacy was marked by the expansion of the church in the central and northern areas of the nation, as well as the training of young pastors both male and female. It is important to highlight that during his episcopacy, the number of female pastors in The United Methodist Church increased. In July 2008, The United Methodist Church of Eastern Central Af-rica held an unforgettable conference at Africa University-Mutare, and more history was made by the election of the first African woman bishop of The United Methodist Church, Bishop Joaquina Filipe Nhanala, who replaced the retired Bishop João Somane Machado in the Mozambican Episcopal Area.

The Expansion of the Methodist Episcopal Church in Central Mozambique

The history of The United Methodist Church in the central region of Mozam-bique began in 1947 in Sofala Province when people from the south, espe-cially Xitshwa-speaking people from Inhambane, traveled to Beira seeking employment. These people worked on the construction of the railway con-necting Mozambique and Rhodesia (today's Zimbabwe). Members of this church joined the United Church of Christ in Sofala and Manica to worship together. Churches with members living in this small ecumenical community from the south felt that there was a need for pastoral leadership to the com-munity. Consequently, pastors from different denominations with members in that community began to be appointed there. The first appointed leader

---

22 According to Rev. Cesar Seventine Pongo.

was Pastor Paulo Matsinhe from the Free Methodist Episcopal Church.[23]

Later on, Methodist members of the church realized that they were not free to carry out what was recommended by their denomination. As a result, they decided to give up worshipping with the ecumenical group and establish their own Methodist community where they would be free to worship in accordance with their own denominational guidelines. There were several factors that contributed to the official emergence of The United Methodist Church. To begin with, there had been some misunderstanding with members of other denominations, especially those who were natives of Sofala. Second, some prohibited Methodist women from wearing the uniform[24] that was being utilized in The United Methodist Church in south Mozambique. Lastly, there was lack of clarity about using funds that were raised by the ecumenical church.[25]

It was in December 13, 1970, that The United Methodist Church members began their own worship as a Methodist denomination in Beira. It is of paramount importance to mention the names of people like Zacarias Macassa Ngotine, Paulo Touó, João Jeque Nhambiho, Aniva Primeiro Tanguane, Elisa Escrivão Zunguze, Helena Pedro Tsevete, and Zaqueu Macie, who were the founders of this denomination in Beira, which became the first circuit. As the church activities were growing along with the membership, there was a need to divide the one existing circuit into two, giving birth to the Manga circuit. To make the work of the church better organized and facilitate the expansion of the church, Beira was elevated to the position of ecclesiastic district in 1979 with only two circuits, Beira and Manga. Rev. Andre Uetela Mulamula was appointed as the first district superintendent. With the dedication of pastors and laity, two new circuits were created: one branched off from Manga, the Dondo circuit, and the other from Beira, the Central circuit.

---

23 "27° Aniversario do Distrito de Sofala 1979 a 2006," (Mozambique Annual Conference), 3.

24 This uniform is comprised of black shoes, red skirt, dark red blouse, and white hat. The uniform is used by women who are full members of the women's fellowship who are ready to dedicate themselves in prayer for other people.

25 27° Aniversario do Distrito de Sofala 1979 a 2006, 4.

The United Methodist Church in Sofala is the first of these churches in all the provinces of the central region. In fact, in Sofala people from south Mozambique who were already Methodist started the churches, and they were the ones who caused them to grow. Other people from the same region, who were scattered in other provinces, felt that they had to follow the same example of starting churches wherever they went. As a result, in 1973 The United Methodist Church emerged in Tete Province under the leadership of Naftal Jossefa Nhambir, Oseia Simão, José Muzonda, and João Candiano Candido, just to mention a few.

At the same time, the churches started in Manica Province, from south Mozambique, were worshipping with other Christians as an ecumenical community. In 1980 they decided to separate from The United Methodist Church, and Mr. Ezequiel Macie and Mr. Faustino Titosse Munhequete became the leaders of that group. At the beginning, this community received supervision from the church in Beira. The first pastor from Beira to visit this church was Rev. Ernesto Gemo Mangumo. In 1982 Rev. Jonas Ndice Sumburane Muhacha was appointed as the first pastor in charge of the church in Chimoio. Then in 1989 The United Methodist Church in Zambézia Province was started by Mr. Alexandre Jaime Mutsuque, his wife Sara Mutsuque, and Armando Gil.

As The United Methodist Church was growing significantly in Sofala and Manica, the denomination decided to create a district composed of two provinces, Sofala and Manica. It was named SOMA, taking the first letters from Sofala and Manica. Later, the same district expanded its mission to Tete Province, and after the church was planted in Tete, the name of the district changed into SOMATE. Meanwhile, the church also reached Zambézia Province, thus establishing The United Methodist Church throughout central Mozambique. The Annual Conference gathered in 1992 and decided that the entire central part of Mozambique would become a district named SOMATEZA, standing for Sofala, Manica, Tete, and Zambézia.[26]

---

26 *Relatorio Oficial da Conferencia Anual da Igreja Metodista unida em Mocambique* (1992), 38.

The Rev. Alfiado Camela Zunguze became the district superintendent.

Very significant evangelistic work was undertaken in SOMATEZA, leading to substantial church growth. Consequently, there was a need to separate each of the provinces into an ecclesiastic district. In 1992 Tete was the first to be separated, and Rev. Fernando Simone Matsimbe was named district superintendent. In 1993 Zambézia separated, and in 1994 the Rev. Jacob Lucas Jenhuro became its first district superintendent. Finally, Manica separated in 1994 with Rev. Pedro Canhavane Monteiro as its first district superintendent, and Sofala stayed on its own as an ecclesiastic district under the leadership of Rev. Alfiado Camela Zunguze as the district superintendent.

The United Methodist Church Reaches the Northern Area of Mozambique

There is no way of talking about The United Methodist Church in Northern Mozambique without touching on the work that was done by the Christian Council of Mozambique. In 1996 the Christian Council took the initiative of expanding Protestantism into the north. At that time, most people were either Muslim—an influence present before Portuguese colonization—or Roman Catholic under colonization.[27] The Protestant "pioneer" was Rev. Felix Cossa of the Presbyterian Church, who was commissioned to go to Nampula in 1968. When he returned to the south in 1978, Rev. Cesar Seventine Pongo of The United Methodist Church was also appointed to Cuamba district in Niassa Province. These two pastors received ecumenical recommendations from the Christian Council of Mozambique, and they were not allowed to start churches specific to their own denominations. The presence of these two pastors in Northern Mozambique helped give people the idea of forming denominational churches in the northern region of the country. The first stage undertaken in Nampula was the creation of a prayer group composed of people from the south. This occurred in 1982, and that group was designated *classe de oração dos irmãos do Sul*, which means "prayer group of

---

27   Mr. António Simione Chibayele, personal communication.

brothers from the South." In 1987 three Protestant denominations emerged from this group in Nampula Province: The United Methodist Church, the Nazarene Church, and the Presbyterian Church.[28]

It is important to highlight that Arnaldo Alexandre Chivale, Carlija Mulandeza (his wife), Eduardo Naene Macuacua, Maria Salomone Banhe, and António Simione Chibayele were instrumental in the process of starting The United Methodist Church in Nampula.[29] Consequently, Mr. Felix António Navesse was appointed as the first local pastor for the church in Nampula. Under his leadership and with the contribution of other church members, The United Methodist Church expanded to other areas in the province. Most important, when people living in the province of Cabo Delgado and Niassa heard the good news about the beginning of The United Methodist Church in Nampula, they did not want to remain behind. They took the initiative and started their own mission, and, in 1988, The United Methodist Church was inaugurated in Pemba, the capital of Cabo Delgado, under the leadership of Mr. André Bahule (a medical doctor who was working there) and his wife Linita Biosse Bahule, Mr. Muhate, and Mr. Alexandre Chivale. In 1989 another small United Methodist community was started in Lichinga, the capital of Niassa Province, through the following people: Raquel Titosse Hlavanguane (a nurse working in Lichinga), Filipe Mazivila, Daniel António Bila, Telma Lucas, Amélia Ngazwane, Pereira Zimba, and Amelia Vilanculos.[30]

In 1990 Rev. João Damião Elias became the first trained pastor appointed in Pemba. Similarly, in 1990 Elias Pechiço Pfungo was appointed as the first catechist in Lichinga. As a result of the existence of The United Methodist Church in Northern Mozambique, in 1990 the first ecclesiastic district of NANICA (signifying Nampula, Niassa, and Cabo Delgado) was created, and the first district superintendent of the new area was Rev. André Uetela Mulamula. Because the church was growing in each of the three provinces, there

---

28 Mr. António Simione Chibayele, personal communication.

29 Mr. António Simione Chibayele, personal communication.

30 Mr. António Simione Chibayele. Amelia Vilanculos is not related to the author of this article.

arose a need to divide the district as a way to accelerate its growth. First, Cabo Delgado was separated as an ecclesiastic district in 1993, and Rev. João Damião Elias was appointed as the district superintendent. Second, Niassa was formed into a district in 2000, superintended by Rev. Júlio André Vilanculos. Nampula remained a district led by Rev. Filimão Punguane Vilanculo. This made The United Methodist Church present throughout Mozambique.

As a result of the church's presence in all provinces, the Africa Central Conference of The United Methodist Church held in Maputo in 2000 approved the division of Mozambique into two annual conferences: the South and North Annual Conferences.[31] The South Annual Conference is comprised of four provinces: Maputo Province and Maputo City, Gaza, and Inhambane. The North Annual Conference is comprised of seven provinces: Sofala, Manica, Tete, Zambézia, Nampula, Cabo Delgado, and Niassa. Both conferences are under the leadership of one bishop, initially Bishop João Somane Machado, followed by Bishop Joaquina Filipe Nhanala. As of 2018, The United Methodist Church in Mozambique in both annual conferences is represented by thirty-two ecclesiastic districts and 150,284 members in the two annual conferences.

Problems and Possibilities in the Present and Future

There is no doubt that since the beginning of The United Methodist Church in Mozambique in 1890 many good things have happened, although the church also faces many challenges. On a positive note, The United Methodist Church is carrying out several programs. The United Methodist Church contributed greatly to the independence of Mozambique through raising the consciousness of people by means of education. Once the people became aware of their real-life situation under Portuguese domination, they worked to change whatever was found lacking. Second, from the time of the arrival of missionaries in Mozambique up to the present day, the church has facilitated projects for human development, which has enabled them to

31 *Mahlahle: Boletim Informativo da Igreja Metodista Unida em Mocambique,* vol. 6 (2006), 3.

acquire secular education and learn new agricultural techniques. Third, the church promoted theological education for women, who later became pastors. The fourth item of note is the church's positive impact on the nation due to important political leaders who have been educated in Methodist mission schools and institutes of high learning. For example, Eduardo Chivambo Mondlane, the first president of FRELIMO—*Frente de Libertação de Moçambique* (Mozambican Liberation Front)—received part of his education in agriculture at Cambine Mission. Graça Machel, who became the first woman minister of education in Mozambique, also has ties to the United Methodist School for Girls in Chicuque.

The fifth, sixth, and seventh positive contributions all relate to education. The United Methodist Church can be found in all provinces of Mozambique, and as new local churches are created, The United Methodist Church in Mozambique is challenged to train more pastors who can be sent to serve the people in different contexts (both rural and urban). Considering the development of the world, where people now are interested in university education, the church in Mozambique needs pastors who have bachelors, masters, and even doctoral degrees to serve local congregations. To alleviate this situation, a United Methodist University of Mozambique was envisioned and dedicated on March 17, 2017. To run a university requires partnerships within and outside Mozambique, and such collaborations will change the face of the country.

Sixth, The United Methodist Church promotes pastors receiving degrees in education and psychology in order to work in clinics as counselors. Last, The United Methodist Church in Mozambique, in partnership with some United Methodist agencies, offers scholarships to laypeople to do advanced studies in agriculture, administration, and social services, among other disciplines. Together, these seven contributions demonstrate the positive influence the church continues to have on the larger society of Mozambique.

Despite the good things that The United Methodist Church has done in Mozambique, the church faces some persistent challenges as well as some crises in its mission. Early on, when missionaries refused to pay salaries for local church workers, this was understood as discrimination by some church members. Muti Sikobele became frustrated and started his own church called *Igreja Luz Episcopal* (the Light Episcopal Church).[32] A number of Methodist members followed him because he was a charismatic man; it weakened the church in Mozambique and took quite some time to recover.

A second challenge involved the Methodist Episcopal Church and the threats it received from *Polícia Internacional de Defesa do Estado* (International Police and State Defense). Some pastors (for example, Rev. Jobe Mbanze, Rev. Zacarias Khofi, and Rev. Andre Machava) were imprisoned and punished for preaching the gospel.[33] The Methodist Episcopal Church was also regarded as an enemy by the Roman Catholic Church and the Portuguese government. This position was promoted by Bishop Barroso of the Roman Catholic Church, who warned, "The Methodist Church constitutes a considerable risk factor against the Portuguese sovereignty in the colony."[34] As a result, the Methodist Episcopal Church was only allowed to operate in the south and not in the north of the nation. Even in the south, the Methodist Episcopal Church buildings were supposed to be built thirty-two kilometers away from any Roman Catholic buildings.

Then, when Mozambique became independent in 1975, another problem emerged. The new government nationalized all hospitals, schools, day care centers, and farms that belonged to The United Methodist Church as well as other Protestant denominations. Many churches were closed, and this situation forced the church to operate underground with worship services and class meetings conducted in the homes of faithful believers. Soon after independence, a civil war erupted. Church properties were destroyed, and some pastors, members, and students in pastoral training were killed. For example, on August 5, 1991, Rev. Jeremias Daragube, Mr. Albazino Simone

---

32 A. Helgesson, *Church, State, and People in Mozambique*, 202.

33 Rev. Francisco Feniche Machava, personal communication.

34 A. Helgesson, *Church, State, and People in Mozambique*, 107.

Hungwe, and Mr. Timoteo Zaqueu Macamo were killed on their way back to Chimoio from Makhate, where they had gone for a thanksgiving service.[35]

When the church completed its centenary anniversary in 1990, the General Board of Global Ministries (GBGM) in New York decided to reduce the financial support to the church in Mozambique. However, the church was not prepared to stand on its own because missionaries had not taught Mozambican Methodists to do so, and the economic status of the country was in shambles due to the civil war. As a result, many pastors suffered, going without salaries, and some abandoned their pastoral careers. To cope with this new situation, the energetic and dedicated Bishop João Somane Machado (now retired) established a new partnership with many annual conferences in the United States such as New York, Virginia, Missouri, and Texas, as well as with some European Methodist churches such as those in Germany and Sweden. These conferences significantly aided the Mozambican Episcopal Area in raising funds for different church projects including schools, chapels, parsonages, salaries of pastors, and scholarships. As a result of this initiative, The United Methodist Church in Mozambique started an exchange program where American teams came to Mozambique as Volunteers in Mission (VIM) to work in different circuits, and Mozambicans likewise traveled to America. The first Mozambican team that went to America under this new partnership was composed of eleven members, who were both clergy and laity, adults and youth, men and women: Bishop João Somane Machado, Nocia Madonela Machado (the bishop's wife), Angelina Abdul, Arlindo Sambo, Arlindo Simbine, Cecilia Jose, Andre Massicame, Humberto Guibunda, Edna Zunguze, and the Reverends Jamisse Uilson Taimo and Pedro Canhavane Monteiro.

Related to the point above, we should highlight that The United Methodist Church in Mozambique remains economically weak. This is why it still depends on donations from overseas to run many of its activities. Arguably, the main reason for this ongoing situation is because the church lacks

35 Mr. Alfeu Julai Mapsanganhe, personal communication.

income-generating projects. In this regard, if one day the friends who are supporting the church in Mozambique stopped their donations, the church would face serious problems. The financial weakness of The United Methodist Church in Mozambique needs to be analyzed from the perspective that the Methodist missionaries brought the gospel to Mozambique, but they did not develop local fundraising for the church and, instead, depended on money from the United States of America. This practice created a relationship of dependency that continues. For example, instruction on tithing was neglected; hence, people contributed only a little amount of money per year and the contributions during circuit conferences were minimal.

There is yet another challenge The United Methodist Church in Mozambique faces. In his dissertation, Lifuna Simush points out that the tension existing between scientific medicine and traditional medicine is a notable problem in the African church.[36] Some United Methodist Church members, when facing illnesses, prefer to consult people who have knowledge of medicinal plants (leaves or roots) with the capacity to cure diseases; worse still, they might go to traditional healers. In most cases, this is done secretly because many Christians believe Christian use of traditional herbs is demonic. On the other hand, some Christians—including myself—do not think it is problematic to use plants, given that some medicines contain herbs and leaves. The Chinese, for example, have long utilized herbal medicines. The concern here is less about the use of traditional medicines and more about the use of traditional healers, a practice that challenges the church significantly when members become syncretistic.

Finally, The United Methodist Church in Mozambique appears to be losing its spiritual and moral discipline. For instance, in the past, the laity respected their pastors, and pastors, in turn, were deeply committed to their pastoral work in caring for the laity. Such discipline now appears to be waning. The cause of this decline might be the fact that the church has a substantial

Traditional medicine and healers

---

36 L. Simush, *The Prosperity Gospel in the Assemblies of God Church: A Case Study of Lusaka, Zambia* (diss., Africa University, 2006), 83.

number of young pastors who are looking for material gain, and as a consequence, the laypeople are not respectful toward the young pastors in general. This situation challenges the church, and it is seeking ways to resolve it.

The Future of The United Methodist Church in Mozambique

Acknowledging that The United Methodist Church in Mozambique faces some challenges in the present leaves the church's future somewhat difficult to predict. However, from a pastoral perspective, the future of The United Methodist Church in Mozambique is not very promising, since there are pastors leaving the church altogether and other part-time pastors working in the public sector where they are paid regularly and, at times, paid at a level consistent with their education. Consequently, bi-vocational pastors are left with little time to serve the church, which undermines good pastoral care. In some respects, these pastors lack courage, since the problems of any institution cannot be resolved from outside but only from within, where together they can advocate for change.

As is true in most parts of the world, United Methodist Church members in Mozambique are leaving for other churches that preach a prosperity gospel, drawn by the promises of riches and happiness to those who believe. However, it is important to point out that many of these members end up returning to The United Methodist Church after realizing that the message preached by those churches is false. Despite this trend, The United Methodist Church in Mozambique is growing significantly, as demonstrated by the increase in new parishes, ecclesiastical districts, and annual conferences. The third Annual Conference of Mozambique has been officially inaugurated. Of course, this increases the challenge noted above, that is, adequate pastoral compensation. The people need strong pastoral leadership to grow in their discipleship as United Methodists.

Another concern for the future, of course, is the financial health of The United Methodist Church in Mozambique. Not only does the church lack money to provide salaries to pastors and other church workers, but the mission and work of the church is underfunded. There is hope in this regard, as the church has been discussing how to initiate projects that will lead to sustainability. If these plans come to fruition, The United Methodist Church will have a joyous and meaningful future in Mozambique.

In conclusion, although The United Methodist Church in Mozambique was established by missionaries from outside Mozambique, the local people have been responsible for the rapid and continuing expansion of the church into different areas of Mozambique. Even though The United Methodist Church began in the nineteenth century, many problems exist today, and each Methodist is called to be part of solving those problems. Yet, despite these challenges, the church is growing in terms of membership and continues to be a part of the people called Methodists.

ASIA AND THE PACIFIC

United Methodist Origins in the Philippines

Luther J. Oconer

The Beginning Years

On Sunday morning, March 5, 1899, just barely a month after the first shot of the Philippine-American War (1899–1903) had rung out, a different type of drama unfolded at *Teatro Filipino*, home to Spanish plays and musicals, in Quiapo, Manila.[1] Taking center stage at the well-known theater was not a Filipino stage actor but Bishop James M. Thoburn (1836–1922), the renowned American Methodist missionary from India. Thoburn intended to establish a Methodist Episcopal Church (MEC) mission in the Philippines, albeit on the coattails of American superior firepower, which ended almost four centuries of Spanish rule and suppressed Filipino aspirations for independence. Oblivious to the ongoing skirmishes between Filipino and American troops in the outskirts of the city, Thoburn proceeded to hold a service that morning. In his diary he wrote:

---

1 James M. Thoburn, 5 March 1899, "Diaries and Journals," 1857–1918, Allegheny College Library, Meadville, PA. See also Homer C. Stuntz, *The Philippines and the Far East* (Cincinnati: Jennings and Pye, 1904), 420–21; cf. Luther J. Oconer, *Spirit-Filled Protestantism: Holiness-Pentecostal Revivals and the Making of Filipino Methodist Identity* (Eugene, OR: Pickwick Publications, 2017), 32.

> At 9:20 A.M. I went to the theatre and found a dozen soldiers at the door and a few others. We went in and somewhat slowly over seventy persons came in and took seats in the main floor while from 30 to 50 Filipinos stood without the railing. Things moved slowly at first but when I began to preach the Spirit wonderfully helped. Seldom in my life have I felt preaching to be a luxury.[2]

The event quickly put into motion the birth of Methodism in the Philippines. The bishop's message was so moving that "Captain Plummer," a Manila resident of twenty years from Albany, New York, broke down into tears. The stevedoring businessman became the main benefactor and one of the founding members of what would later become the MEC "American Church" or Central Church. Also moved, despite language limitations, was an affluent Spanish-speaking Filipino who later invited Thoburn to preach in his home. Though the request was never granted due to the unavailability of an interpreter, it nevertheless underscored the character of early Filipino interest toward the new religion. While the bishop's appeal for a collection elicited some awkward smiles from the audience, the amount they collected helped validate his plans. The ninety-two dollars, mostly foreign currencies, that filled the two hats that were passed among the audience reassured him the "people were ready to support the work."[3]

While Thoburn's visit was the first-ever trip to the Philippines sanctioned by the Missionary Society of the MEC (hereafter MSMEC), the official missionary-sending body of the denomination, we must take into account three other MEC pioneers who preceded the bishop. On August 28, 1898, barely two weeks after Admiral George Dewey's capture of Manila, Chaplain George C. Stull (1858–1933) of the Montana Conference inaugurated what he claimed to be the "first distinctive Protestant religious service" in the country without intending to organize a "Methodist Church."[4] Another MEC

---

2 Thoburn, 5 March 1899, *Diaries and Journals*.

3 Thoburn, "Notes from Manila," 3; "News from Manila," *World-Wide Missions*, Dec.1899, 6. Thoburn's account is also corroborated in Arthur W. Prautch, "Beginning of Methodism in Manila," *The Gospel in All Lands*, Feb. 1901, 59–60. Hereafter designated as *GIAL*.

4 Quoted in Stuntz, *Philippines*, 21–23; George C. Stull, "The Stull Letter," *Journal of the Seventeenth Session of the Montana Annual Conference of the Methodist Episcopal Church* (1903): 21–22.

minister who came before Thoburn was Charles A. Owens (1857–1935), a former missionary from Liberia.[5] Hastily appointed by Bishop Charles McCabe during the Puget Sound Conference, Owens reported organizing a "Methodist Church" among the soldiers on November 24, 1898, preaching "more than forty times" and holding revival services in a borrowed tent attended by soldiers and some locals. Owens's congregation, however, proved to be short-lived, not only because of the temporary nature of troop deployments, but also due to the irregular nature of his appointment. He and his wife were sent home shortly after Thoburn's visit.[6]

On December 17, 1898, another accidental pioneer who arrived in Manila, primarily to cash in on America's new colonial enterprise, was businessman Arthur W. Prautch, the son of German immigrants from Wisconsin and a former MEC missionary who had worked under Thoburn in Bombay. Prautch was recruited by the MEC for mission work in South India, where he would become known for his work among the Gujaratis.[7] Prautch's twelve-year missionary career, however, came to an abrupt halt when he withdrew from the Bombay conference in 1897.[8] Thoburn later reinstated him as a local preacher, putting him and his wife in charge of pioneering MEC work in Manila. The Prautches, with the help of Chaplain Stull, oversaw the English service at the theater and later in a rented hall a few blocks away at Plaza de Goiti, which they named the "Soldier's Institute," a recreational center intended to keep American soldiers away from liquor and other temptations. Aside from Stull, other American Methodists who assisted the Prautches were Jay C. Goodrich of the MEC Newark Conference and agent of the American Bible Society in

---

5 "Charles A. Owens," *Official Journal of the Pacific Northwest Annual Conference of the Methodist Episcopal Church, Eight Annual Session* (1936): 71.

6 "Appointments," *Journal of the Puget Sound Annual Conference of the Methodist Episcopal Church, Fifteenth Session* (1899): 23; Charles A. Owens, "From Manila," *World-Wide Missions*, Sep. 1899, 6; James M. Thoburn, "Bishop Thoburn's Report," *World-Wide Missions*, June 1899, 6.

7 Martin Van Buren Knox, *A Winter in India and Malaysia among the Methodist Missions* (New York: Hunt & Eaton, 1892), 23–26.

8 Note the Gujaratis are a major ethnic group in India. *Official Minutes of the Sixth Session of the Bombay Annual Conference of the Methodist Episcopal Church* (1897), 8, 14.

Manila; First Lt. Edward W. Hearne, secretary of the Young Men's Christian Association (YMCA) in Manila; and a number of military chaplains.[9]

Although Thoburn intended to grow MEC work in the Philippines initially around American soldiers and civilians, Filipinos entered the picture much earlier than he anticipated. On May 28, 1899, at the request of five Filipino Freemasons, Prautch and Chaplain Stull opened a Spanish service for them with the aid of interpreters. This was the beginning of the "First Filipino Church" (later to become Knox Memorial MEC). Among the first Filipinos to join these services were Don Paulino Zamora, a sea merchant, and his twenty-three-year-old son Nicolas Villegas Zamora (1875–1914). On August 6 the young Zamora, who once studied for the priesthood in Manila, eventually became the first Filipino preacher for the congregation. The young Zamora proved to be not only an eloquent preacher but also a crowd-drawer as the nascent congregation grew in numbers. Zamora, together with Prautch, soon opened seven preaching places in and around Manila, where he labored with great success.[10] One of these stations was Malibay, where most of the people and their leaders became Methodists. On the recommendation of the *municipal presidente* (town mayor), the services were held in an old Roman Catholic church damaged during the fighting between American and Filipino forces.[11] Another important point begun by Zamora was Pandacan, a suburb in southeast Manila, where a chapel was dedicated on August 12, 1900, the first Protestant edifice erected in the country.

When Thoburn arrived on March 6, 1900, for a second visit, there were already more than six hundred Filipinos who had thrown their lot behind

---

9   Arthur W. Prautch, "Beginning," 58–61; Francis W. Warne, *Light in the East: India, Malaysia, the Philippines Part II: The Philippine Islands* (Chicago: Missionary Campaign Library, 1900), 54–55; Dionisio D. Alejandro, *From Darkness to Light: A Brief Chronicle of the Beginnings and Spread of Methodism in the Philippines* (Quezon City, Philippines: United Methodist Church Philippines Central Conference Board of Communications and Publications, 1974), 19.

10   Warne, *Light in the East*, 56–57; idem, "Jottings from Manila II," *Indian Witness*, 4 May 1900, 3; Prautch, "Beginning," 60.

11   J. Tremayne Copplestone, *Twentieth-Century Perspectives (The Methodist Episcopal Church, 1890–1939)*, vol. 4 of *History of Methodist Missions* (New York: The Board of Global Ministries of The United Methodist Church, 1973), 196–97.

Zamora and, therefore, virtually stood on Methodism's doorsteps, but without any designated clergy to administer the sacraments to them.[12] Therefore, to address the enthusiastic advance of Filipino work, Thoburn proceeded swiftly to seal Zamora's status within the MEC.[13] A few days later, after organizing the first Philippine Islands Quarterly Conference of the Malaysia Annual Conference, he and his small band of Methodists licensed Zamora as local preacher, and after much discussion agreed to ordain him, although in an unusual manner. After arrangements made by Thoburn, the South Kansas Conference, which was in session at that time, acting on Thoburn's request, voted to admit Zamora on trial, elect him to deacon's orders under "missionary rule," and to transfer him back to the Malaysia Conference. Hence, on March 10, 1900, Thoburn ordained Zamora, making him the first Filipino to be ordained into the Methodist ministry.[14]

Amidst the burgeoning work already started by Zamora among Filipinos in Manila, the first wave of MEC missionaries finally reached the country. On the evening of February 25, 1900, two weeks prior to Zamora's ordination, four missionaries from the Woman's Foreign Missionary Society (WFMS) landed on a dock in Manila, namely Julia Wisner, a missionary from Burma; Mary A. Cody, a teacher from Cleveland; Anna J. Norton, a physician from New York; and Cornelia C. Moots or "Mother Moots," a Woman's Christian Temperance Union worker from Michigan. Dr. Norton was primarily tasked with medical work but later pioneered Sunday school and Epworth League work in the city. Cody and Wisner were responsible for establishing a Methodist Girls School, and Moots was to serve as evangelist and temperance worker among American soldiers.[15] The women's arrival also signaled the coming of the first regularly appointed male missionaries and missionary couples from

---

12 Warne, *Light in the East*, 56–57; idem, "Jottings from Manila II," 3; Prautch, "Beginning," 60.

13 See Thoburn, 6 March 1900, 13 March 1900, *Diaries and Journals*.

14 See Thoburn, 6 March 1900, 13 March 1900, *Diaries and Journals*; Cornelia C. Moots, 26 February 1900, Diaries: January–July 1900, Cornelia Chillson Moots Papers, 1899–1923, United Methodist Church Archives–GCAH, Madison, New Jersey; idem, *Pioneer "Americanas" or First Methodist Missionaries in the Philippines* (Bay City, MI: Cornelia Chillson Moots, 1903), 26–28.

15 Cornelia C. Moots, 26 February 1900, *Diaries: January–July 1900*; idem, *Pioneer "Americanas,"* 12–28.

the MSMEC. The first to arrive was Thomas H. Martin on March 26, 1900, who was briefly tasked to pastor the American Church and later to pioneer MEC work in the Northern Luzon provinces of Tarlac and Pangasinan. On May 9, Jesse L. McLaughlin and his wife, Myrtle Ward, followed. McLaughlin became the first presiding elder of the newly formed Philippine Islands District, which held its first conference on August 20–24, 1900.[16] By 1901, more reinforcements came from both the MSMEC and the WFMS. Notable among them was future bishop Homer C. Stuntz, who became presiding elder, and as pastor of the Central Church (American Church) led an aggressive campaign to build a permanent home for the congregation. On December 23, 1901, the Central MEC chapel was completed on the corner of San Luis and Nozaleda Streets in Ermita, an important section in the city of Manila.

Aside from the Soldier's Institute, the Bethel Seamen's Institute in Binondo, the Chinese section of Manila, also became an important hub for MEC revival work among soldiers and sailors. Moots claimed that Filipinos, often attracted by the sound of loud singing, usually crowded outside the building during their meetings.[17] But they did not have to wait for long as the enthusiasm generated by the meetings finally spilled over to Filipinos when Prautch opened a separate service for them by late 1900. Filipinos singing with "more spirit than tune" attracted passersby; "two soldier ushers invited them in, [and] the place was always packed with thirty or more at the outside door," Prautch recalled. But the testimonies proved to be more powerful than the singing. This was the case for Honorio Feliciano, a fisherman, who "entered one evening by hearing the singing as he was passing along the street. He was interested in hearing his own people testify in his own language, and this led to his conversion."[18] Feliciano would later organize his neighbors at the fishing village of Bancusay, in the nearby suburb of Tondo, and build a

---

16 Jesse L. McLaughlin, "Philippine Islands District," *GIAL*, February 1901, 61–62; William G. Fritz, "Evangelistic Work in Manila," *GIAL*, September 1901, 426–27; Alejandro, *From Darkness to Light*, 24.

17 Moots, *Pioneer "Americanas,"* 53.

18 Arthur W. Prautch, "Methodist Mission Notes from Manila," *GIAL*, May 1901, 228–29; idem, "Reminiscences," *Philippine Christian Advocate*, 20 December 1902, 9. Hereafter designated as *PCA*.

chapel aptly named St. Peter MEC, the second MEC chapel in the country. In addition to Feliciano, Bethel eventually produced about sixteen other prominent preachers for Philippine Methodism, typically from the working class, who supplemented the work of Zamora in and around Manila. Included among them were bookkeeper Felipe Marquez, who pioneered MEC work in northern Philippines; washerman Luis Ocampo and his wife, Nicolasa, pioneer preachers in Bulacan Province; boatman Enrique Cortez and his wife, who also founded Methodist preaching points in Tondo; and druggist José Salamanca, who pioneered MEC work in Cavite Province.[19]

Expansion and Growth

The work of Zamora and the other intrepid Filipino evangelists was pivotal in the spread of Methodism throughout Manila and the nearby towns of Malabon and Navotas in the Province of Rizal. It is also important to note that this early expansion was along the coastal towns and villages around Manila Bay. There were a few Filipino nobility or *principalia* who would convert to Methodism, and most Filipino Methodists came from the lower-middle- to lower-class families. A description given by Presiding Elder Stuntz in 1901 confirms this:

> A large number of the converts are from the middle and lower classes of society. "Not many mighty, not many noble" have yet been called. But they are all sturdily independent. They want nothing but salvation. They are printers, lithographers, washermen, fishermen, clerks, merchants, teachers, and from all the grades of employment in a great city.[20]

On April 26, 1901, the MEC agreed to take the provinces north of Manila as a result of a comity agreement with other Protestant bodies to divide the islands into territories.[21] Thus, Methodist expansion followed the

19 Arthur W. Prautch, "Report of the Soldier's Institute in Manila," *GIAL*, September 1901, 427–28; idem, "Methodist Mission," 228; idem, "Reminiscences," 9; Copplestone, *Twentieth-Century*, 194–96.

20 Homer C. Stuntz, "The Missionary Outlook in the Philippines," *GIAL*, October 1901, 452.

21 Frank C. Laubach, *The People of the Philippines: Their Religious Progress and Preparation for Spiritual Leadership in the Far East* (New York: George H. Doran Co., 1925), 204–6.

Manila-Dagupan Railway, the mass transit that connected Manila and the Province of Pangasinan, a route that took twelve hours to traverse. From train stations, missionaries and their Filipino counterparts would also branch out to nearby towns and barrios that would welcome them.[22] By the end of 1901 and throughout the three years that followed, Methodist congregations had begun sprouting in the provinces of Bulacan, Pampanga, Tarlac, Pangasinan, Bataan, and Nueva Ecija. The most successful of these new churches were mostly accompanied by mass conversions, which came about through the influence of barrio (village) officials and patriarchs or matriarchs from the *principalia* class, mostly freethinkers disillusioned with the Roman Catholic establishment. Some of these freethinkers even began these congregations shortly after hearing the gospel preached in Manila and taking copies of the Bible and other evangelical literature back to their families and communities.[23] Furthermore, there were a few congregations planted from seeds sown by Presbyterian missionaries (prior to the comity agreement in 1901), independent missionaries, American soldiers, and colporteurs (Bible salesmen) of the American Bible Society who ministered to them even before MEC representatives reached them.[24]

Thus, by 1904, the MEC in the Philippines had already outpaced MEC membership rolls in Japan, Korea, Mexico, South America, and Africa, which had all been established decades earlier.[25] The 1904 General Conference also recognized this growth, and it passed an enabling act organizing the Philippine Islands District of the Malaysia Annual Conference into the Philippine Islands Mission Conference. Bishop William F. Oldham, one of the missionary

---

22 John B. Devins, *An Observer in the Philippines* (Boston: American Tract Society, 1905), 300–301; Willard A. Goodell, "From the Provinces," *PCA*, 20 December 1902, 10.

23 See Oconer, *Spirit-Filled Protestantism*, 53–54.

24 See T. Valentino Sitoy, *Several Springs, One Stream: The United Church of Christ in the Philippines, Heritage and Origins (1898–1948)*, vol. 1 (Quezon City: United Church of Christ in the Philippines, 1992), 96–98; Jay C. Goodrich, *Bible Work in the Philippine Islands* (New York: American Bible Society, 1906), 12–14; cf. ibid., 55.

25 Stuntz, *Philippines*, 453–54

bishops in the Southern Asia Central Conference, presided over its first session on March 15, 1905. With fourteen full members, eleven missionaries and three Filipinos, the conference was also divided into two districts: the Manila District, which covered Manila, Rizal, Bulacan, Pampanga, Nueva Ecija, and Bataan; and the Northern District, the predominantly Ilocano-speaking region in the country, which bordered from northern Tarlac, Pangasinan, and all the way to Ilocos Sur and Abra.[26]

As it continued its phenomenal advance, the MEC also sought to consolidate its evangelistic push through the recruitment and training of indigenous workers. Hence, on August 25, 1903, the first Manila Bible Institute, a month-long training institute, was launched. About fifty licensed male local preachers from Manila and as far as Pangasinan participated.[27] This later paved the way for other Bible Institutes in the provinces and was continued as an annual training event in the many years that followed. Clergy education was eventually institutionalized with the establishment of the Florence Nicholson Training School on October 11, 1905, at the mission house in Cervantes Street, Manila, adjacent to the First Filipino MEC. Opening with three faculty members and five students, the school would later operate cooperatively with the Presbyterian's Ellinwood Seminary in 1907, and subsequently in the years that followed, with other seminaries to form the Union Bible Seminary (now Union Theological Seminary in Dasmariñas, Cavite).[28] The training of women workers was also of paramount importance to the blossoming mission, which, therefore, led the WFMS to open the Deaconess Training School to prepare young women for evangelistic work. Recruited from various MEC congregations in Manila and the provinces, ten teenage girls matriculated during the first school year, a modest beginning for what would later become the Harris Memorial Deaconess Training School (now

---

26 Alejandro, *From Darkness to Light*, 59–60.

27 "Instituto Biblico," *PCA*, 1 September 1903, 3–4.

28 See *The Florence B Nicholson Bible Seminary of the Methodist Episcopal Mission, Manila, P.I.* (Manila: The Methodist Press, 1907), 4–5; "Training School for Methodist Preachers," *PCA*, November, 5; Alejandro, *From Darkness to Light*, 125.

Harris Memorial College, hereafter Harris).[29] Aside from Harris, the WFMS also established a similar and yet simplified version of Harris in the north, the Lingayen Bible Training School for Women in Lingayen, Pangasinan. It formally opened its doors on January 3, 1908, to students who were called to serve as "Bible women," mostly to support the expanding evangelistic work in the northern provinces.[30]

The emergence of training institutions meant to reinforce the evangelistic thrust of the denomination was not the only sign of its growth and advance, however. Methodists also actively engaged in social projects as part of their efforts to build rapport with and subsequently reach the masses with the gospel of Jesus Christ. On December 10, 1906, WFMS missionary Dr. Rebecca Parrish opened the Bethany Hospital and Dispensary, which occupied five rooms on the first floor of Harris in Sta. Cruz, Manila. The hospital was renamed the Mary Johnston Hospital when it relocated to Tondo on August 18, 1908. It also opened a School of Nursing that same year.[31] Aside from hospital work, another important aspect of Methodist missions in the country was its dormitories for high school and intermediate students. We should note that the MEC did not endeavor to provide education for the masses in the Philippines as it typically did in other fields because the American colonial government was already providing free education to the public. The first dormitory to emerge was at Lingayen, Pangasinan, in 1907, which was to serve as a "Christian home" for boys attending the provincial high school. That same year, Harris also opened its facilities to seven girls attending schools in Manila, but was later discontinued. Several dormitories were later organized mostly in major centers in the north, in the towns of Tarlac, Lingayen, Dagupan, Aparri, Tuguegarao, and Ilagan, which proved to attract more converts to Methodism. Manila would follow suit in 1912

29 Winifred Spaulding, "The Deaconess Training School," *Third Annual Session of the Woman's Conference of the Philippine Islands' District of the Methodist Episcopal Church* (1904), 64.

30 Alejandro, *From Darkness to Light*, 95.

31 Alejandro, *From Darkness to Light*, 96–97; cf. *Official Journal of the Woman's Conference of the Philippine Islands Mission of the Methodist Episcopal Church* (1907), 10–11.

with the construction of a boys' dormitory, which later became Rader Hall, on Isaac Peral Street, and a girls' dormitory on Nozaleda Street, which later transferred to Sampaloc to become the Hugh Wilson Hall.[32]

Philippine Methodism continued to grow exponentially, and consequently, nine years after the first MEC worship service held in Manila, it reached another important milestone. On March 3, 1908, after having attained the required conditions set forth in the MEC Discipline of 1904, the Philippine Islands Missions Conference unanimously voted to become the Philippine Islands Annual Conference. By this time, there were already twenty-six clergy members, eight of whom were Filipinos; sixteen probationary Filipino ministers; 536 local preachers; 120 chapels; and a constituency of 12,850 full members and 15,502 probationary members from Manila to Vigan and Aparri in the north.[33] By 1913, Filipino MEC members had already exceeded the combined membership of all the other Protestant denominations by more than ten thousand, despite being supervised by a much smaller missionary force.[34]

The Zamora Schism

While Methodism in the Philippines experienced phenomenal success in its early years, it was not immune from internal conflicts that slowed its advance. Just a year after the formation of the Philippine Islands Annual Conference, a major schism ensued and at the forefront of this disaffection was the highly esteemed Nicolas Zamora, whom we have noted earlier. This dissension, however, dates back to the founding of an indigenous missionary society in 1904 known as *Ang Kapisanan ng Katotohanan* (The Truth Society) by leaders from the Tondo Circuit, the most vibrant circuit in the Manila District. Intended as an indigenous version of the American MEC Missionary Society, the *Katotohanan* was composed of laymen who intended to carry the gospel

32 Alejandro, *From Darkness to Light*, 109–10.

33 Alejandro, *From Darkness to Light*, 87–88; *Official Journal of the First Annual Session of the Philippine Island Conference of the Methodist Episcopal Church* (1908), 85–96. All journals of the Philippine Island Annual Conference shall hereafter be designated as *PIAC*.

34 See Anne C. Kwantes, *Presbyterian Missionaries in the Philippines: Conduits of Social Change (1899–1910)* (Quezon City: New Day Publishers, 1989), 152–54.

into districts and towns where Americans could not go. Despite the society's positive implications for the mission and the accolades it received during its inception, missionaries in Manila, nevertheless, increasingly asserted control of the society's affairs in the years that followed. The group's sense of autonomy ran counter to the centralizing tendencies of the MEC mission.[35] Thus, the tenuous relationship came to a head two years later when the group threatened to bolt from the church to protest against missionary control of their work. Bishop Oldham, however, appointed Nicolas Zamora to Tondo to pacify them.[36] Though Zamora was reported to have deterred the disaffection, his appointment to Tondo had an opposite effect.

Eventually, Zamora's nationalistic sentiments and long-standing grievances against missionaries and mission policies would coalesce with the Tondo group's aspiration for ecclesiastical independence. This was further catalyzed by Zamora's sour relationship with Harry Farmer, his district superintendent, which led to a verbal confrontation in early 1909. Thus, on the morning of February 21, 1909, before a congregation of several hundred at St. Paul's Church in Tondo, Manila, Zamora bid farewell and announced from the pulpit that he was withdrawing from the MEC.[37] In a gathering with other Tondo-based local preachers and exhorters that same day, Zamora and two other ordained Filipino clergy decided to surrender their credentials and form the *Iglesia Evangelica Metodista en las Islas Filipinas* (The Evangelical Methodist Church of the Philippines, hereafter IEMELIF).[38] Almost all of the Tondo members and about a hundred more from the neighboring First

---

35 "The Growth of a Circuit," *PCA*, October 1904, 2–3. See also Ruben F. Trinidad, *A Monument to Religious Nationalism: History and Polity of the IEMELIF Church* (Quezon City, Philippines: Evangelical Methodist Church in the Philippines, 1999), 113; cf. Alejandro, *From Darkness to Light*, 44.

36 See the report of Marvin A. Rader in "Manila District," *Official Journal of the Third Annual Session of the Philippine Island Mission Conference of the Methodist Episcopal Church* (1907), 33.

37 See William F. Oldham to Adna B. Leonard, 23 February 1909, *Oldham, W.F., Missionary Files, 1846–1912*, United Methodist Church Archives—GCAH, Madison, New Jersey; cf. Richard L. Deats, "Nicolas Zamora: Religious Nationalist," in *Studies in Philippine Church History*, ed. Gerald H. Anderson (Ithaca, NY: Cornell University Press, 1969), 335; "The Defection in the Philippines," *The Christian Advocate*, 29 April 1909, 7.

38 Isaac B. Harper, "The Zamora Defection," *PCA*, March 1909, 3; cf. Richard L. Deats, "Nicolas Zamora," 335; cf. William F. Oldham to Adna B. Leonard, 23 February 1909.

Filipino Church joined them.[39] The movement initially spread among the Tag-alogs and Spanish-speaking Filipinos, but soon met success in some churches north of Manila and even among Ilocanos in Nueva Ecija. Of the estimated thirty thousand Philippine Methodists at that time, approximately fifteen hundred joined the secession.[40]

Holiness-Pentecostal Revivals and Moral Crusades

While early MEC evangelistic work in the Philippines had been highly consistent with Methodist heart religion, it was, however, engulfed by anti–Roman Catholic themes. In a country that never knew any form of Christianity except Roman Catholicism, Methodists pragmatically presented themselves more as Protestants than Wesleyans to easily distinguish themselves from Catholics, as was evident in their early publishing endeavors. As standard staples encouraged among their preachers and adherents, Protestant principles co-existed with, if not surmounted, Methodist essentials to help dictate Filipino Methodist identity. Though Methodists retained their zeal for evangelism by heavily relying on street preaching, they vigorously preached, in most instances, the Reformation message of *sola fide* to counter long-held beliefs and customs of Roman Catholics. Evangelistic passion often easily gave way to bellicose attacks against Roman Catholicism, which won more people to Methodism, especially those who were already predisposed to Protestantism prior to the arrival of Protestant missionaries.[41]

Although anti-Catholic polemics would persist among Filipino Methodists for years, Methodist missionary attitudes toward Catholicism, to some extent, improved over time.[42] Relative to this growing détente was a realization among missionaries of the need to shift from a crusade against Catholicism to a crusade against sin as missionaries lamented the perennial lack of

---

39 See Alejandro, *From Darkness to Light*, 102.

40 See Deats, "Nicolas Zamora," 336.

41 For examples of Methodist anti–Roman Catholicism, see Oconer, *Spirit-Filled Protestantism*, 70–54.

42 Kenton J. Clymer, "Methodist Missionaries and Roman Catholicism in the Philippines, 1899–1916," *Methodist History* 18, no. 3 (1980): 177.

spiritual quality among Filipino Methodists even as it continued to grow by leaps and bounds. In 1901, for instance, Stuntz complained that "the social life of the convert is beset with difficulties. Smoking is a universal habit. Women, men, and children all smoke," and one affluent convert (referring to Simeon Blas of Malabon) who even built a MEC chapel at his own expense was the owner of a local cock-fighting pit. "The remainder of the Sunday he spends at the cockpit gate taking his entrance money from the crowds that throng the places," Stuntz lamented.[43] But in the years that followed, there was an increasing concern to raise the standards of membership from that of merely enrolling converts to that of "building them up towards righteousness."[44] Such feeling ultimately reached its peak shortly after the Zamora Schism in 1909, which missionaries easily dismissed not only as misplaced jingoism but also as a lack of membership quality or true conversion among early converts. There was a strong consensus among them that they were merely producing Protestants and not Methodists.

Consequently, this shift resulted in the vigorous promotion of holiness revivalism in the fabric of Philippine Methodist life and culture by bishops and missionaries who were influenced significantly by myriad manifestations of the Holiness Movement in the United States and India. At the forefront of this move was Bishop William Fitzjames Oldham (1854–1937), who experienced his sanctification in Singapore in 1907.[45] Oldham, who was born in India to British parents, quickly set into motion a new spiritual direction at the beginning of his second term in the country. "There is a full salvation which lifts men to the highest plane of personal worth and effectiveness. . . . I trust we may reach the end of the quadrennium with increased number and a deeper tide of religious life," he sanctioned.[46] The official appeal

---

43 Homer C. Stuntz, "Missionary Outlook in the Philippines," *GIAL*, October 1901, 452.

44 *PCA*, November 1904, 2.

45 William F. Oldham, "God Keeps: A Personal Testimony of Experiences," *The Christian Advocate*, 29 November 1917, 1266.

46 "Letter from Bishop Oldham," *PCA*, October 1908, 17.

for holiness spirituality was accordingly met with support and complemented first in Manila through several revival meetings conducted by Charles William Koehler (1875–1955), who arrived at the close of 1907. A graduate of Iowa Wesleyan and a former Southern Illinois Conference evangelist (1906),[47] Koehler conducted "Pentecostal services" (or Pentecostal meetings) for the YMCA at Fort McKinley, a military base near Manila, resulting in hundreds of conversions in 1908. That year, Koehler also led Pentecostal meetings in half a dozen points in and around Manila as well as in the Bible Institute and District Conference.[48] Also known for his proficiency in Tagalog, Koehler quickly gained a reputation among his Filipino counterparts for his evangelistic skills and piety. By 1910, he reported that Filipino preachers were conducting their own Pentecostal services by "faithfully" copying his mannerisms, his movements, and the same songs sung in his meetings, albeit with little success.[49]

Oldham further reinforced his promotion of holiness spirituality by inviting Holiness evangelist Henry Clay Morrison, president of Asbury College in Wilmore, Kentucky. Morrison took Philippine Methodism by storm by conducting a series of Pentecostal meetings in all of the morning services during the Annual Conference of 1910 at the First Filipino Church (also called Knox MEC) and at the special evening meetings at the American Central Church. Morrison testified: "The altar was filled every morning with people seeking the Lord for pardon, restoration or full salvation. Missionaries and natives flocked together to the mercy seat and prayed and sobbed out their heart longings into the ear of our compassionate God and he blessed them."[50] In the aftermath of the conference, Oldham attested that Morrison's coming

---

47 See Koehler's obituary in "Charles W. Koehler," *Official Record and Minutes, One Hundred Twelfth Session of the Iowa–Des Moines Annual Conference* (1955), 138.

48 Harry L. Farmer, "Manila District,"*PIAC* (1909).

49 Charles W. Koehler, "Evangelistic Outlook in the Philippines," *PCA*, July 1910, 9.

50 Detailed accounts of these meetings are found in *PIAC* (1910), 11–21; Henry C. Morrison, *World Tour of Evangelism* (Louisville, KY: Pentecostal Publishing, Co., 1911), 203–13; idem, "Our World Tour of Evangelism Chapter 30: In the Philippines," *Pentecostal Herald*, 4 May 1910, 8; idem, "Our World Tour of Evangelism Chapter 32: Upon the Stormy Deep," *Pentecostal Herald*, 18 May 1910, 1.

has "practically fixed the holiness idea as the birthright of every man in the Methodist Church" in the Philippines.[51] Indeed, "revival meetings of the Holy Spirit type," as one missionary labeled them,[52] persisted in Manila and northward to other provinces for decades, although in varying intensities and frequencies. Morrison's visit, as Bishop Dionisio Alejandro later attested, had made the term *culto Pentecostal* ("Pentecostal meetings") the "watchword" in early Philippine Methodist life and culture; services lasted "from one week to ten days and continued until the outbreak of World War II."[53]

In the next three decades, many Filipino workers and male and female missionaries would essentially emerge as evangelists in Pentecostal meetings, making impassioned appeals to their hearers to receive the "baptism of the Holy Spirit" for spiritual empowerment and holiness. This baptism, they promised, would lead to victory against the temptations of gambling, alcohol, tobacco, and other vices.[54] These holiness- and Pentecostal-themed revival meetings, ironically, helped win some degree of respect for the denomination for publicly demonstrating Methodism's ability to reorder and discipline the lives of its adherents. Consequently, the persistent ritualizing of morality in the ubiquitous Pentecostal meetings also helped shape Philippine Methodist self-identity and behavior in the society. This fact is substantiated by annual conference reports from 1911 to 1924, which addressed the need for the church to further engage in revivals, rid its ranks of immorality, and condemn perceived public "evils" such as cockfighting and other forms of gambling, liquor saloons, tobacco use, dance halls, boxing, prostitution, and the heavily disdained *cine* (movie theaters).[55]

Consequently, Filipino Methodists in the public sphere responded to the call for a crusade against social evils. Chief among them was Justo Lukban (1863–1927), mayor of Manila from 1917 to 1920, who gained the admiration

---

51 Quoted in Morrison, *World Tour*, 213.
52 Edwin L. Housley, "Pampanga," *PIAC* (1910), 45.
53 Alejandro, *From Darkness to Light*, 106–7.
54 For details, see Oconer, *Spirit-Filled Protestantism*, 70–138, 163–65.
55 Oconer, *Spirit-Filled Protestantism*, 126–27.

of his fellow Methodists for his uncompromising, yet controversial, approach to prostitution. From October 16 to 25, 1918, he had the police round up about 170 women of "ill repute" from the city's red-light district in Gardenia Street in Sampaloc. Then, he had them hustled into two coastguard steamboats and shipped to Davao in the Island of Mindanao, supposedly with the intention of providing them employment in hemp farms.[56] Another Methodist to carry such moralizing impulse was Miguel Binag, the representative of Isabela Province in the fifth Philippine Legislature. In 1922, he introduced a bill that would abolish cockfighting in the country.[57] Congress did not pass the bill, but this did not deter Pio Valenzuela, the Methodist governor of Bulacan, who was known for his "strong aversion" to gambling, including *jueteng*, a widely popular illegal numbers game in the Philippines. During his second term he waged a campaign to rid the province of vice by ordering the police to conduct raids on gambling joints and the arrest of local *jueteng* operators.[58]

In the 1930s, Jorge Bocobo (1886–1965), the president of the state-owned University of the Philippines (hereafter UP), became the face of the Methodist moral crusade in the public square. In 1936, he added a leaf to cover the private parts of the university-commissioned The Oblation, a nude statue of a young man with outstretched arm meant to serve as the symbol of the university.[59] Whereas Bocobo was seen as a strict moralist, his crusade was far from simplistic. His morality was very much connected to his robust sense of justice and human rights. He was a well-known nationalist who advocated for the country's independence from the United States.[60] Additionally, he was one of the few Filipinos who did not turn a blind eye to distressing developments in Europe. On November 19, 1938, more than a week after

56 Marvin A. Rader, "Editorial," *Philippine Observer*, January 1919, 2; Laubach, *People of the Philippines*, 408–9; *Zacarias Villavicencio et al. v. Justo Lukban et al.*, G. R. No. L-14639 (Republic of the Philippines Supreme Court 1919).

57 Perry N. Cedarholm, "The Cagayan District," *PIAC* (1920), 47; "Minutes," *PIAC* (1922), 26, 30.

58 Joshua F. Cottingham, "Central District," *PIAC* (1924), 43; Isabelo T. Crisostomo, *Dr. Pio Valenzuela: Misunderstood Patriot* (Quezon City, Philippines: J. Kriz Publications, 2001), 238–39.

59 Balares and Co, "Oblation: The Truth Behind the Leaves," *Oble*, 2 March 2011, para. 4.

60 Apilado, *Revolutionary Spirituality*, 228–30.

the *Kristallnacht* (Crystal Night) when Nazi mobs destroyed synagogues and looted Jewish-owned businesses in Germany, Bocobo was the main speaker at an indignation rally at the Ateneo de Manila campus in Intramuros. His efforts, as well as that of other individuals, served as an impetus for President Manuel Quezon to allow the settlement of twelve hundred German Jews in the Philippines in the months that followed, at a time when many countries, including the United States, refused them.[61] In 1947 he led the commission that produced the New Civil Code of the Philippines, which included among its features the "liberalization of women's rights" and the "implementation of social justice."[62] Philippine Congress enacted it and President Elpidio Quirino signed it into law through Republic Act No. 386 on June 18, 1949.[63] Bocobo continued with his moral campaign for years and, for his many efforts, was honored with The Moral Leader of the Decade Award during the Citizens for Moral Crusade Conference in 1961.[64]

The Stagg Schism

The public reputation of prominent Filipino MEC laypersons helped reinforce not only non-Methodists' perception of their religion but also Filipino Methodists' expectation of themselves. The high moral standard perpetuated by this public image was soon to backfire against them through another major upheaval, the Stagg Schism. While nationalist impulses were the primary *raison d'être* for the Zamora schism, for the Stagg Schism, however, it was mainly a moral issue. In 1928 Melecio de Armas, minister for sixteen years in the Manila District, was accused of immorality. Initial investigation exonerated de Armas, but was revived by the Manila District two years later upon pressure by Samuel W. Stagg, the young and popular pastor of Central MEC. The

---

61 From an interview with Racelle Rosenblatt Weiman, director of the Dialogue Institute at Temple University. See Wilson Lee Flores, "How President Quezon and Two Cigar Makers Saved 200 Jews," *The Philippine Star*, January 6, 2013.

62 Juan F. Rivera, *Father of the First Brown Race Civil Code* (Quezon City, Philippines: University of the Philippines Law Center, 1978), 91.

63 Rivera, *First Brown Civil Code*, 1–2, 81–82.

64 Rivera, *First Brown Civil Code*, xxiv.

church, by this time, had become the Central Student Church, an upscale congregation, which catered to Filipino students, a nascent American-educated Filipino intelligentsia, including well-known government dignitaries. The ensuing investigation and controversies would pit Stagg against the senior missionaries. Stagg later dismissed the investigation as a "travesty" and proceeded to carry the fight in the court of MEC public opinion.

Stagg presented evidence and vilified "corrupt" missionaries and their Filipino allies through a series of mimeographed open letters but not without irritating others and raising doubts as to his intentions.[65] Nonetheless, Stagg's mimeographed assaults did pay off. The case was elevated to the Annual Conference session of 1932, which finally found de Armas guilty of adultery and expelled him from the ministry. However, when de Armas's camp appealed the decision before the General Conference, its appellate court overturned the decision based on a technicality.[66] In the ensuing fallout following the reversal, Stagg positioned himself as a champion of morality, working to "clean up" the mission as he unleashed vitriol against his senior colleagues.[67] While Stagg's attempts resulted in the recall of one senior missionary, his strategy backfired—the missionary board also recalled him. Notwithstanding, Stagg, with the support of his loyal members at Central, defied the order. He further widened his range of attacks against his bishop, Bishop Edwin Lee, and the missionary board secretaries in New York. He managed to remain in the country until the Annual Conference and take a prominent role in the events that were to unfold.[68]

65　The sequence of events surrounding the de Armas case is summarized in Romeo L. Del Rosario, "The Schism in the Methodist Episcopal Church in the Philippines in 1933" (PhD diss., Boston University, 1982), 387–426. Among a number of documents from Stagg detailing the case, see, for example, Samuel W. Stagg to the Board of Foreign Missions, 2 February 1933, Stagg, Samuel Wells (Rev. & Mrs.), 1922–1933, Folder 5, Missionary Files (Microfilm Edition), United Methodist Archives Center—GCAH, Madison, New Jersey.

66　See Del Rosario, "Schism," 405–16.

67　See Samuel W. Stagg to Ernest E. Tuck, 16 September 1932, "To the President and Secretary of the Annual Conference," TDS; Stagg Samuel Wells (Rev. & Mrs.), 1922–1933, Folder 5, Missionary Files (Microfilm Edition), United Methodist Archives Center—GCAH, Madison, New Jersey.

68　See Samuel W. Stagg to John R. Edwards, 5 January 1933; Samuel W. Stagg to the Board of Foreign Missions, 2 February 1933. For details, see Del Rosario, "Schism," 426–51.

The full ramifications of the General Conference decision did not become apparent until the first day of the Conference session on March 22, 1933, in San Nicolas, Pangasinan, when de Armas's name was restored to its rolls by order of visiting Bishop Herbert Welch, who presided in the absence of Lee. Subsequent motions and appeals made by Stagg and Cipriano Navarro, a well-respected Filipino clergy from Pangasinan and one of Stagg's associates, produced little results that day. By the fourth day, after hearing closing arguments on the matter, the die was cast when the bishop reiterated his incapacity to ignore the General Conference's decision. This led Navarro to announce his withdrawal and move "that we here and now declare ourselves independent from the American General Conference." Navarro and Stagg left, along with forty-three other ministers (from a total of 106 present), seventeen deaconesses and Bible women, four WFMS missionaries, and a number of laypersons.[69] This was the beginning of what would later become the "Philippine Methodist Church." The biggest fallout was at Central, where a significant number of the congregants, under the leadership of Stagg and Navarro, left to form what would later become the "Cosmopolitan Church."[70]

Shortly after the conference where de Armas filed his resignation, one of the seceders rejoined the MEC. "Really, I don't know of any more reason now to split the Church, because the original cause, namely, the moral issue, is already settled," he reasoned.[71] Not all followed suit, nevertheless, since de Armas's withdrawal did little to appease other deep-seated issues that had nothing to do with the moral issue, such as antagonism between seceding and loyalist missionaries, resentment of seceding nationals toward certain missionaries, infighting among nationals, and varied attitudes about autonomy, among others.[72] A year later, only nineteen clergy remained with the

69 "Daily Proceedings," *PIAC* (1933), 10–28; Cf. Del Rosario, "Schism," 460–74.

70 Del Rosario, "Schism," 475–85.

71 Eusebio Manuel, "Why I Stay in the Mother Church," *Philippine Observer*, June 1933, 5.

72 The "background causes" are summarized in Del Rosario, "Schism," 640–50.

"New Movement," while the rest returned to the MEC. It was also estimated that the MEC lost more than sixteen hundred members to the schism.[73] In May 1948, the seceding denomination joined the Presbyterians, Congregationalists, United Brethren, Disciples, and other small Protestant groups to form the United Church of Christ in the Philippines.[74]

The Philippines Central Conference

As the de Armas controversy weighed heavily upon the Methodist Church in the Philippines, membership records tell a different story. Despite losing sixteen hundred members in 1933, the denomination gained over twenty thousand new members during the same period (1928–34).[75] It was in the midst of this rapid growth that the General Conference of 1932 authorized the division of the Philippine Islands Annual Conference into two separate conferences. Hence, on February 16, 1936, almost four years later, the Philippine Islands Annual Conference worshipped for the last time as one body at the Central Student Church in Manila after five days of conferencing under the leadership of Bishop Lee.[76] The next morning the newly named Philippine Annual Conference and Philippine North Annual Conference convened separately in the same church to conduct their respective organizations. The former comprised the Manila-Bulacan, Pampanga-South Tarlac, Bataan-Zambales, and Nueva Ecija-Tarlac districts. The latter, on the other hand, comprised the Cagayan-North Isabela, Ilocos Sur, Nueva Vizcaya-South Isabela, and Pangasinan districts.[77]

Among the actions taken during the united session was a memorial requesting the General Conference to establish a central conference in the

---

73 Del Rosario, "Schism," 510–13.

74 Floyd T. Cunningham, "Diversities within Post-War Philippine Protestantism," *The Mediator* 5, no. 1 (2003): 68. For an extensive account on the beginnings of the United Church of Christ in the Philippines, see Sitoy, *Several Springs*, 485–502.

75 See Bienvenido A. Bibay, "Membership and Statistical Records of the Methodist Church in the Philippines, 1913–1963" (BD thesis, Union Theological Seminary, Manila, 1965), 144.

76 "Daily Proceedings," *PIAC* (1936), 13–29.

77 "Daily Proceedings," *PIAC* (1936), 20–21, 29–44.

Philippines, separate from the Southeastern Asia Central Conference, as a step toward further indigenization. This was also in line with the recent establishment of the Philippine Commonwealth more than a year before when it was signed into law by US president Franklin D. Roosevelt as a path toward the full independence of the Philippines after a ten-year transition period. The conference memorial argued: "In view of the setting up of the Philippine Commonwealth and the attendant interest aroused thereby, the authorization for a Central Conference for the Philippines alone will be of real psychological value." This memorial was also followed by a request for the said central conference to elect its own bishop "during the ensuing quadrennium."[78] Hence, on May 18, upon the recommendation of the Committee on Episcopacy, the General Conference meeting in Columbus, Ohio, passed two enabling acts that allowed for the creation of the Philippines Central Conference and the election of its own bishop but with the proviso that there will be no more than one bishop during the quadrennium.[79]

While the way had been paved for the establishment of a Filipino central conference, it took almost four years before this became a reality. From February 29 to March 2, 1940, the first session of the Philippines Central Conference convened at Central Student Church, just ten months after the Uniting Conference of 1939 that created the new Methodist Church. With thirty-four lay and clergy delegates, Bishop Lee, now resident area bishop, presided over the inaugural session. At this point, the Methodist Church in the Philippines had a total of 324 churches, 94,774 full and preparatory members, and 89 clergy full members.[80] As for the election of its own bishop, the absence of a central conference session during the four years immediately following the 1936 General Conference naturally prevented them from electing one. Hence the Philippines and Philippines North conferences, meeting

---

78 "Daily Proceedings," *PIAC* (1936), 24–25.

79 *Journal of the Thirty-Second Delegated General Conference of the Methodist Episcopal Church* (1936), 410–11.

80 Alejandro, *From Darkness to Light*, 173–74.

separately, issued a similar memorial asking the 1940 General Conference to renew its previous enabling act by allowing them to elect a bishop for the 1940–44 quadrennium, which they argued was a fitting precursor to the full independence of the Philippines in 1946. However, out of respect for Bishop Lee, they also coupled this with a seemingly conflicting memorial to retain the highly esteemed bishop for the same quadrennium, "until such a time" as the Philippines Central Conference elects its own bishop.[81] The Philippine delegates to the 1940 General Conference in Atlantic City later clarified this in a joint statement by reiterating the request to retain Bishop Lee but also with the understanding "that they shall have the right to elect a Central Conference Bishop at the close of the quadrennium just before the next General Conference."[82]

Electing a Filipino Bishop

As the General Conference that met on May 1940 voted to adopt the two memorials,[83] the Filipinos kept to their desire to retain Bishop Lee for the new quadrennium. Ten months later, on March 5–6, 1941, a second session of the Philippines Central Conference, now with forty-three lay and clergy delegates, did not exercise its right to elect its own bishop.[84] They could have never guessed the unintended consequences in the months that followed. On December 8, 1941, eight months after the central conference session, the Japanese Imperial forces began their campaign to occupy the Philippines. Five months later, after the protracted battles of Bataan and Corregidor, American and Philippine defense forces finally surrendered to the Japanese. Within the next three years, the "Religious Section" of the Japanese Imperial Army pressured Filipino Methodists to fully disentangle themselves from the American Church as they increasingly herded most of the remaining American

---

81 *Journal of the Philippine Annual Conference of the Methodist Church* (1940), 57–58, 65.

82 *Journal of the First General Conference of the Methodist Church* (1940), 394–95.

83 *Journal of the First General Conference of the Methodist Church* (1940), 555.

84 *Journal of the First General Conference of the Methodist Church* (1940), 176–77, 189–90.

missionaries in the country into prison camps. The Religious Section was a corps of Japanese Roman Catholic priests and Protestant ministers, including Methodists, tasked to "discredit American missionaries, unite the churches, and Filipinize them."[85] It eventually succeeded in persuading a number of prominent Filipino church leaders from other Protestant denominations to form the Federation of Evangelical Churches in the Philippines on October 10, 1942, in which the Methodists reluctantly participated. The Federation dissolved six months later and out of it came the Evangelical Church in the Philippines. The Methodist Church did not join this union.[86]

The Methodists were relentlessly pressured by the Religious Section and the leaders of the Evangelical Church to elect their own bishop and join the united church, but their leaders kept making excuses despite the risks involved.[87] Juan Nabong, a prominent lawyer who was acting chair of the central conference executive committee, explained, "No Methodist would follow what was not in their Discipline."[88] But when efforts to pressure them intensified in mid-1943, this eventually led him and the executive committee to convene an adjourned meeting of the second Philippine Central Conference at Central Student Church on January 21–22 at the Knox Memorial Methodist Church in Manila with Dionisio D. Alejandro presiding.[89] In his report on behalf of the executive committee, Nabong convinced the delegates to move from "technicality" or "hesitation" and proceed with the election of a bishop by arguing on the basis of 1936 and 1940 enabling acts of the General Conference.[90] Thus, after a recommendation from the Committee on Election, the delegates proceeded with the election. After the fourth balloting, they unanimously elected Alejandro, thereby making him the first Filipino to

---

85 Alejandro, *From Darkness to Light*, 182–86.

86 Sitoy, *Several Springs*, 440–49.

87 See Alejandro, *From Darkness to Light*, 188–96.

88 Juan C. Nabong Jr., *Gird Life with the Truth: A Filipino Father's Life's Episodes* (Victoria, BC, Canada: Trafford Publishing, 2008), 18.

89 Alejandro, *From Darkness to Light*, 191–94; Nabong, *Gird Life*, 17–18.

90 Nabong, *Gird Life*, 18.

be elected to the episcopacy of the Methodist Church. A "service of induction and dedication" conducted by a body of elders for the new bishop was held the day after the conference at Central Methodist Church in Manila. There was no laying on of hands, though, because there was no Methodist bishop present. As for the question on church union, the delegates approved the recommendation of the Committee on Church Union that argued that the central conference has "no authority" over the matter because the two annual conferences were the only bodies authorized to decide on the matter. This was in essence a repudiation of the appeals made on the floor by the leaders of the Evangelical Church and the head of the Religious Section. In the months that followed, none of the two annual conferences that met separately voted toward union despite the presence of Japanese observers in their midst.[91]

Japan's intrusion into Methodist life, however, quickly dissipated after the decisive American victory at the Battle of Leyte, which opened the way for a series of campaigns that finally routed the Japanese. Overall, the war left scores of Methodist Church sanctuaries around the country in ruins and hundreds of Methodist Church members and workers dead.[92] A comparison of the statistics from the two annual conferences in 1941, the last conference sessions before the war, and 1947, when membership statistics became available again, shows that the Methodist Church may have lost more than eleven thousand members during the war due to death or dislocation. Consequently, with "liberation" also came the difficult task of rebuilding through the help of returning and newly arrived missionaries and American Methodist chaplains and military personnel. Chaplains and soldiers not only helped rebuild Methodist churches and chapels in Manila and in the provinces but were also involved in extensive evangelistic work that won many new converts to the Methodist Church.[93]

---

91 Alejandro, *From Darkness to Light*, 192–200.

92 For a summary, see Alejandro, *From Darkness to Light*, 200–206.

93 Alejandro, *From Darkness to Light*, 206–7, 213–15.

On March 22–23, 1946, the Philippines Central Conference gathered for its third session at the Harris Memorial School chapel in Sampaloc, Manila, with Bishops Alejandro and Lee presiding. Since Bishop Alejandro had not been consecrated in 1944, the conference unanimously voted to affirm his election. At five o'clock in the afternoon of the first day, Bishop Lee consecrated Alejandro with the assistance of eight district superintendents. The next morning, the conference gathered again for another episcopal election since the bishop's term was only effective up to the 1946 Conference. On the second ballot, Alejandro gained the needed two-thirds vote to elect him. Requesting the newly reelected bishop to join him in front, Bishop Lee announced that Alejandro would "now assume full responsibility as Bishop of the Philippines Central Conference." Lee's gesture, according to Alejandro years later, in effect signaled "the transfer of episcopal supervision from the hands of American bishops to those of Filipino bishops." It also seemed analogous to America's forthcoming granting of full independence to the Philippines three and a half months later. While the transfer of episcopal power does not quite measure up to independence, it still marked an increased degree of autonomy for the Methodist Church in the Philippines. Forty-seven years after Bishop Thoburn's worship service in Manila in March 5, 1899, Filipino Methodists were now at a greater liberty to chart their own course.

Fast-forward seventy-two years later, United Methodism in the Philippines continues to maintain the same dynamics that was begun in 1748 in terms of its relationship with the US church. The Philippines Central Conference now has a total number of twenty-six annual conferences, three episcopal areas, more than 220,000 professing members, and almost 2,000 ordained clergy.[94] It has also elected a total of eighteen Filipino bishops since Bishop Alejandro's election to the episcopacy in 1944.[95]

---

94   Membership and clergy data is based on statistical reports from 2016. See "2020 General Conference Delegate Distribution by Annual Conference Now Available," UMC.org, accessed February 27, 2018, http://www.umc.org/news-and-media/2020-general-conference-delegate-distribution-by-annual-conference-now-avai.

95   See The Book of Discipline of The United Methodist Church (Nashville: The United Methodist Publishing House, 2016), 4–9.

A Brief History
of Korean Methodism

An Autonomous Methodist Church

Chan-Hie Kim

Modernization of Korea, 1866–1883

Korea has been known as the hermit kingdom for many centuries. It has been invaded frequently by neighboring countries like China, Mongolia, and Japan and plundered by Japanese pirates. Things changed, however, in the second half of the nineteenth century. Along with China and Japan, Korea could no longer survive without opening up to the world, particularly to the Western powers that had been advancing toward the last bastion for trade in the Far East after colonizing most of Southeast Asia. Western influence happened to China first after the opium war (1842), and then to Japan after the collapse of the Tokugawa shogunate (1868), and finally to Korea after the downfall of Daewongun's regency (1873). France and Great Britain were striving to move north after colonizing Southeast Asia. Russia had ambitions to exert political influence on the Far East. The United States was trying to become a major power in the venue of the Pacific Ocean. Newly westernized and industrialized Japan was eager to expand its territory and colonize Korea. They were all pressing hard on Korea.

In the second half of the nineteenth century, Korea was the precious prey of powerful neighbors. Alarmed by the Japanese advancement to the Korean peninsula and learning of the US desire to have a commercial and diplomatic treaty with Korea through Japan, Li Hongzhang, the well-known politician and diplomat of the Qing dynasty, made an arrangement with US Admiral Robert Wilson Shufeldt stationed in China to pursue a treaty between the United States and Korea mediated by China. By doing this, he tried to maintain Chinese influence on the Korean peninsula. On May 22, 1882, a treaty called the "Treaty of Amity and Commerce Between the United States of America and Corea" was signed, and then enacted on June 4, 1883.[1] Unlike other Asian countries, it was the United States that had prompted Korea to open the door widely to the Western world. Consequently, American influence on Korean life has been definitive and absolute, even today, in many areas of culture, economy, and politics. With this treaty, Korea became the last Asian nation to open its door to the West.

After the treaty was proclaimed, the US government appointed Gen. Lucius H. Foote as the "Envoy Extraordinary and Minister Plenipotentiary to Corea" on March 7, 1883. He arrived in Seoul on May 13, 1883, and opened the legation. Robert Samuel Maclay (1824–1907), a veteran missionary to Asia, confesses about the treaty as follows: "The negotiation by Admiral Shufeldt of this treaty with Korea was a trumpet call to immediate efforts for the evangelization of the Korean nation which Protestant Churches, and in particular the Methodist Episcopal Church, could not suffer to pass unheeded."[2] Surely he could not miss this great opportunity and visited Korea in the summer of 1884 to explore the possibility of a Methodist mission there.

Beginnings of Korean Methodism, 1883–1885

Soon after the treaty, King Kojong dispatched a team of eight envoys headed by Min Young-ik. This was a courtesy visit. The envoys sailed for San Francisco

---

1 A more comprehensive and detailed description of the event can be found in my article, "Robert Samuel Maclay (1824–1907): The Pioneer of the American Protestant Mission in Korea," in *Methodist History* 39, no. 3 (April 2001): 167–80.

2 Robert S. Maclay, "A Fortnight in Seoul, Korea, in 1884," *Gospel in All Lands* 22 (August 1896): 357.

and arrived there on September 2, 1883. From San Francisco, they traveled by train toward Washington to make a call on President Arthur. During this journey a very historic event in the history of the Korean Protestant mission took place. Dr. John Franklin Goucher (1845–1922), an ardent supporter of foreign missions and a member of the Missionary Society of the Methodist Episcopal Church, happened to be on the same train. He was very interested in these foreign guests and invited them to visit his home in Baltimore after their tour in Washington. About two months after encountering these dignitaries from Korea, he made a request to the General Missionary Committee of the Methodist Episcopal Church to "aid in commencing missionary work in Korea."[3] He mentions this in his letter to Robert Maclay, dated January 31, 1884, saying, "Under date of November 6, 1883, I wrote to the Missionary Committee that if they deem it expedient to extend their work to the Hermit nation, and establish a mission in Korea under the superintendence of the Japan mission . . . I shall be pleased to send my check for, say, two thousand dollars toward securing that result."[4]

About a week after receiving Goucher's letter, the General Missionary Committee voted that "$5,000 be appropriated to the Japan Mission for the purpose of opening Mission Work in Corea of which $2,000 is a special donation by Rev. J. F. Goucher."[5] In the fall of 1884, after Maclay returned to Tokyo from his trip to Seoul, Goucher offered an additional $3,000 "to be used in purchasing a suitable site for our mission operations in Seoul."[6] With this financial support, Maclay was able to make arrangements for the Korea mission and purchased land in the Chung-dong area of Seoul, the birthplace of modern Korea.

---

3 November 1883, Appenzeller correspondence quoted by Everett N. Hunt Jr., *Protestant Pioneers in Korea*, American Society of Missiology Series, no. 1 (Maryknoll: Orbis Books, 1980), 11.

4 Robert S. Maclay, "Korea's Permit to Christianity," *The Missionary Review of the World* 9 (n.s.), no. 4 (April 1896): 287f.

5 "Minutes, General Missionary Committee," vol. C: 33, quoted by Wade Crawford Barclay, *History of Methodist Missions* (Board of Missions of the Methodist Church: 1949), 742.

6 "Minutes, General Missionary Committee," vol. C: 33, quoted by Wade Crawford Barclay, *History of Methodist Missions*, 742; see also L. George Paik, *The History of Protestant Missions in Korea 1832–1910* (Pyongyang: Union Christian College Press, 1927; reprint, A Series of Reprints of Western Books on Korea, no. 6, Seoul: Yonsei University Press, 1971), 82.

Robert Maclay always kept an eye on the Korean peninsula, waiting for an opportunity to open a Methodist mission there. The letter from Goucher made him realize the decisive moment had come.[7] He left Japan for Seoul, accompanied by his wife, on June 8, 1884, and entered Seoul on June 24. About a week later on June 30, he met Kim Ok-kyun with whom he got acquainted while in Japan and handed over to him the petition he had written in Japanese to be presented to the king. Kim Ok-kyun was on the king's court as a secretary at the time. He was very aware of what Christianity had brought to Japan as it accelerated its modernization program. Since the petition contained the request to grant permission for "medical and educational work" in Korea, he was very supportive of the request.

After waiting a few days for the king's decision, Maclay visited Kim on July 3. He reported about the historic opening of the Korean mission as follows:

> He [Kim Ok-kyun] received me very cordially, and at once proceeded to inform me that the king had carefully examined my letter the night before, and in accordance with my request had decided to authorize our society to commence hospital and school work in Korea. "The details," continued Mr. Kim, "have not been settled, but you may proceed at once to initiate the work." The king's favorable response to our appeal was so prompt and complete, that I could not fail to recognize it as from the Lord, and after tendering to Mr. Kim hearty thanks for his good offices in our behalf, I took my leave, repeating to myself, as I rode through the crowded streets of the city, "The king's heart is in the hand of the Lord, as the rivers of water. He turneth it whithersoever He will."[8]

The date July 2, 1884, is a historic date not only for Korean Methodism but for all Protestant missions in Korea. Maclay relates the event honoring Goucher's contribution as follows: "The opportune proposal of Rev. John F. Goucher, D.D. of Baltimore, to give liberal aid in founding the Korea Mission, was cordially accepted by the missionary authorities of our Church. My visit

---

7 Maclay writes in "Korea's Permit," 288.
8 Maclay, "Korea's Permit," 289.

to Seoul was the result of this proposal; and thus it became my high privilege to lay the first foundation for a Christian mission in Korea."[9]

Soon after receiving permission from the king, the Methodist mission board was actively engaged in recruiting missionaries to send to Korea. The first residential missionaries the Methodist Episcopal Church found and appointed to the mission were Rev. William Benton Scranton, MD (1856–1920)[10] and his wife, Luisa Wyeth Arms; Mrs. Mary Fitch Scranton (1832–1909),[11] the mother of Dr. Scranton; and newly married Rev. Henry Gerhard Appenzeller (1858–1902)[12] and his wife, Ella J. Dodge.

Bishop Fowler's letter to Maclay dated February 23, 1885, and sent from San Francisco indicates the formal organization of the Korea Mission as follows: "We desire you to act as superintendent of Korea and Brother H. G. Appenzeller as assistant superintendent under your direction. Dr. Scranton will act as treasurer of Korea Mission."[13] While the party was temporarily staying in Japan, the Korea Mission was thus organized. These five persons became the trailblazers of Korean Methodism. Their accomplishments were remarkable in laying down a firm foundation for the future Korean Methodist Church.

From Missions to the Autonomous Church, 1885–1930

As the church promised the king, the missionaries devoted themselves to doing mainly *educational* and *medical* work. Dr. Scranton joined and helped Dr. Horace N. Allen, the first Presbyterian medical missionary, and the elder Mrs. Scranton and Rev. Appenzeller initiated educational work. Although the Korean government was prohibiting propagation of foreign religions at the

---

9 Maclay, "A Fortnight," 357f.

10 He was appointed in October and was ordained deacon and elder on December 4, 1884.

11 Unlike Dr. Scranton and Rev. Appenzeller she was sent by the Woman's Foreign Missionary Society of the MEC.

12 He was appointed to be a missionary on December 20, 1884, while on his honeymoon and was ordained by Bishop Charles Henry Fowler as an elder in San Francisco on February 2, 1885, just a day before his departure for Korea.

13 Robert S. Maclay, "Commencement of the Korea Methodist Episcopal Mission," *Gospel in All Lands* 22 (November 1896): 502.

risk of capital punishment, it tacitly allowed the evangelizing activities of the missionaries because of the benefits Christianity was bringing to the nation and its people. Traditionally, Korea had been a Buddhist country, but since the Yi Dynasty (1392–1897) Confucianism had become the national religion.[14]

Medical Work

Dr. Scranton's own ministry began in his home on September 10, 1885,[15] after assisting Dr. Allen for about two months in Seoul. The following year, after renovating a Korean house, he opened a "hospital," where his main focus was on the poorest and neediest people. In order to get closer to them, he opened dispensaries outside the West Gate in Aogae (Aheon), at the East Gate, and near the South Gate in Sangdong, where the well-known Methodist churches were founded and still exist today.[16] Due to a significant increase in demand for more doctors, the MEC sent Drs. Meta Howard, Rosetta Sherwood, and William McGill to help the Methodist medical work. In subsequent years many more doctors were sent by the Mission Board and Woman's Missionary Society of the MEC.

Educational Work

Long before organizing local churches, the missionaries were gathering young people in their private homes to teach them English and other subjects. Rev. Appenzeller started his educational enterprise with two students on August 3, 1885. But the school for boys called Paichai Hakdang had officially started on June 8, 1886.[17] This was the first Western-style school and the beginning of the secondary education system in Korea.

After securing a suitable property, Mrs. Mary F. Scranton started recruiting and teaching girls. Her first student was a concubine of a high-ranking

---

14 Actually, the dynasty lasted until 2010 when Japan had completely colonized Korea. In 1897 Korea declared that it was an empire, installing the king as emperor. There were virtually no changes in the government; only the name of the nation was changed from "Korea" to "Korean Empire."

15 *68th Annual Report of the Missionary Society of the MEC for the Year 1886* (January 1887), 268.

16 Those churches are Aheon Methodist Church and Sangdong Methodist Church, respectively.

17 *68th Annual Report of the Missionary Society of the MEC for the Year 1886* (January 1887), 267.

official who wanted her to learn English so that she could become the interpreter for the queen.[18] This was also the beginning of the first modern secondary education system for girls in Korea. The school was given the name Ewha Hakdang later by the king. It officially opened on May 31, 1886. In 1910, the woman's missionary society opened a woman's college called Ewha College for Women. This was the first college established for women in Korea. The college, which is now known as Ewha Women's University, has developed into the largest women's university in the world today.

Evangelistic Work

The missionaries' educational ministry incorporated some evangelistic elements into their teachings. The elder Mrs. Scranton in her report in 1886 witnessed:

> He [a student] knows now, and I tell him all I can about God and the Bible, and what it can do for a nation or an individual. Were he a bolder man he would become a student of the Bible. Now he reads when he thinks he is not observed. It is dangerous for this people to have anything to do with a "new religion," and we must be slow in condemning them if they hesitate to put their lives in jeopardy.[19]

During the first few years of the mission, they accomplished their goal, which was the "evangelization of the people" through medical as well as educational institutions.

Planting Churches

The interdenominational worship gathering of the missionaries was the first Christian religious activity carried out on Korean soil. It was held on June 21, 1885, at the home of Dr. Allen. Beginning the following Sunday, June 28, they met at the American consulate. They had the first Protestant communion service in Korea on October 11, 1885. This gathering was later developed

---

18   Mary F. Scranton, "Woman's Work in Korea," in *The Korean Repository* 3, no. 1 (January 1896): 3.

19   Mary F. Scranton, *Woman's Foreign Missionary Society 17th Report* (1886), 47.

into the Seoul Union Church. Strictly speaking, this was not a Korean native church even though a few Koreans were attending the service. On July 24, 1887, Appenzeller baptized a Paichai student by the name of Park Joong Sang, who became the first Korean Methodist ever baptized on Korean soil.[20] The first native church called Bethel Chapel—the predecessor of the present-day Chungdong First Methodist Church—was born on October 9, 1887. Appenzeller reports about it as follows: "In September we purchased a small house (bethel) a chapel, if you please, for that is the use to which we are putting it. To it seekers are invited, and on Sundays religious services are held there. October 9 I held the first public service for Koreans. Four were present besides myself, and the meeting was one of peculiar interest to us all."[21] Within two years, the missionaries had made great progress in converting people as he reports: "In Seoul and in the country I baptized 27, and received on probation, 29; and into full membership, 2; . . . Present number of members, 9; probationer, 36; . . . local preachers licensed, 2."[22] The progress they made is amazing, for they had already organized the first quarterly conference—charge conference—within five years of their arrival in Korea:

> At a regular meeting (monthly) of the Mission in December we organized the first Quarterly Conference ever organized in Korea. This we did according to the recommendation of Bishop Andrews. We have now one church, or, as we call it, circuit regularly and formally organized, and can now transact all our business according to the law of the Church. It is less than five years since your first missionaries left their homes for Korea.[23]

Publishing Enterprise

Because of the philanthropic medical and educational activities of the missionaries, they received favorable support from the government that was very interested in modernizing Korea. Appenzeller opened Tri-Lingual Press in

---

20 The first Korean Methodist was Tchi Ho Yun, who was baptized by MEC, South in Shanghai, China, in April of the same year. See note 24 below.

21 *69th Annual Report of the Missionary Society of the MEC for the Year 1887* (January 1888), 314.

22 *71st Annual Report of the Missionary Society of the MEC for the Year 1889* (January 1890), 292.

23 *71st Annual Report of the Missionary Society of the MEC for the Year 1889* (January 1890), 292f.

1890 at Paichai for propagation and distribution of Christian literature in three different languages: Korean, English, and Chinese. The first Korean language Christian newspaper, *Korean Christian Advocate*, was published, and the journals of *Korean Repository* (1892–1898) and *Korea Review* (1901–1906) were also published in English. Beginning in 1900, they published a biblical and church monthly magazine for Korean readers called *Sin-Hak Wol-Po*, edited by George Heber Jones. Beginning in the early twentieth century, Korean Methodists themselves started publishing various kinds of Christian journals, books, and tracts.

Laying the Foundation for Democracy

Seo Jae-pil (*aka* Philip Jaisohn, 1864–1951), a medical doctor trained in America, returned home in December 1895 and started teaching the democratic decision-making process to Paichai students by instructing them how to debate in deliberative assemblies and small meetings. Later, in the early 1900s, Tchi Ho Yun was also involved in promoting Robert's Rules of Order for the church as well as for the general public by publishing its summary in 1908. Both of them taught Western democratic principles for the first time in Korean history. These are just a few examples of the way Korean Methodism exerted influence on the cultural as well as social transformation of Korea. The church was instrumental in the modernization process of Korea as it was slowly evolving from an old traditional society and culture to a modern one.

Bible Translation

The first interdenominational work the missionaries engaged in was the Bible translation project. Under the leadership of Horace G. Underwood and Henry G. Appenzeller, a Permanent Bible Committee was organized in early 1887, and with the help of Korean scholars they started translating the whole Bible into Korean. As soon as any single book of the Bible was completely translated, they were sold and distributed through the colporteurs who were not only salespersons but evangelists at the same time. The Bible translation project was a joint project sponsored by the Scottish, British, and American Bible societies. The official translation of the New Testament was completed in 1906. The Old Testament section was completed in 1911 and was published together with the New Testament in the same year. Its revised edition is now widely used by Korean Protestant churches today along with the New Korean Standard Version published in 1993, which has also been revised several times.

The contribution of the Bible translation to Korean Christianity and Korean culture is enormous. First, it helped Koreans understand better the invaluable cultural treasure they had in their 571-year-old script called Hangul, which is not a pictographic script like Chinese and Japanese characters but an alphabet. Traditionally, learned Koreans used to employ Chinese characters in their literary work and communications denigrating the Hangul script. But the new Korean Bible, written in the vernacular with the Hangul alphabet, showed its beauty, convenience, and value as never before realized. The advancement of Hangul is appreciated even more in this computer age. Second, the mass of people could easily get in touch with the Christian message. This is one of the reasons for the rapid growth of Korean Protestant churches.

Leadership Training and Theological Education

As the membership of the church was increasing, the demand for native pastoral leadership was also growing. Like the early settlers in America, the missionaries were envisioning a higher learning institution in the form of a theological department or school. They started training pastoral leadership in 1893 at Paichai Hakdang with twelve students. They met two or three times a week every afternoon to study Bible, preaching, soteriology, and other pastoral subjects. In August 1893 the annual Missionary Conference officially adopted a four-year course of study for training local preachers. Along with the course for local preachers, they also designed courses for exhorters and class leaders. But as early as 1901 the conference for the first time ordained Chan-shik Kim and Kibum Kim as deacons, i.e., provisional elders. They were the first native Korean clergy. The majority of early preachers emphasized the uniqueness of Christianity and its superiority over traditional native spiritual-ity and indigenized religions like Buddhism and Confucianism.

Establishment of an undergraduate-level theological school was first sug-gested at the 1907 joint meeting of the MEC and MEC, South. It became operational in 1910 and produced its first graduates in 1911. The school is now known as the Methodist Theological University and still stands at its original location in Seoul. Currently there are two other Methodist theologi-cal schools in Korea, the Hyupsung University and Mokwon University theo-logical colleges and graduate schools.

Opening of the Mission of the Methodist Episcopal Church, South

About ten years after the northern Methodist Church opened a mission in Korea, the Methodist Episcopal Church, South, initiated its mission in 1895, and opened it officially in 1896. The person who was instrumental in help-ing the Foreign Mission Board of the MEC, South (MECS) was Tchi Ho Yun (1865–1945), who was educated at Vanderbilt and Emory Universities.[24] Mr. Yun and President Candler made a request to the mission board of the MECS to have Bishop Eugene R. Hendrix visit Korea along with Dr. C. F. Reid (1849–1915), missionary in China, to explore the possibility of opening a mission. They came to Korea in October 1895. When it was decided to open a mission, they were able to purchase a property with the help of Mr. Yun. The follow-ing year on August 14, 1896, accompanied by his family, Dr. Reid moved to Korea as the presiding elder of the Korea District of the China Mission Con-ference. The district became an independent Korea Mission of the MECS in 1897. In October 1897 the Woman's Foreign Missionary Society also joined the mission and sent Mrs. Josephine P. Campbell to Seoul from China. Since many other American denominational churches were well established in key areas of Korea, the MECS had to initiate their work in Songdo and Wonsan, which were areas away from the major cities.

---

24 While in exile in Shanghai he was converted and baptized into the MEC, South, on Palm Sunday, April 3, 1887, thus becoming the first Korean Methodist.

Expansion of the Missions

The evangelistic efforts of the missionaries of both the northern and southern Methodist Churches were so successful that in 1905—only twenty years after the opening of the mission in Korea—the northern MEC upgraded the Korea Mission to the Korea Missionary Conference. Within three years, it was organized into a full Korea Annual Conference. Such rapid growth of Korean Methodism was due to many factors. First, as mentioned above, the Korean alphabet Hangul made it easy for people to be readily exposed to Christian literature, including the Bible. Second, in the midst of political turmoil caused by surrounding foreign powers competing to swallow up helpless Korea, people saw hope in the Christian message for the future of their nation. The liberation from Babylonian exile was one of the favorite biblical themes at the time. Third, newly enlightened people were attracted by Western culture and advanced learning that came with Christianity. Whatever the reason may have been, by 1910 Methodism was deeply rooted in Korean soil, and a sizable number of Koreans found their faith in Christianity.

Loss of Independence in 1910

It was Japan among the neighboring countries that finally won the battle for Korea. Japan took away diplomatic autonomy from Korea in 1905, and in 1910 it had completely annexed and colonized the nation. The powerless people of this poor land were like the Judeans of the Babylonian period. The only hope that Christians without a country had was the coming kingdom of God. Consequently, apocalypticism became the main theological trend during this period. Church leaders, both lay and clergy, firmly believed in the goodness and justice of God, and they fearlessly proclaimed the message that someday God would take away the shackles of Japanese colonial power and restore the nation.

Since Christian churches had strongly resisted the colonization, Japan started persecuting Christians immediately after it annexed Korea. Beginning in 1911, they arrested and tortured seven hundred or more Christians, and finally, in 1912 imprisoned 105 key leaders, the majority of whom were Christians, including prominent Methodist leaders. They fabricated the charge that these leaders attempted to assassinate the governor-general of Korea, a Japanese army general. Their main target was influential Methodist leaders. This incident is now well known in Korea as the "105 Person Incident."

However, the real nationwide independence movement took place in the spring of 1919. The nonviolent demonstrations known as the March First Independence Movement started on March 1, 1919. Here again the key leaders were religious leaders, including many Methodists. The demonstrations should be registered in world history as the first nonviolent resistance movement for independence and liberation involving millions of people and lasting several months. The movement was triggered by the ruthless draconian military rule of Japan. Even though the movement had failed, the burning fire of yearning for liberation from Japanese domination was never quenched in the subsequent years.

The Church until the End of World War II, 1930–1945

The most notable bastion of the independence movement was the Sangdong Methodist Church. Its Epworth Club was a gathering of young people burning with patriotism. It was an enduring beacon of the movement. The membership of the club included not only political activists, but prominent scholars and social reformers as well. Some of the members were imprisoned for many years. Because of anti-Japanese activities the Korean Methodist Church and other denominational churches were constantly harassed and persecuted by the Japanese authority until the end of colonial rule on August 15, 1945.

Becoming an Autonomous Methodist Church in 1930

Within forty-five years after Methodism was introduced to Korea, the Korean Missionary Conferences became one autonomous Methodist Church on December 2, 1930. This came to fruition through the joint efforts of both the northern and southern Methodist Episcopal Churches. It is to be noted that the event took place nine years before the joining of the two American Methodist Episcopal Churches in 1939.

In June 1926, the Korea Conferences of the two Methodist denominations each adopted the resolution that Korean Methodism should become a single unified Methodist Church. An equal number of five from each denomination formed a study committee on the autonomous Korean Methodist Church. Reverend Joo Sam Ryang, the first general superintendent of the Korean Methodist Church, summarizes the subsequent event as follows:

> In 1927, realizing the need of closer fellowship and a united front in the operation of work, a joint petition to their respective General Conferences had been framed, asking for authority to unite the two Annual Conferences into an autonomous Methodist Church of Korea. In 1928 the General Conference of the Methodist Episcopal Church, in 1930, the General Conference of the Methodist Episcopal Church, South, approved the plan and each appointed five commissioners to carry out the plan together with the ten commissioners who were to be appointed by the two Annual Conferences in Korea.
>
> So from Nov. 18th to 29th 1930, the twenty members of the Joint Commission together with the eleven coopted members met in the Union Methodist Woman's Bible Training School in Seoul and prepared a Proclamation, suggested some necessary legislations and called the First General Conference on December 2, 1930. This General Conference which was composed of one hundred members met in the Union Methodist Theological Seminary, Seoul, until the evening of December 12th and adopted a constitution and the Discipline for the Church, which has been named "Ki Dok Kyo Choseun Kamni Hoi," or the Korean Methodist Church.[25]

They elected Rev. Joo Sam Ryang not as a lifetime bishop but as "general superintendent" for a term of four years, renewable only once. The episcopacy was introduced only in the late 1940s, and this tradition of term limits continues in Korean Methodism.

---

25 J. S. Ryang, "Historical Sketch of the Church," *Hand Book of the Korean Methodist Church for 1931–1932* (Seoul: General Board of Korean Methodist Church, 1932), 2f. (English section).

Theological Orientation

"A Statement of Faith" adopted by the new autonomous church at its General Conference is now contained in the *Hymnal* of The United Methodist Church (884). As reflected in the creed, the church was and is evangelical in the Wesleyan tradition but progressive at the same time. It endeavored to make the Christian gospel continually relevant to the ever-changing society and culture. However, the reality of everyday Christian lives was not quite consistent with the expression in this statement until the latter part of the twentieth century. In the early days it was much closer to fundamentalism in its classic definition. As Spencer Palmer has rightly noted, "Under the impetus of a program directed by American missionaries of 'Puritanic zeal and Wesleyan fervor,' fundamentalism held sway in the peninsula."[26] Strict observance of the Sabbath and abstaining from dancing, smoking, gambling, and drinking were strongly urged by the church. These behaviors were condemned as grievous sins. Although Korean Methodism is nowadays less strict in observing these rules, the evangelical fervor with a strong Biblicist current is still retained and has been the prevailing theological climate to this day. Yearning for the apocalyptic second coming of Christ, indifference to political and social issues, and the sincere desire for entering into the kingdom of God—the paradise after death—were popular beliefs among ordinary Christians in those days up until the early 1980s. Of course, we can still find such theological beliefs among many Christians today, but it is not the major nor dominant theological tenet. It must be emphasized that along with these popular Christian beliefs a more sophisticated theological understanding of the Christian faith as expressed in the Statement could be found among the learned pastors and theologians of this period.

Statistics on the Status of the Church

In June 1931, statistics were reported to the joint conference as follows: a total of 55,448 adherents; 239 men and 68 women full-time ministers—ordained

---

26 Spencer J. Palmer, *Korea and Christianity*, Royal Asiatic Society Korea Branch Monograph Series, no. 2 (Seoul: Hollym Corporation, Publishers, 1967), 26.

clergy, local preachers, Bible women, etc.; 722 churches and 169 prayer places; 3 annual conferences with 23 districts.[27] The church also had a Manchuria Mission Conference for the Koreans residing in the region with two districts and 4,898 adherents. It is remarkable that the church had grown this much within a period of forty-five years, given Korea's history.

Before and During World War II

In 1937 Japan invaded and occupied Manchuria, a region in the northern part of China. It was a prelude to the attack on Pearl Harbor. All Koreans were coerced to attend Shinto shrines and offer prayers there. But the Christians strongly resisted it. Those who refused to attend were constantly harassed. In 1938 Korean language was prohibited in all schools. In 1939 Koreans were ordered to change their names by adopting Japanese names. Particularly during World War II, the oppression of the church was severe. Sunday worship services were constantly under surveillance by Japanese police. Many of the local churches were forced to sell their properties including sanctuaries and lands in order to support the war against the United States. As Japanese militarism intensified, so did the oppression against Koreans. All churches were pressured to use Japanese in their worship services. Unfortunately, there were a few church leaders who collaborated with Japanese authorities during the war, even encouraging young Korean men to join the Japanese army. This would become an issue in the church after the war.

In the early 1940s, the Japanese government forced all Korean Protestant churches to be united under an umbrella called the United Church of Christ in Korea—similar to what was done in Japan—in order to oversee and control the churches more easily. While under the same organizational structure, the Methodists learned about the ministry of "ruling elders," who were laypeople in the Presbyterian Church, and adopted it as an office of the ministry of Methodism. It has now become institutionalized as a hierarchical

---

27 J. S. Ryang, "Historical Sketch of the Church," 33.

structure of the highest ranking for laypeople, together with the "exhorters" and "stewards" in the Korean Methodist Church today.

Aftermath of World War II and the Korean War, 1945–1970

The liberation from Japanese colonization was joyfully celebrated, and the church thanked God for the promise and subsequent liberation, not unlike the promise to the Jews during the Babylonian exile. But in the first few years after the end of the war, the church was in turmoil because of those who had collaborated with the Japanese during the war. The church was divided into two factions. The collaborators insisted that they had no choice but to cooperate with the Japanese authorities to protect the church. But the pastors who were expelled from the church and even imprisoned did not accept their arguments. However, because of the outbreak of the Korean War the issue did not surface again.

The Korean War

The joy of liberation and independence was short lived. Korea was divided in half along the thirty-eighth parallel of latitude immediately after the war. This nation, which had been one country and one ethnic group and had spoken the same language for more than a thousand years, was divided by foreign powers—the United States and the Soviet Union—on August 15, 1945, and each side established its own government in 1948. On June 25, 1950, instigated by Stalin and Mao, North Korea invaded South Korea. The war had devastating effects on the whole country, destroying families, industries, infrastructures, and forests. It also caused millions of families to be separated. Human casualties were enormous: many Methodist ministers, including the first general superintendent Rev. Ryang, were kidnapped and murdered; more than five million lives—about 10 percent of the total population—were lost or wounded. During the war, a couple of million people, many Christians among them, escaped the North and fled to the South. Christians and their churches were purged and completely wiped out in North Korea. Not a single visible church exists in the North today. Pyongyang, the capital of North

Korea once known as the Jerusalem of Asia, has now become the citadel of the Communist dictatorial regime.

The armistice was signed on July 27, 1953, after the three tragic years of war, but no peace treaty has ever been signed. Thus, Korea is still technically at war. It is a fragile peace on the Korean peninsula, which has been constantly threatened over the last seven decades. It is the only country in the world today that remains divided as a result of war.

Reconstruction

The war made Korea one of the poorest countries in the world without any hope for recovery from the extreme poverty and devastation. The leaders of the church had to focus their efforts and ministry on refugee relief and foreign aid. They appealed to world Christian relief organizations, particularly the United States, and millions of dollars' worth of goods poured into Korea to help the suffering people. But the country was in turmoil, and the government was not able to function properly. Such a situation and political chaos called for strong leadership that led to a military coup d'état headed by Gen. Park Chung Hee on May 16, 1961. Gen. Park, who became the president soon after the coup, was a benevolent dictator—an oxymoron. During his eighteen years of rule, he laid the foundation for economic recovery and growth unlike anything Korea previously experienced in its history, and such prosperity continues today. Even though Koreans lost the political freedom they had yearned for since the turn of the century, in exchange, they earned economic freedom from grinding poverty.

Oppression and Human Rights Issues

As expected, human rights were oppressed and grievously violated under Gen. Park's regime. The public media was under the control of the government. Those who opposed dictatorship were thrown into prison. Here, the churches became the key leaders of the resistance. One notable theology we find at this period was the birth of a Korean liberation theology. Being influenced by Latin American liberation theology, the so-called Minjung theology developed. This theology insists that Minjung—the grassroots mass of the people—should be the driving agent for the nation and not any social or political group, including the military. But the theology did not get much attention from the church at large.

In this period under Gen. Park's control, church membership also grew. People found consolation in the church, realizing that the church was the bulwark of the nation's democracy and individual freedom. Many people took refuge during the difficult times of oppressive military rule. The rapid growth of church membership reached its zenith in the 1970s through the 1990s.

Ordination of Clergy Women

The newly established autonomous church declared in 1931 that "the Korean Methodist Church has abolished all the discriminating features between sexes, so any woman who meets the requirements may be licensed to preach, ordained as a minister, and received into an Annual Conference as any man."[28] Even so, it was not until 1955, a quarter century later, that the church for the first time in its history finally ordained two unmarried women, Milla Jeon and Whayong Myung, and gave them conference membership at the same time. It is interesting to note that the first woman admitted to provisional membership in any annual conference in the Methodist Church was Dr. Maud Kiester Jensen, a long-time missionary to Korea, alongside her husband. It was possible because the 1956 General Conference of the Methodist Church had finally granted full ministerial rights and conference membership to women. Korean Methodism was at least a year ahead of the mother church in admitting clergywomen to annual conference membership.

Foreign Missions

Even though the church had limited financial resources, it did not lose the vision for foreign missions. Already in the mid-1960s, the Korean Methodist

---

28   J. S. Ryang, "How Two Methodisms Unite," *The Missionary Voice* 21, no. 10 (October 1931): 14.

Church was involved in sending missionaries to Bolivia and Pakistan. The first official denominational mission work was initiated by the Chungdong Church, who sent a missionary family to Sarawak, Malaysia, in 1965. The opening of a foreign mission was planned in 1964 as an eightieth-anniversary project of the Korean Methodist Church. Since then, the Korean Methodist Church has dispatched thousands of missionaries all over the world. No other country except the United States has sent so many foreign missionaries as Korea has to date. The majority of these missionaries are sponsored and supported by local churches rather than denominational organizations.

The Church under Economic Prosperity since 1970

Along with the unexpected upheaval of the economic and political climate, the Korean Methodist Church had shifted its message to ride on the changing culture of Korea beginning with the early 1970s. In this period, South Korea had gradually evolved from a country of abject poverty to an industrialized nation. In a few decades, the nation accomplished both the introduction of representative democracy and an economic miracle. Korea ended its unfortunate time of a government controlled by military leaders. In 1960, the per capita Gross Domestic Product (GDP) of South Korea was around eighty dollars—about one thousand dollars in today's value. By 2017, GDP had grown to almost thirty thousand dollars and, in terms of its purchasing power parity, it is worth about thirty-nine thousand dollars. Among nations with a population over fifty million and per capita GDP over thirty thousand dollars, South Korea ranks sixth in the world today. This figure alone indicates that South Korea has now become an affluent industrialized nation that the world has never seen before. But this changing phenomenon made people indifferent to religion. The people became full of confidence and very optimistic about the future of Korea, despite the constant threats from North Korea.

In this rapidly transformed country, the message from the pulpits has also shifted from the otherworldly message of "believe in God and go to heaven" to the "this-worldly" message of "believe in God and get rich here on earth." It is regrettable that the church seems to be more interested in preserving the status quo and in amassing more wealth. Like a large corporate business enterprise, the Korean Methodist Church is more interested in investing in buildings and expanding operational budgets. In some senses, the secular world and the development of Korean society have corrupted the church. Indeed, at the turn of the twenty-first century, the Korean Methodist Church membership began to decline because the church had lost its prophetic voice and potency. The church is no longer a bulwark of democracy and advocate of underprivileged people.

In particular, the authoritarianism of clergy leaders is rampant. Since the collapse of the connectional system that was replaced by the congregational-type system in the Korean Methodist Church, the real power of appointment-making has moved from the bishops to the congregations. Bishops still read the appointments at the annual conferences, but it is no more than a rubber-stamping ritual. Thus, it has become a common practice of some large local church pastors to pass on the churches they had been serving to their sons after retirement. Such a practice is possible only because current pastors exert absolute influence and authority on the congregations they serve. This is a serious problem the Korean Methodist Church is now facing.

At present, Methodists make up about 2.8 percent of the total population of South Korea and about 10 percent of the total Christian (Catholics and Protestants) population. There are 6,344 local churches and 10,833 ministers of various kinds as of 2016.[29] According to the Pew Research Center, 29.4 percent of Koreans are Christians and 46.4 percent of Koreans do not have any religious affiliation or connection.[30] These are the people the church must reach. They should be the major target of the evangelistic mission of the church in the future. If the church can regain momentum in this direction, it is quite possible that it can revive the faith community through inviting the

---

29 According to the 2016 statistical report of the Korean Methodist Church, the total number of the Methodists are 1,375,319. Cf. https://kmc.or.kr/about-kmc/states-of-church.

30 Pew Research Center, "The Global Religious Landscape, January 2012 Chapter," 49.

unaffiliated to the church. The Korean Methodist Church is a praying church. Many of the church members get up early in the morning and go to church to pray. This practice is a unique phenomenon found in Korean churches. It is the source of a dynamic force that can move the church forward again to build the Kingdom of God on Korean soil and across the world.

EUROPE
AND EURASIA

Methodism
in Continental Europe

Anglo-American Mission Approaches
and Connectional Developments[1]

Ulrike Schuler

I t is challenging to focus on Christianity in Europe, especially Methodism, because the continent is enormously diverse. Although it is the world's second-smallest continent[2] with a population density of about 700 million in a relatively small area, Europe includes forty-eight nations, twenty-three official languages, more than a hundred spoken languages, and innumerable dialects. The geographic area called "Europe" has changed over the centuries and is not clearly defined. To the north and west, Europe is bordered by the Arctic and North Atlantic Oceans, and to the south the Mediterranean Sea. To the east there is no clear natural division from the continental mass of Asia, though the Ural Mountains are often cited.

Over the past two centuries, national boundaries within Europe have often changed because of war or political circumstances. Even the names of

---

1   This essay is based on my much broader chapter, "Methodism in Northern and Continental Europe," in *T & T Clark Companion to Methodism*, ed. Charles Yrigoyen (London: Continuum, 2010), 166–87.

2   Strictly speaking, Europe is only a subcontinent of Eurasia. Because of its special historical and cultural background, it is common to speak about Europe as a continent.

several nations have been altered. An example in the recent past is the fall of the Soviet Union in 1991. The following true story told in a radio interview by an old farmer can illustrate the situation: "I was born as a subject of the Austrian emperor and Hungarian king, went to school in Czechoslovakia that I finished in Slovakia. I was a farmer in Hungary and served in the Red Army Faction of the Soviet Union. Today I am retired in the Ukraine. Beside my military service, I have never left my home village."[3]

Whole books could be written about specific European countries, each with specific historical, social, political, economic, and religious developments. Currently, "Europe" is considered the coalescence of those states that identify themselves in the historical and cultural traditions rooted in Greece and Rome. Europe occupies a prominent place in the Western world since it is usually considered the birthplace of Western culture. Its influence has extended to other continents through colonialism, the slave trade, Christian missions, and other forces that we are questioning critically today.

Europe has also played an important role in the history of the Christian church—its organization, theology, and doctrine. The three basic traditions of Christianity—Roman Catholic, Eastern Orthodox, and Protestant (Lutheran and Reformed)—were born and developed in the geographic and cultural boundaries of Europe. The strong awareness that, in God's world order, the coherence of a commonwealth can only be thought and guaranteed in its religious unity led to the social model of the *"Corpus Christianum,"* which was adamantly defended for centuries. This forced a long tradition of interplay of church and state fighting for dominance in the West while in the Eastern Orthodox hemisphere a hierarchical form of government, the *"Caesaropapism,"* with a clear understanding of the church's subsidiary role, was instituted.

---

3 The former bishop of The United Methodist Church in Eurasia, Dr. Rüdiger Minor, told this story. The Karpatho Ukraine is a historical area in the very west of the Ukraine with the boundary to Rumania, Hungary, Slovakia, and Poland. It belonged to the "k.u.k. (imperial and royal) monarchy" (Austria/Hungary) up to the end of World War I. In 1920 it became part of Czechoslovakia. In 1938 the German Reich and Italy decided to give it to Hungary. In 1939 it was occupied by the Germans, given to Slovakia, then totally to Hungary up to 1944; in 1944–45 back to Czechoslovakia; from June 1945 on to the Soviet Union; then in 1946 to the Ukraine Soviet Republic. Since 1992 the Ukraine has been independent, but as of 2014 parts of the country (Crimea and East-Ukraine) are again places of ongoing dispute with Russia.

Those established relationships were significant when—following the Enlightenment—the demands for a separation of church and state increasingly took shape in European countries and also when Methodists became connected and began mission work. The call for the abolition of established churches as well as freedom of faith, conscience, and creed led in the nineteenth and twentieth centuries to a variety of constitutional systems in European countries. For example, France and Portugal have a complete separation of state and church (laicism). Germany, Italy, and Spain have a kind of partnership or cooperation in public affairs with a system of agreements with churches (a concordat with the Roman Catholic Church or with Protestant churches). A "unity system" where the head of state is also the head of the church, exists in Norway, Denmark, and England (up to the year 2000 that was also the case with Sweden). Separation of church and state has also led to the suppression of religious practice. The strongest of that type was realized in Albania, where from 1968 to 1990 state atheism was in effect.

Europe not only was the scene of major Christian expansion but also witnessed some of history's most brutal religious persecutions. These include the medieval Inquisition, Protestant campaigns against the Anabaptists during the Reformation era, and for centuries, anti-Semitism of the pogroms, and Christian complicity in the Holocaust. All these resonate in Europeans' thinking and acting.

A number of developments were especially important for the unfolding of Christianity in more recent centuries. Among the most significant were the Enlightenment, the Industrial Revolution, two world wars followed by the Cold War (and Iron Curtain), the fall of the Soviet empire, and the creation of the European Union. Each of them left its mark on the Christian faith and European churches including Methodism. An important development for the churches is the influence of the confessional "mixture"[4] that arose mainly

---

4   Because of the legal rule of the Peace of Augsburg (1555), *"cuius region, eius religio"* ("whose region, whose religion"), through the centuries the areas were largely homogeneous according to the confession of the inhabitants.

after World War II and forced the churches to become more knowledgeable about each other and gave rise to a growing ecumenicity.

When the Soviet Union collapsed, a number of middle and eastern European countries became independent.[5] From the 1990s on, all of them became members of the European Union,[6] a cooperative of sovereign nations committed to freedom, security, participatory democracy, justice, and solidarity. Europe is now in the early stages of growing together and recognizing that its religious identity is defined by three lines of tradition: Greco-Roman antiquity, the Jewish-Christian tradition with a Latin and Orthodox imprint, and the Enlightenment. With all these different aspects[7] as the context, we turn to the Methodist missions that brought Christianity in a transformed form back to the "cradle of the Reformation"—trying to support renewal and reform and dedicated to continuing the reformation that Pietism advocated.

Methodist Missions to European Countries[8]

The beginning of Methodism's influence on old, traditional Europe extends from the late eighteenth century to the middle of the nineteenth century.

---

5 Soviet Union (1922–1991), a federal state made up of fifteen republics (sixteen between 1946 and 1956): Armenia, Azerbaijan, *Belarus*, *Estonia*, Georgia, Kazakhstan, Kyrgyzstan, *Latvia*, *Lithuania*, *Moldova*, *Russia*, Tajikistan, Turkmenistan, *Ukraine*, Uzbekistan (italicized states are European states); other communist governments in Europe existed after World War I or II up to the 1990s: the Czech Republic (1918–1992), Poland (1945–1989), Yugoslavia (1945–1963, later independent from the Soviet Union–socialistic), Hungary (1949–1989), Bulgaria (1944–1989), Rumania (1947–1989), Albania (1948–1992); under communist influence, from 1952 with socialist governments: East Germany/German Democratic Republic (1949–1990).

6 The European Union was originally founded in 1951 by six Western European countries basically to advance collective economic interests. It emerged with enlarged political interests (e.g., establishment of a European parliament in 1979) and more member states (today twenty-eight states without Switzerland, which declared neutrality since 1647, Macedonia, Kosovo, Albania, Montenegro, Bosnia and Herzegovina, Turkey). In 2012 the EU was awarded the Nobel Peace Prize "for over six decades [of having] contributed to the advancement of peace and reconciliation, democracy and human rights in Europe."

7 The aspects listed are very striking only to make clear the specific situation that reflects mission circumstances. The particular local situation is much more complicated—a combination of different factors—social, political, economic, and cultural.

8 The explanation below depends largely on Patrick Ph. Streiff, *Der Methodismus in Europa im 19. und 20. Jahrhundert* (Stuttgart, Medienwerk der Evangelisch-methodistischen Kirche, 2003 [EmKG.M 50]) [in English: Patrick Ph. Streiff, *Methodism in Europe: 19th and 20th Century* (Tallinn, Estonia, 2003)]. Based on secondary literature, conference minutes, and mission board reports he produced a remarkable survey of European Methodist history. His overview requires more detailed research on various regions and raises many important questions. In addition, lectures of European Methodist Historical Conferences with topics focusing on European Methodism are published in monographs by the "Studiengemeinschaft für Geschichte der Evangelisch-methodistischen Kirche" as: Michel Weyer (Hg.), *Der kontinentaleuropäische*

During that period Methodist missions must be recognized in light of renewal movements that influenced different parts of Europe as a late extension of Pietism, followed by revivalism, the Holiness Movement, and Pentecostalism. All these movements primarily affected Western Europe. Eastern Europe had no similar cultural conditions that launched drastic changes in churches.

Methodism in Europe began with people sharing stories of faith with one another. Migrants, sailors, soldiers, travelers, and others who had been touched by Methodist people on their journeys outside of Continental Europe, primarily to Great Britain and the United States, and who had been transformed by the Methodist message eagerly talked about the gospel message that revolutionized their lives. As others were drawn by this faith-sharing, small informal Methodist gatherings were sometimes formed. The official beginning of a mission among those interested by a Methodist mission board or conference followed much later, sometimes several decades later. Often the local people supported small Methodist gatherings until denominational officials offered formal support and supervised further organization.

Methodist missions to Continental Europe were linked to migration. People immigrated to Great Britain and the United States for a variety of reasons. They came into contact with Methodists in those countries, were converted, and reported this back home (or in some cases actually took their newly found faith back to their native lands). Recognizing the potential of church growth among European immigrants, Methodists in the United States organized foreign-language annual conferences. These annual conferences were an important factor in the spread of Methodism in Europe by initiating missions, providing financial support, and nurturing personal contacts with family

---

Methodismus zwischen den beiden Weltkriegen (Stuttgart: BGEmK 36, 1990); Michel Weyer, *Heiligungsbewegung und Methodismus im deutschen Sprachraum. Einführung in ein Kapitel methodistischer Frömmigkeitsgeschichte und kleine Chronik einer Bewegung des 19. Jahrhunderts* (Stuttgart: Anker Buch & Medien, 1991) [BGEmK 40]; Patrick Ph. Streiff (Hg.), *Der europäische Methodismus um die Wende vom 19. zum 20. Jahrhundert. Referat der historischen Konferenz der EmK in Europa vom 10. bis 15. August 2004 in Tallinn, Estland. Stuttgart 2005* [EmKG.M 52]; Ulrike Schuler, *Methodismus in Europa nach dem Zweiten Weltkrieg (1945–1964)* (Frankfurt am Main: Evangelisch-methodistische Kirch—Referat fr effentlichkeitsarbeit, 2018). The last-named conference papers were also published in *Methodist History: Methodism in Europe after World War II (1945–1964)*, Methodist History 1, nos. 1 and 2 (October 2012 and January 2013).

and friends "back home." For decades there developed communication between European Methodists in Britain and the United States and those in their
home countries through European-language books, periodicals, letters, and
personal contacts. At first, the main concern of Methodist missions was to
support the renewal of the established Protestant state churches in Europe.[9]

Where the Orthodox Church was strong in Europe, the situation was very
different. In Bulgaria, for example, the Ottoman Sultan officially sanctioned an
autonomous Bulgarian Orthodox Church in 1849. He also invited other confessions for work.[10] While Methodism's first expressed mission effort (1857)
was to enliven the Orthodox Church, the (Islamic) government's motivation
was much more to destabilize the Orthodox Church as well as to provide for
Christian plurality.[11] That situation provoked strong Orthodox resistance that
precluded the idea of cooperation with other churches. In areas where Orthodox churches were strong, it was difficult to extend the Methodist mission
and to establish their brand of Protestantism as "genuine Christianity." Also,
the social-cultural situation made it difficult for male missionaries to connect
with women who were mainly responsible for Christian education.[12]

Different still were missions to countries where Roman Catholicism was
dominant. In those countries Methodism encountered strong and aggressive
opposition in its attempt to break the Catholic stronghold[13] and to bring the

---

9   For example, France, where the Wesleyan Methodists cooperated with the minority Reformed Church around
    Nimes or Paris, or in French-speaking Switzerland. It was also the case in Germany, Norway, Sweden, and
    Finland with the Lutheran Church and in German-speaking Switzerland with the Reformed Church.

10 That was also true in Macedonia where a Congregational mission (The American Board of Commission-
    ers for Foreign Missions) had been founded and in 1921 was ceded to the MEC (in that year Macedonia
    became part of Yugoslavia).

11 That is how Streiff interprets this advance. See Streiff, *Der Methodismus in Europa*, 58.

12 Research about the role of women in Methodist missions in a Roman Catholic and Eastern Orthodox con-
    texts: Paul W. Chilcote and Ulrike Schuler, "Methodist Bible Women in Bulgaria and Italy," in *Methodist
    History* 55, nos. 1 and 2 (October 2016 and January 2017): 108–27; Paul W. Chilcote and Ulrike Schuler,
    "Methodist Women Missionaries in Bulgaria and Italy," in *Methodist History* 55, no. 3 (April 2017): 180–
    95. Paul W. Chilcote and Ulrike Schuler, ed., *Women Pioneers in Continental European Methodism, 1869–
    1939*, Routledge Methodist Studies Series (New York: Routledge, 2018).

13 Including Portugal, Spain, Austria-Hungary, France, and Italy. After the 1848 Italian Revolution, with the
    formation of the national Italian Union and the annexation of the Vatican State (1861), buoyant con-
    sideration was given to entering for the purpose of converting liberal Roman Catholic priests (which
    really happened) and introducing Methodism. A growing and lay piety developed in Roman Catholicism

Reformation to completion. Numerically the greatest success of Methodist mission occurred in the German-speaking countries and Scandinavia.[14] Yet, Methodist congregations were organized all over Europe. Typically, the organizational strategy included forming classes and Sunday schools, translating and publishing a Methodist hymnbook and Discipline, and establishing a periodical.[15] Later, in some places a publishing house[16] was founded, a training center for circuit preachers instituted,[17] and deaconess "mother houses" created.[18] Nursing care facilities, hospitals, children's schools, and other social institutions followed.[19]

The Methodist objective was to spread social holiness across the continent, and as part of this mandate, Methodist missions deliberately supported the very poor in rural and urban areas with educational and other social service ministries. Those missions were extremely expensive. The need for

---

because of the pressure in some states (e.g., the "Kulturkampf," a struggle between the Catholic Church and the Prussian state, 1872–1887, similarly in Switzerland, and in Austria where the power struggle succeeded more moderately). The results of Vatican Council I, the founding of Roman Catholic political parties, and growing Ultramontanism were viewed very skeptically by Protestants and raised fear of Roman Catholic imperialism. At the beginning of the twentieth century a very aggressive "Los-von-Rom-Bewegung" [exempt-from-Rome-movement] began. It was rooted in Austria and carried by Protestants and Old-Catholics to other countries.

14 For this reason, this article mainly focuses on these areas with short notes about the other European countries where detailed historical research is needed.

15 Here are some examples with no claim to be complete: Bulgaria, 1864 *Zornitza* (MEC); Italy, 1870 *Il Corriere Evangelico* (WM); Denmark, 1873 *Missionstidende* (MEC); Sweden, 1868 *Lilla Sändebudet* (MEC); Germany, 1850 *Der Evangelist* (MEC), 1863 *Der Evangelische Botschafter* (EA), 1873–1889 *Methodisten-Herold*, 1890–1897 *der Sonntagsgast* (WM), *Die Geschäftige Martha/ Der Deutsche Telescope/ Der Froehliche Botschafter*, 1883 *Der Heilsbote* (UBC); France, 1853 *Les Archives du Méthodisme*, later *L'Evangéliste* (WM); Norway, *Kristelig Tidende* (MEC).

16 E.g., Germany, 1850 Bremen (MEC), 1871 Nürtingen (EA); Norway, 1867 (MEC); Sweden, ca. 1874 (MEC); Switzerland, 1895 (EA); and Norway, 1867 Oslo (MEC).

17 E.g., Germany, 1858 Bremen (MEC), 1864 Waiblingen (WM), 1877 Reutlingen (EA), 1952 Bad Klosterlausnitz/GDR (EA/MC); Switzerland (French-speaking area), 1850s Lausanne (MEC with the Free Reformed Church), Sweden, 1874 Orebro, Stockholm, Uppsala (MEC); Denmark/Norway, 1874 Oslo (MEC); Finland, 1897 Tampere, Helsinki (MEC); Göteburg for all Scandinavian countries, 1924 (MEC); Italy, 1893 Rome (MEC); France, 1889 Paris (WM); Baltic States, 1994 Tallinn, Estonia; Russia, 1991–1995 Moscow; Austria, 1986 Graz, Waiern; Belgium, 1950 Protestant Theological Faculty Brussels (MC and two other Protestant denominations; Czechoslovakia, 1950 "Comenius Faculty Prague" (MC and other Protestant denominations; Poland, 1983 (UMC).

18 Centers were founded in Germany and spread out to other countries: Germany, 1874 Bethanien-Verein Frankfurt a.M. (MEC), 1886 Bethesdaverein für allgemeine Krankenpflege zu Elberfeld (EA), 1889 Martha-Maria-Verein Nürnberg (WM); Norway, 1897 Sosternhjemmet Bethanien (MEC); Sweden, 1900 Diakonissenschwesternschaft (MEC); Denmark, 1895 Bethanienverein (MEC).

19 For example, there were different types of schools for girls (later for boys) in Italy, Spain, Portugal, Hungary, Yugoslavia, Macedonia, Bulgaria, and a residential school in Albania.

financial support of these missions existed for decades, often up to the present.

The policy of British Methodists was to delay the initiation of more mission projects than they were able to support financially. Their mission philosophy also included departing from a mission field as soon as it could become fully autonomous, which was often possible with the cooperation of other denominations. Sometimes the mission work was handed over to the mission of the Methodist Episcopal Church if there were growing congregations in their context. Financial support of its European missions facilitated by Methodists in the United States was generally significant not only from congregational giving, but sometimes through the large generous gifts of individuals. It was not rare, however, for mission projects to be abruptly abandoned because of financial exigency. Such situations caused deep disappointment to those who were involved in these ministries and those who benefitted from them. They cultivated a sense of abandonment.

Organizationally, United States Methodism created an international connectional structure by integrating mission fields while giving them increasing administrative and financial accountability. Typically, a "mission conference" was formed. If the work developed to become approximately twenty-five ordained ministers (the benchmark was boosted to thirty-five in the twentieth century), the mission conference became an Annual Conference with the same responsibilities (rights and duties) as annual conferences in the United States. They also instituted an intermediate step, a "provisional conference" (minimum ten ordained ministers), for those locations where a mission conference was not possible.[20]

Responding to its international expansion and a growing self-understanding as an international church,[21] and counteracting worldwide national tendencies aiming for autonomy at the turn of the nineteenth to the twentieth

---

20 In Europe today there are the Austria Provisional Annual Conference, Bulgaria-Romania Provisional Annual Conference, Hungary Provisional Annual Conference, Serbia-Macedonia Provisional Annual Conference, Finland-Swedish Provisional Annual Conference. In Eurasia there are the Eastern Russia and Central Asia Provisional Annual Conference, Northwest Russia Provisional Annual Conference, Southern Russia Provisional Annual Conference, Ukraine-Moldova Provisional Annual Conference—all United Methodist Churches.

21 This was based on a rediscovery of John Wesley's understanding of a "world parish."

centuries,[22] "central conferences" were created beyond the United States in 1884 by the General Conference of the Methodist Episcopal Church (MEC).[23] Central conferences today perform basically the same functions as The UMC's jurisdictional conferences. Delegates elected by annual conferences normally gather every four years to elect bishops, choose persons to serve on denominational boards and agencies, and conduct other routine business. After appropriate meetings and discussion,[24] a European Central Conference of the MEC was founded in 1911.[25] Nine years later the 1920 General Conference decided to divide the European Central Conference into three. As a result of political circumstances and The UMC union in 1968,[26] the country composition of the European Central Conferences changed several times.[27] The current three central conferences in Europe are the Northern Europe and Eurasia Central Conference, the Central and Southern Europe Central Conference, and the Germany Central Conference.[28]

---

22 In times of national aggrandizement insistence on independence from foreign influences is easily aroused.

23 The Methodist Episcopal Church was founded in 1784 in Baltimore, Maryland, according to the need of the Methodists in the newly created United States of America (1776)—now being independent from the Church of England—to administer the sacraments.

24 In 1893 a central council for the MEC in Europe was initiated (Zentralrat der Konferenzen und Missionen der Bischöflichen Methodistenkirche in Europa). It met in Berlin in 1895, in Zurich in 1903 under the name Methodist Episcopal Church Congress, and Copenhagen in 1907. Today the autonomous Methodist churches like the British Methodist Church are also members of the European Methodist Council (EMC).

25 The first MEC bishop, William Burt, was stationed in Europe in 1911 in Zurich. In 1912 Bishop John Nuelsen, a German-American, was elected and stationed in Europe until 1940—from 1924 on as bishop of the Middle European Central Conference. In 1928 the MEC General Conference gave its central conferences the right to elect their own bishops.

26 In 1968 the Methodist Church (after a union of the Methodist Episcopal Church, the Methodist Episcopal Church, South, and the Methodist Protestant Church in 1939) and the Evangelical United Brethren Church (in 1946 the United Brethren in Christ and the Evangelical Church—former Evangelical Association—united) united to The United Methodist Church.

27 The most painful shift happened in 1936 when, due to difficult political situations, Germany organized a single German Central Conference with an episcopal leader. See Urs Schweizer, *Mit dem Feuer der ersten Liebe und dem tiefen, stillen Wasser des bewährten Glaubens. 50 Jahre Zentralkonferenz von Mittel- und Südeuropa der Evangelisch-methodistischen Kirche* (Zurich: German Central Conference, 2005). As a consequence of the Iron Curtain a second German Central Conference for the GDR was established in 1970.

28 The North European and Eurasia Central Conference (Belarus, Denmark, Estonia, Finland, Kazakhstan, Kyrgyzstan, Latvia, Lithuania, Moldavia, Norway, Russia, Sweden, Tajikistan, Ukraine, Uzbekistan), the Central and Southern Europe Central Conference (Albania, Algeria, Austria, Belgium, Bulgaria, Croatia, Czech Republic, France, Hungary, Republic of North Macedonia, Romania, Poland, Serbia-Montenegro, Slovak Republic, Switzerland, Tunisia), and the Germany Central Conference (the only central conference of one nation and language).

The Evangelical Association (EA)[29] had a similar structural arrangement; in 1922 a central conference for Europe was organized. It included all the EA's European missions in Germany and Switzerland, dividing it into three annual conferences: North-German, South-German, and Switzerland.[30]

Overview of Anglo-American Methodist Missions to Europe
British Methodist Missions [31]

The chronological beginning of Wesleyan Methodist (WM) mission from Great Britain in Europe originated and developed as follows: (* = Catholic territories).

Catholic Territories	Year of Initial Contact	By Whom	Year Adopted by Mission Society
Gibraltar*	1769	British soldiers	1808
France*	1790/1791	tradesman	1818
Belgium*		British soldier/lay preacher	1816
Spain*	ca. 1825	missionary from Gibraltar/ propagating the Bible	1854/1868
Sweden	1809	manufacturer	1826
Germany	1830	returning emigrant	1859
Switzerland	1840	minister from Great Britain, having begun in France	
Austria*	1870	preacher from Germany	

29 Although the name was changed in the United States in 1922 to Evangelical Church due to a union, no such union was needed in Europe. The church maintained the title Evangelische Gemeinschaft. The same happened at the time of the EUBC union in 1946—the name Evangelische Gemeinschaft retained only with a subtitle "Evangelical United Brethren Church." Changing "Evangelical Church" would have implied problems in a German-speaking context since that is the name of the principal Protestant church in Germany.

30 Unlike the MEC, the EA retained its border-crossing conference in the time of German National Socialism.

31 British Methodist missions to Continental Europe were only begun by Wesleyan Methodists. A minister from the Wesleyan Methodist Association (a separation from the Wesleyan Methodists in 1836) was sent to an English-speaking congregation in Hamburg; that work was marginal and was later assimilated into the MEC mission.

Catholic Territories	Year of Initial Contact	By Whom	Year Adopted by Mission Society
Italy*	1861	converted Catholic priest	1861
Portugal*		layperson	1871

Methodism's spread from Great Britain to the European continent was simple in its beginnings; it was connected to individuals and their Christian experience. Sometimes the work initiated by individuals faded away when there were no successors to carry on mission work. Because of Methodism's self-understanding as a renewal movement within the Church of England, John Wesley did not encourage missions abroad. Extensive mission work was mainly organized by others, Thomas Coke being the early leader in this endeavor.

In the first half of the nineteenth century, Wesleyan Methodism (WM) as a reform movement within the Church of England changed, and Methodism was increasingly rejected. That also influenced the approach to missions abroad, which, especially in Protestant areas, was considered extremely inappropriate with overtones of proselytism. At the same time an anti-Catholic disposition grew among WMs that encouraged them to consider mission to Catholic areas. British Wesleyan Methodists were skeptical about evangelizing in Protestant regions, but repeated requests to send a Methodist preacher for a growing mission work started by a layperson forced them to argue for this work as a springboard into traditional Catholic territories.[32]

An example of this is the start of the WM mission to Germany in 1830 by Christoph Gottlob Müller,[33] a butcher and German immigrant who was

---

32 This is well described in an unpublished dissertation by the Nazarene scholar Helen Wright in "The Wesleyan Methodist Missionary Society and its Mission to Germany and Austro-Hungary, 1859–1897" (PhD diss., Brunel University, London, 2006).

33 Christoph Gottlob Müller (1785–1858) was a butcher who left Germany to avoid the Napoleonic conscription in 1806 and became a WM in London, a class-leader, steward, and lay preacher. In 1831 he returned to Germany (Winnenden/Kingdom Württemberg) where his class meetings and Sunday schools generated an awakening that later spread to the Black Forest. At the time of his death, the work he began encompassed 1,040 members with eighty-two preaching places. Müller is the founder of Wesleyan Methodism (Wesleyanische Methodistengemeinschaft) in Germany. Karl Heinz Voigt wrote more than 150 articles about Methodists with helpful source notes. Articles on all of the persons mentioned below will be found in an Internet encyclopaedia (www.kirchenexikon.de).

converted in a Methodist congregation in London. After a long correspondence with relatives and friends in his hometown of Winnenden in Württemberg, he went back as a lay preacher, spoke in pietistic meetings, and founded
classes.[34] He repeatedly asked the WM mission society for support. Modest
annual funding was finally approved by the society after considerable correspondence. After Müller's death in 1858, the mission board sent an official
superintendent, John Lyth.[35] In 1863 Lyth published the periodical *Der Sonntagsgast*, a hymnal (*Die Zionsharfe*), and a Sunday school song book. Also
in 1863 the first chapel was built in Prevorst. Lyth trained the first German
Methodist ministers and campaigned for religious freedom against Lutheran
restrictions. Not until the arrival of Lyth's successor, John Cook Barratt,[36] was
a Methodist society formally organized in 1865. Under Barratt's leadership,
German Methodism began to grow. Classes were formed, Sunday schools
founded, a Discipline and a periodical (*Methodist Herald*) published, a training center for preachers established in Waiblingen/Württemberg,[37] and a
deaconess facility (Martha-Maria-Verein Nürnberg) planted in Nürnberg/Ba-
varia in 1889. Barratt also applied for the status of an incorporated society
(Verein) according to newly enacted laws in the kingdom of Württemberg[38]
and in Bavaria.[39]

---

34 The whole story is well documented in Friedemann Burkhardt, *Christoph Gottlob Müller und die Anfänge
    des Methodismus in Deutschland* (Göttingen: Vandenhoeck and Ruprecht, 2003 [Arbeiten zur Geschichte
    des Pietismus 43]).

35 John Lyth (1821–1886) was an apprenticed bookseller and lay preacher who was later ordained in 1843
    in the Methodist Conference. After appointments in Great Britain he was sent as general superintendent
    to Germany in 1859. In 1865 he returned to Great Britain beginning regular circuit work. Biographical
    information about WMs in Britain is available via Internet in the *Dictionary of Methodism in Britain and
    Ireland*, edited by John Vickers. See www.wesleyhistoricalsociety.org.uk; see also www.kirchenlexikon
    .de.

36 John Cook Barratt (1832–1892) was educated as a landscape gardener and became a lay preacher and
    Methodist missionary to the West Indies (1855–1864). From 1865 to 1892 he was general superintendent
    for the WM German district. Barratt organized and led the Methodist mission later to be acknowledged
    by the state. Under his guidance the mission spread to Bavaria and Austria.

37 The provisional training center moved from Waiblingen to a new building in Cannstatt in 1875. The his-
    tory of the German Methodist preacher training institutions is described in Ulrike Schuler, ed. *Glaubens-
    wege–Bildungswege. 150 Jahre theologische Ausbildung im deutschsprachigen Methodismus Europas.*
    (Reutlingen, 2008 [EmKG 29/2008, 1–2]).

38 In 1872, which granted state approval.

39 Granted status in 1885 as a Privatkirchengesellschaft (private church society).

Beginnings of missions in Continental Europe initiated by members of the Wesleyan Methodists from Great Britain can be located in France, Belgium, Italy, Spain, Sweden, Germany, Switzerland, and Austria. As mentioned previously, the main WM strategy was to encourage the mission to become independent from the mission board as soon as possible for organizational and financial reasons. For example, in 1897 the mission work of the WM in Germany and Austria was formally combined with the mission work of the MEC in Germany.[40] In other European countries WM mission work was also transferred into MEC missions. That happened in 1852 with the France-Switzerland Conference; in 1898 with the mission among the Portuguese on Madeira; in 1900 with the French-speaking mission in Lausanne, Switzerland; and in 1946 with the mission in Italy.

In other European countries some Methodist societies founded by the British WMs became autonomous as in Belgium, Portugal, and Spain. Some went into a communion with other Protestant churches. In Belgium WMs went into the Eglise protestante de Belgique in 1963, which after further unions with two Reformed churches became the Eglise protestante Unie de Belgique in 1978. In Spain the WMs merged in 1955 with an existing union that had been founded in 1869, the Iglesia Evangélica Española. In Italy the United Methodists merged with the Waldensians in 1979 to form the Chiesa Evangelica Valdese.

Missions from the United States

In addition to what has already been said about the origin of Methodist beginnings in Europe being "narrative," it must be noted that the mission also arose out of a situation particular to the United States. In the nineteenth century there was extensive immigration to North America from Europe[41]

---

40 This transfer was enabled by the financial gift of the Austrian Baroness Amelie von Langenau, who also played an important role in Austrian Methodist history. See Paul Ernst Hammer, *Baronin Amelie von Langenau*, Methodistenkirche in Österreich (Wien, 2001). There will be a chapter about her in the new book about Women Pioneers in Continental European Methodism (see 12).

41 Statistics published from 1820 on verify the enormous immigration from Europe to the United States. See the graphic in Ulrike Schuler, *Die Evangelische Gemeinschaf: Missionarische Aufbrüche in gesellschafts-politischen Umbrüchen* (Stuttgart: Medienwerk der Evangelisch-methodistischen Kirche, 1998 [emk studien 1]), 361.

as people fled revolutions, wars, and pogroms.[42] Americans drew their own conclusions from the experiences of those immigrants. Revolution, many believed, meant opposing God's established order and showed the distance between the people and God, and the need to continue reforms that began with the Reformation. Church periodicals regularly outlined the main problems: the spiritual situation that followed the Enlightenment and the onset of liberal theology. Furthermore, letters were published from "positive" ministers including the "impromptu" by Johann Hinrich Wichern[43] concerning the need for home missions given the social circumstances created by the Industrial Revolution. All this information heightened the desire of American Methodists to support missions to the people of Europe, whether in the United States or on the continent.

Methodist Episcopal Church (MEC) Missions

As a result of the large influx of immigrants arriving in the United States, domestic MEC missions were first initiated in their native languages.[44] These foreign-language missions later played an important role when supporting mission work in the immigrants' native countries. There was thus a dynamic interdependence between home and foreign missions. This work was also substantially supported by the Woman's Foreign Missionary Society, founded in 1869.

Mainly driven by the Scandinavian immigrants and of special importance is the *Bethel Ship* mission. It was located in the New York harbor, Brooklyn, Pier 11. The ship was appropriately named *John Wesley*. The *Bethel Ship*

---

42 In 1789 the French Revolution; between 1804 and 1815 the wars between France, Prussia, and Russia; between 1812 and 1813 the Balkan War; 1818 the Russian Revolution; 1820 Revolution in Spain and Portugal; 1821–1829 war and independence in Greece; 1830 Revolution in Belgium; 1830–1831 Revolution in Poland; 1847 Risorgimento in Italy; 1848 German Revolution and the February Revolution in France; 1853–1856 the Crimean War; 1859 War of Sardinia and France against Austria; 1864 Austrian and Prussian War against Denmark; 1870–1871 Franco-German War.

43 Johann Hinrich Wichern (1808–1881), famous German theologian, pedagogue, founder of the Protestant home mission (Innere Mission) in Germany in 1848, and prison reformer.

44 German-speaking mission in Cincinnati, Ohio, in 1935; founding of three German-speaking Annual Conferences in 1864; mission to people from Scandinavia in Illinois, Wisconsin, Iowa, Minnesota; first Swedish Conference in 1876; Welsh Conference in 1830; Portuguese Conference in 1880; Italian Conference in 1880; Spanish Conference in 1890. See Streiff, *Der Methodismus in Europa*, 41–43.

mission functioned from 1845 to 1876.[45] It was heavily influenced by the holiness movement and focused on immigrants who regularly arrived in the port and were in danger of being defrauded in their new homeland and forced into financial dependence by unscrupulous villains. In some cases, would-be employers paid the immigrants' passage to the United States in exchange for cheap labor after their journey from Europe. Several converted at the *Bethel Ship* mission—mainly sailors—returned to Scandinavia, and began to evangelize in Sweden, Denmark, Norway, and Finland. From Finland this evangelism spread to Russia.

The Swedish missionary Olaf Gustaf Hedstrøm[46] supervised the evangelical and social service work of the *Bethel Ship* mission. He was a pioneer of the Scandinavian mission in the United States as well as in Sweden where he effectively preached on a visit in 1863. He also assisted the Norwegian sailor Ole Peter Petersen[47] to find Christ and be led into the ministry. Peterson became the pioneer missionary to Norway as well as a minister to Norwegian immigrants in the United States.

The founder of Methodism in Denmark was Christian Willerup,[48] a Dane who had immigrated to the United States, converted, and was ordained in the MEC in 1850. He served for a short time at the *Bethel Ship*, where he met Ole Peter Petersen and Olaf Gustaf Hedström. After having had an appointment

---

45 Nuelsen states that in that time about two hundred thousand Scandinavians arrived in the US. See John Nuelsen, *Geschichte des Methodismus von den Anfängen bis zur Gegenwart* (Bremen: Buchhandlung und Verlag des Traktathauses, 1929), 737.

46 Olaf Gustaf Hedstrøm (1803–1877) was born near Karlskrona, Sweden. He was a sailor converted in the United States in 1845 at the *Bethel Ship* mission. Hedstrøm went back and forth from the United States to Sweden on several occasions visiting family and meeting with the people he had met at *Bethel Ship*. Finally, he permanently resettled in Sweden.

47 Ole Peter Peterson (1822–1901), a Norwegian sailor who was converted at the *Bethel Ship* mission, returned to Norway and began preaching in 1849. Peterson returned to the United States and became a missionary among Norwegian immigrants in Iowa. Meanwhile those people who were awakened in Norway by his preaching came under the influence of Mormons. In 1853 Peterson was ordained and sent to Norway by the MEC. After other missionaries were sent Peterson went back to the United States in 1858 and worked at the *Bethel Ship* mission. He was appointed as superintendent in Norway from 1869 to 1871.

48 Christian Edvard Baltør Willerup (1815–1886), a salesman, immigrated to the United States and worked in Savannah, Georgia, for a Methodist employer. He was the founder of a Norwegian Methodist congregation in the United States, founder of Methodism in Denmark, and was appointed superintendent for Scandinavia by the MEC.

in Cambridge, Wisconsin, Willerup was appointed superintendent for all ministries in the Scandinavian countries (Norway, Sweden, and Denmark[49]). He and his family arrived in Copenhagen in 1856 and stayed there briefly. He was sent by the mission board to support Ole Peter Peterson in Norway. Willerup lived and worked in Norway for two years during which three congregations were founded. In 1858 he returned to Copenhagen, Denmark, where he held the first Methodist service. A congregation was founded there in 1859.[50]

The counterpart to the *Bethel Ship* mission was the German mission that strategically began in Bremen in 1849.[51] Bremen was the chief port of embarkation to the United States. It was also one of the few cities in Germany that possessed a constitution guaranteeing full religious freedom. So Bremen offered a unique opportunity to evangelize emigrants. Letters from Germany to American Methodists requesting support, articles in periodicals describing Methodist prospects in Germany, and a visit and report by the German-American Methodist leader Wilhelm Nast[52] in 1844 encouraged Methodist work among the Germans. After the German Revolution of 1848 and the launching of religious liberty,[53] Ludwig Sigismund Jacoby[54] started

---

49 For centuries Finland was part of Sweden. Beginning in the eighteenth century, Sweden increasingly lost land in Finland to Russia. Finland became independent in 1917.

50 For more about Scandinavia, see the following paragraph in the text on the Holiness Movement.

51 The beginning of this mission is described in Karl Heinz Voigt, *Warum kamen die Methodisten nach Deutschland. Eine Untersuchung über die Motive für ihre Mission in Deutschland* (Stuttgart: Christlickhes Verlagshaus, 1975 [BGEmK, Beiheft 4]).

52 Wilhelm Nast (1807–1899) studied theology in Blaubeuren and Tübingen, immigrated to the United States in 1828, and worked as a language teacher and librarian. He was converted to Methodism, became a lay preacher, and in 1835 was appointed MEC missionary among Germans in the United States. He was founder of the German branch of the MEC beginning in Cincinnati, Ohio, and publisher from 1839 of the periodical *Der Christliche Apologete*, a periodical for German immigrants. In 1844 Nast visited Germany to examine the possibility of a MEC mission to Germany. Nast visited Christoph Gottlob Müller (see note 33 above), concluding that lack of religious freedom made a German mission inadvisable. Nast was co-founder of the German Wallace College in Berea, Ohio, where he became president in 1865.

53 Later that impression proved wrong. The first attempt to install a democratic national state collapsed in 1849 and most of the liberal laws were withdrawn.

54 Ludwig Sigismund Jacoby (1813–1874) was educated in the Jewish tradition, converted at the age of twenty-three, baptized a Lutheran, and was apprenticed for commercial employment. In 1838 he immigrated to the US, was converted to Methodism, and became a lay preacher. In 1841 Jacoby was appointed by the MEC to work with German immigrants, and in 1849 he was sent to Germany, where he became the founder of the MEC in Continental Europe. After organizing European Methodist mission work, Jacoby returned to the US in 1871, where he died.

mission work in Bremen in 1849 with the support of the German-speaking conference of the MEC and the denomination's mission board. Under his supervision the mission broadened rapidly and strategically. Jacoby founded the Traktathaus Bremen (publishing house) and published a periodical, *Der Evangelist*. In 1858 Jacoby established a seminary for Methodist ministers (Bremer Missionsanstalt) and became its director until 1868.

Before leaving Bremen for America, some became Methodists as a result of the mission work in Germany. Others, such as Ernst Gottfried Mann,[55] instead of departing for the west, went back to spread the gospel as Methodist preachers in their homeland. Mann returned to the Palatinate, caused an awakening in that area, and founded the "Pirmasens and Alsace mission." He became a circuit minister and was the first of the MEC appointed to Lausanne, Switzerland, in 1856 after he had suffered persecution and punishment in Alsace for preaching despite official prohibition.[56] From Bremen, therefore, the MEC mission work also expanded into other German and German-speaking areas (such as Switzerland).[57]

Independent of the Bremen mission, in another part of Germany, namely Thuringia and Saxony, a mission was started by the witness of a returning emigrant from the United States, Erhard Friedrich Wunderlich.[58] In 1865 this

---

55 Ernst Gottfried Mann (1830–1915). In the turmoil of the 1848 German Revolution, Mann decided to immigrate to the US. At the port of Bremen his life was revolutionized by a Methodist Bible peddler. He went back to his family in Pirmasens, the Palatinate, and led a spiritual awakening. In 1855 Mann was appointed Methodist circuit minister, sent to Alsace, and in 1856 sent to Lausanne, where he worked cooperatively with WMs; the mission spread to other Swiss cities. In 1867 Mann finished his work as minister and founded a commercial enterprise. He was accountable for a kind of state-acknowledged Privatkirchengesellschaft of the MEC in Bavaria in 1883.

56 In 1856 the general conference formed the German-Switzerland-Mission Conference.

57 In 1856 the MEC general conference formed the Germany-Switzerland Mission Conference. At that time Germany was composed of thirty-nine autonomic states (empires, kingdoms, dukedoms, princedoms, and free imperial cities) with different laws. There was no religious freedom, which seriously complicated the mission. Persecution by state authorities coerced by state church ministers was a daily occurrence (e.g., banishment, penalty, and other punishment).

58 Erhard Wunderlich (1830–1895) immigrated to the US in 1849 and was converted to Methodism in Dayton, Ohio. Returning to his native place, Rüßdorf, Thuringia, in 1850, he worshiped and preached at his parents' estate with his family and workers. He expanded his evangelical ministry when a regional awakening began. After enduring persecution, imprisonment, fines, and other punishment he returned to the US in 1853. Wunderlich was then ordained and worked among German immigrants. His brother Friedrich continued the mission work that was soon integrated into the MEC mission under the supervision of Ludwig Sigismund Jacoby (see note 54).

work was integrated into the MEC mission. Converted laypeople of the MEC gave testimony of their renewed faith and started classes and mission work in Sweden, Norway, Denmark, Finland, Germany, Switzerland, France/Alsace, Italy, Bulgaria, Macedonia, and Serbia.

The following is a chronological list of the MEC missions in the particular European countries.[59] (* = Catholic territories).

MEC Missions	Year of Initial Contact	By Whom	Adopted by Mission Society
Sweden	1833	*converted sailors (Bethel Ship)*	1854
Norway	1849	*sailors (Bethel Ship)*	1853
Germany	1840	*correspondence of immigrants*	1849
	1850	*returning emigrant (in Thuringia/ Saxony)*	1865
Switzerland[60]	1856	*preachers from Germany*	1886
Denmark	1857	*returning emigrant*	1858
Bulgaria		*request of the American Board*[61]	1857
Finland	1859/80	*laypersons (Bethel Ship)*	1880
France/ Alsace	1855/68	*contact to German-speaking people in German-speaking Alsace*	
Macedonia[62]	1867	*American Board*	1921
Italy*		*decision of the mission board*	1871
		decision of an Italian Annual Conference of the MEC in the United States to open a mission in Trieste (at that time Austria)	1898

---

59 The first date marks the initial contact by laypersons and the date in parentheses gives the date of official acceptance by a denominational mission board.

60 Work among Italian-speaking foreign workers in Switzerland.

61 The American Board of Commissioners for Foreign Missions (or American Board) was the first American Christian foreign mission agency (non-denominational). It was officially chartered in 1812.

62 Macedonia was part of the Ottoman Empire from 1371 to 1913. After the second Balkan War it was related to Greece. After WW II Macedonia again became a nation but was marked by violent relocations and displacements. After WW I and during WW II, Macedonia occasionally came under the Bulgarian statute of occupation; in 1944 it was part of Yugoslavia. In 1991 Macedonia became independent with the problem of uniting an ethnically diverse patchwork of citizens.

MEC Missions	Year of Initial Contact	By Whom	Adopted by Mission Society
Serbia[63]		contact with German settlers in the south of Austria-Hungary (today North Serbia)	1899

Evangelical Association (EA) Missions

The largest immigrant population to the United States came from Germany. The two German-speaking denominations, the Evangelical Association (EA) and the Church of the United Brethren in Christ (UBC), had retained a strong German identity. The UBC opened several English-speaking annual conferences, but that was not normal for the EA in the United States, which had only a few until after World War I.[64] Members of both denominations kept in touch with relatives and friends in Germany. Through these contacts and their church periodicals, members were well informed about social, political, and religious developments in their homeland.[65]

The EA celebrated its fiftieth anniversary in 1850. Their denomination's general conference minutes and denominational periodical reported that the American members of the EA desired to express their thanks to their homeland and the land of Reformation. They thoughtfully considered all the information received regarding the situation in Germany as well as Wichern's well-known "impromptu." In 1850 a major financial campaign

---

63 From 1459 to 1804 Serbia was part of the Ottoman Empire. In 1882, after revolutions and wars, it became an autonomous kingdom. At the end of WW I the kingdoms of Serbia, Croatia, and Slovenia constituted Yugoslavia. After further conflicts and World War II, Serbia became one of six partial republics of Yugoslavia later called Socialistic Republic Serbia. After 1991 Serbia became independent as did the other republics. After further wars (e.g., the Kosovo War) and federation era with Montenegro, Serbia became an independent republic in 2006.

64 In several states in the United States, speaking German was forbidden and names were anglicized.

65 The *Christlicher Botschafter* was the EA's periodical—an excellent source of news from Germany where letters, mission reports, and other information about the church was published. It was the longest published church newspaper in German (1836–1946). *Die Geschäftige Martha*, the periodical of the UBC, had a complicated history. First published in 1841, it was discontinued in June 1846, and from 1846 to 1848 it appeared as *Der Deutsche Telescope*. In 1849 it was again named *Die Geschäftige Martha*, and in 1851 it changed yet again to *Der Fröhliche Botschafter*.

was begun to send two missionaries to Germany.[66] As a result of the campaign, Conrad Link[67] was dispatched as the first official EA missionary to Germany. The mission joined with a class meeting organized by Sebastian Kurz,[68] a returning immigrant from the United States to Germany who wrote about his work in the EA periodical (*Evangelischer Botschafter*), asking for EA support in 1846. The main mission goal of what followed was not the founding of a new church, but the support of orthodox theology, ministry, and renewal in Protestant churches that already existed. Those involved in the mission were clearly aware that theirs could only be a humble contribution to much-needed wider mission work.[69] They joined with the mission taking place in those areas that already had strong pietistic development, that is, the kingdom of Württemberg, which was mainly a rural area. Even so, the EA mission soon gained ground in cities.[70] By 1911 they had established congregations in twenty-eight of forty-one principal German cities.[71] The key features of the EA mission were evangelism, education, and medical treatment (in a time when it was not compulsory for the state to provide medical care).

In 1865 after a long period of negotiation and chicanery by the state churches, an EA annual conference was organized under the direction of Bishop John J. Escher as Deutschland-Konferenz der Evangelischen Gemeinschaft. Nine preachers for Württemberg, Baden, and Switzerland were appointed. The mission work spread largely through personal connections

---

66 The creative Zehn-Thaler-Plan is described in Schuler, *Evangelische Gemeinschaft*, 124–27. Nicolai's plan is printed in *Christlicher Botschafter*, No. 22 (November 15, 1849): 170–71; also in Schuler, 362–64.

67 Johann Conrad Link (1822–1883) immigrated to the United States in 1836–1837 and became a member of the EA and minister of the West Pennsylvania Conference. In 1850 he was appointed a missionary to Germany. Together with Johannes Nikolai (1818–1912), the second missionary sent, Link became the founder of the EA in Germany. After disagreements with the denomination, Link left to become a Baptist minister.

68 Sebastian Kurz (1789–1868) immigrated to the US in the early 1830s and became a ministerial member of the EA in Pennsylvania. He returned to Germany in 1845, began class meetings, wrote letters that were printed in the *Christlicher Botschafter*, and later became a colporteur for the MEC.

69 See the article by C. G. Koch, *Christlicher Botschafter* 24 (December 15, 1849): 188.

70 E.g., Preußen Mission (Prussian mission; a mission among coal miners).

71 J. Steven O'Malley, *On the Journey Home: The History of Mission of the Evangelical United Brethren Church, 1946–1968* (New York: General Board of Global Ministries, The United Methodist Church, 2003), 36.

such as friends and family. It spread from Germany to Switzerland in 1866, to Alsace-Lorraine in 1868, and to East Prussia in 1895. From its churches in East Prussia,[72] the EA began a mission to the German-speaking people in Latvia in 1911. All mission work in Europe was exclusively in German and conducted by German people; in that manner the EA mission differed from the mission philosophy of the MEC.

Listed here are the EA missions in Europe with chronological detail.

EA Missions	Source of Introduction	Year Adopted by Mission Society
Germany	letter connections of emigrants with relatives and friends	1850
Switzerland	personal contacts between Germans and people in the German-speaking Switzerland	1866
Alsace-Lorraine[73]	1865 personal contacts between Germans and and people in Alsace-Lorraine; relatives	1868
East Prussia	personal connections, also from immigrants in the United States, expanding to West Prussia and Pomerania	1895
Latvia	ministers from East Prussia	1911

Beginning with the initial meeting of the Ecumenical Methodist Conference in London in 1881, delegates of the MEC, EA, and WM also held regular meetings on their common work in Germany. They agreed not to begin a

---

72 East and West Prussia, in late medieval and Reformation times the territories of the Teutonic Knights, became in the sixteenth century part of Ducal Prussia (later Kingdom Prussia). From 1871 to 1945 Prussia was part of the German empire, then after World War II under Polish respectively Soviet control; since 1992 the area is part of Poland while the northerly part of East Prussia belongs to Russia. The EA reported revival and emerging congregations in East and West Prussia from the beginning of the twentieth century to the 1930s. A report in 1945 speaks of forty-two emerging congregations, but twenty-three church buildings were occupied and German inhabitants were banished.

73 The Alsatian people lived in a boundary area between Germany and France that was occupied several times from both sides—always followed by the change of the main language and persecution. From 1871 to 1918 Alsace and Lorraine were considered an administrative district–Alsace-Lorraine–of the German Empire (Deutsches Reich). Today the territory is part of France.

mission in a German region if another Methodist church already had started mission work.[74]

Church of the United Brethren in Christ (UBC) Missions

The UBC began a mission in Germany in 1869. Unlike other Methodist missions to Europe, the intention of the UBC general conference was to learn more about Germans because of shrinking German conferences in the United States.[75] There was also an expectation to enlist ministers in Germany for the German-speaking conferences in the United States. These expectations arose by observing the MEC and EA missions and the interdependence between their German-speaking home missions and missions abroad.

The UBC mission in Germany was opened by Christian Bischoff,[76] a former butcher, innkeeper, and cattle dealer who immigrated to the United States, converted to the UBC, and was sent back to Germany as a lay preacher. He started preaching in Naila, Franconia—a Catholic area without religious liberty. The mission extended north to Thuringia, Saxony, Pomerania, and Posen—all German regions. The mission was not as prosperous as anticipated. Although a publishing house and book store were founded in Zeitz, the mission remained small and was finally integrated into the MEC's German mission in 1905.

Methodist Episcopal Church, South (MECS) Missions

World War I left an extraordinary amount of destruction in European countries, which was only exceeded by that which remained after World War II.

---

74 For more details about these meetings, see Ulrike Knöller and Doris Sackmann, *Erste Zusammenkünfte von Vertretern der drei Gemeinschaften methodistischen Ursprungs in Deutschland: Sitzungsprotokolle 1881–1885* EmKG 28/2, 2007, 83–86.

75 There is an important discussion about this matter as reason to open a mission in Germany at the UBC general conference in 1869. See *Proceedings of the Fifteenth General Conference of the United Brethren in Christ, held in Lebanon, Pennsylvania, May 20 to June 1, 1869* (Dayton, OH: United Brethren in Christ Church, 1869), esp. 175f, 183f.

76 Georg Christian Heinrich Bischoff (1829–1885) was a member of a pietistic Lutheran congregation in Naila, Franconia. His brother immigrated to the United States and wrote letters about his conversion. Bischoff followed his brother to America in 1867, became a member of the UBC, was ordained in 1869, and was sent as a missionary to Germany. He evangelized unremittingly. Bischoff is considered the founder of the UBC in Germany.

The Methodist churches in the United States and Great Britain immediately started an impressive, wide-ranging relief campaign. The Methodist Episcopal churches (MEC and MECS) prepared to celebrate the centenary of their foreign mission work in 1919. The MEC's goal for this "Centenary Movement" was to raise $40 million over five years to expand its mission outreach and to spend more than $3 million to enlarge mission work in Europe.[77] In consultation with the MEC, the MECS decided to help with reconstructing post-war Europe. They already supported European foreign-language annual conferences in the United States and had received requests for widening their missions in Europe. For example, Czech ministers and students urged them not to forget Bohemia and Moravia,[78] which, they argued, was the cradle of Moravianism, which led to John Wesley's conversion to living faith. Therefore, materially supporting that territory was a way of giving thanks for its contribution to Methodism's origin.[79]

As a part of the Centenary Movement, the MECS wanted to extend its current mission fields and open new missions. In cooperation with the MEC, which at that time had missions in seventeen European countries, both churches cooperatively sent a committee to Europe to study the social and religious situation. Upon the return of the MECS representatives, their

---

77 Streiff, *Der Methodismus in Europa*, 168.

78 Bohemia and Moravia are the two historical areas today in the Czech Republic. After the collapse of the Austro-Hungarian Empire after World War I, the independent republic of Czechoslovakia was created in 1918. This country incorporated regions of Bohemia, Moravia, Silesia, Slovakia, and the Carpathian Ruthenia with significant German-, Hungarian-, Polish-, and Byelorussian-speaking minorities. In 1993 this area emerged as the states of the Czech Republic and Slovenia.

79 See details in Vilém Schneeberger, *"Der Methodismus in der Tschechoslowakei,"* in Friedrich Hecker, Vilém Schneeberger, and Karl Zehrer, *Methodismus in Osteuropa: Polen–Tschechoslowakei–Ungarn* (Stuttgart: Medienwerk der Evangelisch-methodistischen Kirche, 2004 [EmKM 51]), 40.

denomination decided in 1920 to start missions in Poland,[80] Czechoslova-kia,[81] and Belgium.[82]

With enormous effort, mission work was initiated in Poland. A building with eight floors was constructed as a church center with a chapel, apartments, a flourishing language school, and a soup kitchen that daily served about 2,600 students and workers. A pharmacy and medical clinic were also established. Between 1922 and 1925, ten schools were opened as well as a Bible school.[83]

A similar initiative shaped the mission to Belgium beginning in 1922. Among the facilities built were an orphan house, a boarding school for girls, a headquarters building with a book store and a Bible house, a center from which colporteurs could distribute Bibles and Christian literature, a hospital and nurse's training school, and a Bible school that also provided theologi-cal training for ministers.[84]

Help for the mission in Czechoslovakia was not as forthcoming as in Po-land and Belgium. Nevertheless, the mission fed a hundred students daily. Together with the Red Cross, social work among very poor children and refugees from Russia was undertaken. A successful tent evangelization was promoted. A publishing house distributed tracts among the population and a Bible school offered Bible study, theological education, and an English lan-guage class.[85]

---

80 Poland's history is shaped very tragically beginning with the seventeenth century. It is marked by divisions (by Austria, Prussia, and Russia), occupations, oppression, and fighting for freedom and independence. The details are much too complicated to explain in a footnote. In parts of Poland, Methodist missions were started but did not survive. A UBC mission was begun in 1880 in Pomerania; however, there is no information about what happened to this mission. The WM mission in Silesia opened in 1876 but was abandoned for the lack of a preacher; a Moravian Congregation was affiliated with the MEC in 1914. The MEC based in north Germany evangelized Polish areas (details can be found in Hecker, Schneeberger, and Zehrer, *Methodismus in Osteuropa*, 9–29).

81 The story of Methodist missions in Czechoslovakia is linked to the conversion of a theater director, Václav Pázdral (1845–1919) in 1879. Details are found in Hecker, Schneeberger, and Zehrer, *Methodismus in Osteuropa* 30–166.

82 Instead of Belgium they first had decided to go to south Russia, but political development changed this plan. The MECS already had a mission in Congo, Africa, that was at that time a Belgian colony.

83 Streiff, *Der Methodismus in Europa* 210 ff.

84 Streiff, 218 ff.

85 Streiff, 214 ff.

Those who energetically and financially initiated MECS missions found that their labors had to be curtailed or abandoned when the goals of the Centenary Movement were not achieved and funds were lacking. Furthermore, the global economy crisis in the late 1920s exacerbated the problem. The same fate occurred to the projects that were enthusiastically started by the MEC. After the union of the MEC, MECS, and Methodist Protestant Church in 1939, the MEC and MECS missions were more modestly continued by the Methodist Church (MC).

Turning Points in European Methodism in the Twentieth Century

Influence of the Holiness Movement

The holiness movement that reached European shores and inland in the last quarter of the nineteenth century focused on a central Methodist tenet, namely, the holy life. This movement was critically viewed by the European churches of the Reformation who generally viewed holiness with skepticism. Furthermore, even in Methodist churches the Wesleyan holiness doctrine had lost theological stature at the time the holiness movement evolved. Not until the holiness movement was underway was holiness doctrine again recognized as a spiritually inspiring feature of Methodism. After a period of uncritically embracing holiness doctrine and of exaggerating the doctrine of Christian perfection, and an intense period of schismatic activity, Methodist churches on the whole chose to distance themselves from the holiness movement and began to work on a rigorous, theologically based definition of scriptural "justification, holiness and Christian perfection."[86] Sympathetic writings by supporters of the holiness movement, e.g., FA bishops William W. Orwig and John J. Esher, encouraged a new interpretation in the 1902 EA Discipline. There followed subsequent work by other writers and theologians.[87]

---

86 Karl Steckel proves this very clearly in his article, "Die Veränderung des Traktats zur, Christlichen Vollkommenheit' in den verschiedenen Kirchenordnungsausgaben der früheren Evangelischen Gemeinschaft (1809–1968)," *Mitteilungen der Studiengemeinschaft für Geschichte der EmK* 11, no. 2 (1990): 5–27.

87 That led at least to a more precise definition in *The Discipline of The United Methodist Church* (1968).

When the Methodist societies on the European continent are considered, the holiness movement only seems to have affected Germany, Switzerland, and Scandinavia. When the holiness movement appeared, it was at first trans-confessional as a result of the Anglo-Saxon-German relationship, as were the societies that were established at the same time (like the Evangelical Alliance).[88]

In Germany and Switzerland there were different holiness society meetings involving Methodists in 1874–1875 under the leadership of Robert Pearsall Smith. Very clearly an increasingly ambivalent situation arose: Methodists were very well informed about the holiness movement in the United States and England, following the reports that were published in periodicals in the United States and Germany. They were touched by the holiness emphasis and naturally worked, in some cases leading to large revival-like gatherings. German Methodist minister and hymn writer Ernst Gebhardt with Robert Pearsall Smith became the musicians of large holiness assemblies. More and more conflicts arose from the criticism and suspicion by state church clergy. It is important to remember that at that time Methodism's legal situation was uncertain. As mentioned before, religious freedom was given in some German territories. In the 1870s MEC, EA, and WM made use of their rights, after the conflicts[89] with the state churches continued. In that tense situation there was considerable suspicion that Methodists sought to benefit from the dissolution of the state church by stabilizing and consolidating their own community from those initially raised by Lutheran ministers and congregations. In fact, Methodists did express a hope of greater acceptance and recognition by representatives of the state church as the holiness emphasis became more accepted, and they certainly hoped for missiological cooperation.

Based on overly enthusiastic and exaggerated reports of experiences of Christian perfection, and the recognizable schismatic impact of the holiness

---

88 Voigt describes this relationship in his monograph *Die Heiligungsbewegung zwischen Methodistischer Kirche und Landeskirchlicher Gemeinschaft. Die Triumphreise von Robert Pearsall Smith im Jahre 1875 und ihre Auswirkungen auf die zwischenkirchlichen Beziehungen* (Wuppertal: Brockhaus Verlag, 1996).

89 This included prohibitions from celebrating the sacraments, conducting funerals in church yards, etc.

movement (including the Pentecostal movements), Methodists in Germany increasingly dissociated themselves from the whole movement deliberately and distinctively. This was necessary because German Methodists were generally identified with the holiness movement through their doctrines. However, they wanted to protect themselves and their important ministry from the criticism of Lutheran theologians and clergy. These combined efforts weakened a holistic understanding of "holiness" including "social holiness" in Germany.[90]

Methodist churches in the United States and Scandinavia, however, absorbed this holiness impulse. The mission in Scandinavia was directly affected by the holiness movement through the *Bethel Ship* mission.[91] During the following years there emerged a distinctive social work under the influence of the holiness movement.

In Denmark, Methodists engaged in social holiness projects with problem drinkers using the model of the Methodist Central Halls in Great Britain that were centers for homeless, unemployed, and chronically poverty-stricken people. Danish Methodists developed a comprehensive program of social work: treatment for alcoholism, a children's home for sick mothers and small children, a home for elderly and poor persons, provision for basic needs support such as food, clothes, shelter, and health care, an office for adoptions, an orphanage, and a holiday home in the country for boys and girls. There the work also gave rise to a temperance movement that sought to influence secular society.

In Norway the holiness movement influenced Methodism and the secular women's movement. Women argued for the right to preach and were successful in the campaign for women's suffrage. Furthermore, Methodists advocated for religious tolerance, temperance, and religious education.

---

90 To learn more about the Holiness Movement in the German-speaking area, see Michel Weyer, *Heiligungsbewegung und Methodismus im deutschen Sprachraum. Einführung in ein Kapitel methodistischer Frömmigkeitsgeschichte und kleine Chronik einer Bewegung des 19. Jahrhunderts* (Stuttgart: Christliches Verlagshaus, 1991 [BGEmK 40]).

91 These and other findings are specified in Streiff, *Der Methodismus in Europa* and Streiff, *Der europäische Methodismus um die Wende* vom 19. zum 20. Jahrhundert. Referat der historischen *Konferenz der EmK in Europa vom 10. bis 15. August 2004 in Tallinn* (Stuttgart: Estland, 2005 [EmKG.M 52].

Leaders of trade unions, temperance organizations, and the Labor Party were members of Methodist churches, which leads us to remember the powerful social-political dedication at the beginning of the Methodist movement.

In Norway a Pentecostal movement evolved inside the MEC guided by superintendent Thomas Ball Barratt,[92] who was influenced by the movement in Los Angeles. Barratt was finally suspended by the Norwegian Annual Conference. He later relinquished his certificate of ordination. Barratt went on to work as an independent evangelist, becoming the "father" of the Norwegian Pentecostal movement.[93]

Two World Wars: 1914–1918, 1939–1945

Both World Wars left their marks all over Europe with enormous death and destruction. People suffered physically and mentally. There was massive damage to buildings, infrastructure, and cultural identity. Many felt hopeless and feared the future. The collapse of European society cannot be painted darkly enough to describe the situation that people—guilty or through no fault of their own—experienced.[94] Empires and kingdoms collapsed while new republics and states advanced.

Methodism made no general survey of the European situation, although the Methodist mission organizations and the denominational General Conferences (EA, EUBC, and MC) tried to take stock. In The UMC archives in Madison, New Jersey, there is a very large collection of photographs. Many

92 Thomas Ball Barratt (1862–1940), minister, evangelist, and founder of the Norwegian Pentecostal movement and European Pentecostalism, was born in Great Britain and studied theology, arts, and music (at Edvard Grieg). He went to Oslo, Norway, to become a minister of the MEC. He wrote songs and poems. In 1902 he became superintendent of the supra-denominational Christiana City Mission and experienced the "second anointing" in 1906. Up to 1916 Barratt was a Methodist speaker and writer in the Pentecostal movement. He published a Pentecostal periodical, *Korsets Seier*, in Swedish, Finnish, Russian, German, and Spanish.

93 Research on Methodist attitudes toward European Pentecostalism are in their infancy. Three recent articles are concerned with that matter: Christoph Raedel, *Der Methodismus und das Aufkommen der Pfingstbewegung in Deutschland*; Peder Borgen, *Der Methodismus und die Anfänge der Pfingstbewegung in Norwegen*; and Jorgen Thaarup, *Der Methodismus und die Pfingstbewegung in Dänemark*. These are published in Streiff, *Der europäische Methodismus um die Wende vom 19. zum 20. Jahrhundert*.

94 S. Ulrike Schuler, "Crisis, Collapse, and Hope: Methodism in 1945 Europe," in *Methodist History* 51, nos. 1 and 2 (2012): S. 5–27.

of those photographs were taken in European countries after the wars to promote fundraising to support immediate relief programs and to convey the desperate circumstances of European Methodists and their neighbors. After World War I, help came directly and less bureaucratically than after World War II when many different agencies first had to be authorized by the US government and had to work with the occupying armies. Both periods need more careful research.

Perhaps this is a good place to offer a few general conclusions. At the end of World War II, the EA and MC experienced severe interruptions in their European work—the death or imprisonment of preachers and church members and major damage or complete destruction of buildings.[95] This devastation produced a crisis. Should the denominational work in Europe continue? Would the devastating effects of the conflict allow reconstruction? The EA and MC in Europe were again deeply dependent on their parent churches.

Support was provided by the churches in the United States, Switzerland, and even Scandinavia: shipments of food, clothing, kitchen utensils, and bicycles for routine travel. Donated spare parts and raw materials could be sold to raise funds for the reconstruction of churches, schools, and hospitals. In some cases, complete wooden churches with furniture were sent to be constructed on appropriate plots. Changing state laws made it necessary to transfer monetary donations directly. This material assistance came under an evangelistic mission program that started in both denominations prior to the end of the war: the Kingdom Advance program of the Evangelical United Brethren Church (EUBC),[96] and the Crusade for Christ program of the Methodist Church (MC).[97]

In 1945, in addition to the Methodist programs, in Germany there was

---

95 For detailed statistics on Germany, which had the greatest problem, see the article by Ulrike Schuler, "Methodisten in Deutschland nach 1945," *KZG* (2/2000): S. 429–55.

96 The EUBC developed the Kingdom Advance Program in 1946, which merged the Kingdom Service Fund of the EA and the Advance Program of the UBC (Schuler, *Die Evangelische Gemeinschaft*, 221–62).

97 S. Ulrike Schuler, "Crusade for Christ–Ein 'methodistischer Kreuzzug' in der Mitte des 20. Jahrhunderts? Ein Forschungsbericht," *ThFPr*, Nr. 1–2 (28/2002): 94–111.

a relief organization founded by the churches called Hilfswerk der Evange-lischen Kirchen. It was the first time that free churches were officially included in the work of the main Protestant church[98] in Germany. This was not be-cause of the increased interest of free churches but was something that re-sulted from ecumenical initiatives in the United States where, among others, Methodist churches as mainline denominations were able to give advice on how to cooperate with other free churches in Germany. It also arose out of consideration of the future help that could be delivered by the free churches in the United States. How this worked in other European countries is a ques-tion open to further examination.

After World War II an awareness of the larger European Methodist com-munity emerged. A conference of European Methodist churches was held in 1950 to coordinate mission work and other collective concerns. In the 1990s a European Commission on Mission was formed in which British Method-ists were also involved. A European Methodist Youth Council was created in 1970 and composed of the autonomous churches of south Europe. In 1966 the Council of European Central Conferences (MC) met and invited the British Methodists as observers. In 1990 a Fund for Mission in Europe was established with the collaboration of the British. After years of consultative work, the Eu-ropean Methodist Council expanded in 1993 by including the autonomous Methodist churches in Europe—the British Conference, the Irish Conference, the Methodist Church in Portugal, the Opera for the Evangelical Methodist Churches in Italy, the Spanish Evangelical Church, and the Church of the Naz-arene. The goal was to develop a stronger Methodist witness in Europe by building connections, coordinating mission and ecumenical projects, engag-ing in theological studies, and giving financial support for mission in Europe.

Finally, an association of United Methodist Theological Schools in Europe was organized in 1999.[99] Its stated intention was to support an interchange

---

98 Evangelische Kirche in Deutschland (EKD) at that time had twenty-seven autonomous Protestant (former state) churches (Lutheran, Reformed, Uniate).

99 Participating institutions included Centre Méthodiste de Formation Théologique, Lausanne, Switzerland (today Strasbourg, France); Eesti Metodisti Kiriku Teologilinke, Tallinn, Estonia; Hoyskolen for Kistendom,

of professors, organize joint conferences, exchange information, cooperate in a doctor of ministry program, and form a corporate effort for accreditation and theological education in Europe. It is agreed that the deans of all the theological schools meet every other year and the professors every fourth year to coordinate Methodist theological education in Europe.

Since financial support from The UMC General Conference has been lacking, some of the East European theological schools have experienced difficulty. A newly designed collective European theological education was started with the founding of the European Methodist e-Academy in February 2008. "The Methodist e-Academy began as a project of the United Methodist Seminaries in Europe with the aim of providing internet-based distance learning courses for people preparing for the ordained ministry in European countries where The United Methodist Church had no seminary. The intention was to supplement the theological education that was available in these countries."[100] It is now the tenth year and the third group of students from all over Europe began in the 2017–18 winter semester.[101]

Ecumenical Concerns and Participation

While being one of the European minority churches,[102] the Methodist churches in Europe are considered a "bridge" between former state churches and the free churches. In this function Methodists are highly esteemed. On the one hand, this situation is explained by Methodism's connectional church structure. The majority of free churches are organized congregationally, which hinders closer authoritative agreements with other churches as well as their

---

Metodistkirkens Studiesenter, Bergen, Norway; Theological Seminary of the Russia United Methodist Church, Moscow, Russia; Theological Training Center for the Balkans, Graz-Waiern, Austria (no longer exists); Theologisches Seminar der Evangelisch-methodistischen Kirche, Reutlingen, Germany (since 2008 Reutlingen School of Theology); and Wyzsze Seminarium Teologiczne in Jana Laskiego, Warsaw, Poland. (For the situation today see http://mgefld.wixsite.com/mgefld-europe).

100 For a description of the intention of this program, see http://www.methodist-e-academy.org/.

101 Always two seminar courses complete the session: Methodist history, Methodist doctrine, and Methodist ecclesiology.

102 All "Free Churches" (independent from the state) total about 1 percent of all Christians in Europe (according to the total population that calls itself Christian).

participation in ecumenical dialogues.[103] Furthermore, Methodists also practice an ecumenical spirit that allows them to be among the founding members of all the principal European ecumenical institutions including the World Council of Churches (1948), the Conference of European Churches (1964), the Community of Protestant Churches in Europe (1973), as well as—on the level of free churches—the "Free Church Association" (1926) that is organized at the federal state level. Methodist Churches in Europe also signed the Charta Oecumenica, a joint document from the Conference of European Churches (CEC) and the Council of European Episcopal Conferences (CCEE, Consilium Conferentiarum Episcoporum Europae), which contains twelve guidelines and self-commitments for the growing cooperation among the churches in Europe.[104]

Methodists have a long tradition of quality educational work. In recent decades more and more Methodist theologians have been recognized and accepted in scholarly theological dialogues.[105] Methodist work in evangelism, education, and social service is also well known. In spite of its small size, Methodism operates a large number of hospitals, health-care institutions, residences for the elderly, child care services, and other community facilities.

Conclusion and Important Questions

The rationale for all Methodist mission is soteriological and ecclesiological. It arises out of a concrete theological focus on a holistic holiness doctrine supported by a connectional church structure. Both doctrine and structure create a deep understanding of the oneness of the church as Christ's body, rooted in work of the Trinitarian God. They place humanity in a vital, living,

---

103 See Ulrike Schuler, *Chancen und Grenzen freikirchlicher Organisationsstrukturen im ökumenischen Prozess*, in Holger Eschmann, Jürgen Moltmann, and Ulrike Schuler, eds., *Freikirchen—Landeskirchen. Historische Alternative—Gemeinsame Zukunft?* (Neukirchen-Vlyn: Neukirchener Verlag, 2008 [Theologie interdisziplinär, Bd. 2]), 36–56.

104 The statement is originally written in German. An English translation can be found at https://web.archive.org/web/20121225040803/http://www.ceceurope.org/current-issues/charta-oecumenica/.

105 The Reutlingen School of Theology (affiliated with The United Methodist Church) was the first theological institute of the free churches that became officially recognized by the state in Germany (2005).

ongoing relationship with God, in a perpetual covenant with God and other people. The combination of Methodist theology and ecclesiology can open a dialogue that is trans-confessional and multicultural; this seems ideally suited to the European reality.

The Methodist way of living is continually confronted with other theologies, traditions, and cultures. This inevitably leads to conflict. Methodism has to coexist with and appreciate the reality of other scriptural concepts of what it means to be the church. It has to find creative ways to work and coexist with other churches as something always new and dynamic by reflecting scripturally on its own actions in each new situation.

Methodism in continental Europe went through several phases. New emphases and structures were sought in each new context, sometimes without careful reflection on more traditional ones. Whenever scriptural reflection was undertaken, erroneous trends could be recognized and sometimes partly corrected. So, class meetings as centers of Methodist missions were understood as communities in which to live and learn. Spiritual living and learning belonged to a discipline, and the truths of faith were acquired through musical and poetic form by the singing of hymns. Christian publications and a Christian education program for all ages and for responsible members were developed alongside social service work undertaken by either individuals or institutions. All of this formed a part of the life-changing process that the believer adopts in becoming Methodist.

The desire "to spread scriptural holiness across the nation" with other faithful people must always become concrete in each new context. Reversals and frustrations never justify either weakening or discarding mission. History shows that the cooperative ecumenical missionary work developed in the twentieth century could progress and develop. In Europe the Methodist churches created their own distinctive organizational structures: some chose autonomy; some joined in church unions with other confessions; still others stayed in a worldwide connection of one church, working together so that the experience of God's grace could become more widely and convincingly known.

153

Methodism in Europe is an ongoing history of migration. An example of our days shall underline this finding: There was no official mission to the Netherlands till the end of the twentieth century. Nevertheless John Wesley had visited this country three times and had connections with a lot of different faithful people. Also some of his articles and main tracts (like the Character of a Methodist and also the General Rules) were translated into Dutch. Holiness churches settled in the Netherlands—among others the Salvation Army and the Church of the Nazarene as well as a Pentecostal Methodist group from Scandinavia. But it was not before the end of the twentieth century that missions from West India (Caribbean) and Ghana officially began to work in the Netherlands because of migration. Both homelands were former Dutch colonies. Both decided to do mission in this secularized country after they had become independent and autonomous Methodist churches: 1961, The Methodist Church Ghana; 1967, the Church in the Caribbean and the Americas. Both also became members of the WMC. The declared reason was for the Caribbean to connect with their emigrants in the Netherlands within the "Methodist Church in the Caribbean and the Americas" (1989). For Ghana, the articulated goal was to do mission outside the Ghanaian communities in the Netherlands with the help of the immigrants already settled in the Netherlands (1996). Methodist missions continue across Europe with faithful people fulfilling God's commission to spread scriptural holiness across the nations.

Methodists in Russia (1889–2018)

A Brief Overview

Sergei V. Nikolaev

I n this chapter I examine the history of the Methodist Church in Russia primarily through the work of three prominent Methodists in northwest Russia in the period beginning with the organization of the first Methodist church in 1889 and ending with the death of Russian Methodist Julius Hecker in 1938. In the epilogue, I give a brief overview of the reemergence of Methodism in Russia in the 1990s and some current developments.

Frequently, historical essays dealing directly with religious matters often fall into two wide camps, being either hagiographical, triumphant "lives of the saints," or critically oriented material of the character-assassination type. My aim in this essay is to avoid falling into either of these camps. My approach is to position my narrative, on the one hand, as a critical analysis of Russian Methodist history and, on the other hand, as an evaluation that helps us understand the value this part of Methodist history provides for the present and future of people who claim to be truly Russian and truly Methodist.

Historical Background

Methodism entered Russia in a historically significant way in 1889 as a mission of the Methodist Episcopal Church.[1] On a visit to St. Petersburg with Bishop Charles H. Fowler after multiple requests from Russia and several preliminary trips, Bent August Carlson (1833–1920), an American born in Sweden and a presiding elder of the Finland District of the Sweden Annual Conference, organized a small Methodist congregation with seven probationary members to serve the Swedish population.[2] Over the next sixteen years, the number of Methodists in Russia did not increase much because Russia still had a legal prohibition against conversion to non–Russian Orthodox Christianity in the late imperial period, although less stringently enforced than earlier due to the rapid social and economic change Russia was undergoing. Nonetheless, conversion among non–Russian Orthodox traditions typically required permission from the state.[3] Because of its entry into Russia as a confession serving a "foreign minority," Methodist services could not be advertised in newspapers. Methodist evangelism had to be aimed at the Swedish and Finnish populations in the St. Petersburg area during private

---

1   There are references to earlier Methodist work with Russians dating back to 1860 but with no Methodist community emerging as a result. Frederick William Flocken (1831–1893), a Russian-born member of the New York Conference and missionary to Bulgaria, reported baptizing four Russian children in Tultcha, Bulgaria (later Romania). Donald Karl Malone, "A Methodist Venture in Bolshevik Russia," *Methodist History* 18, no. 4 (1980): 239; Wade Crawford Barclay, *History of Methodist Mission: The Methodist Episcopal Church, Widening Horizons*, vol. III (New York: The Board of Missions of the Methodist Episcopal Church, 1957), 1019. Also, for reference to F. W. Flocken see Paul W. Chilcote and Ulrike Schuler, "Methodist Bible Women in Bulgaria and Italy," *Methodist History* 52, no. 2 (2014): 101.

2   Malone, "A Methodist Venture," 239–40; John Dunstan, "George A. Simons and the Khristianski Pobornik: A Neglected Source on St. Petersburg Methodism," *Methodist History* 19, no. 1 (1980): 23–24; John L. Nuelsen, Theophil Mann, and J. J. Sommer, "The Methodist Church in Finland, Russia, and the Baltic States, 1880–1928," trans. from the German by S. T. Kimbrough Jr., in *Methodism in Russia and the Baltic States: History and Renewal*, ed. S. T. Kimbrough Jr. (Nashville: Abingdon Press, 1995), 31–32; Barclay, *Widening Horizons*, 978; Nolan B. Harmon, ed., "Russia," in *The Encyclopedia of World Methodism*, vol. 2 (Nashville: The United Methodist Publishing House, 1974).

3   The Russian Empire had great interest in regulating confessional affiliation because in addition to ideological reasons, it relied on confessional records for determining the age and legitimacy of children, inheritance rights, eligibility of exemptions from military draft and for entering state service, as well as conferring rights on the place of residence and access to education and certain occupations. Paul W. Werth, "Arbiters of the Free Conscience: Confessional Categorization and Religious Transfer in Russia, 1905–1917," in *Re-Bounding Identities in Russia and Ukraine*, ed. Blair Ruble, Dominique Arel, and Nancy Popson (Washington, DC: Woodrow Wilson Center Press, 2006), 182.

visits to people's homes. In 1904, there were only twenty officially recognized Methodists in Russia.[4]

After 1905 the situation changed considerably in two important ways. The Russian Empire passed a series of legislative measures in 1905, including the Edict of Toleration, liberalizing its religious order and granting its subjects freedom of conscience.[5] These measures allowed Methodist meetings in Russia to be implicitly recognized by the state from 1905 on.[6] Thus, in 1907 the Russian-born and Finnish-trained pastor Hjalmar F. Salmi, who could preach in Russian, Finnish, and Swedish, as well as communicate in English, was able to obtain state permission to hold religious meetings in St. Petersburg Province.[7] Within a year he reported over 150 Methodist converts in the Khandrovo Circuit of six preaching stations.[8]

George Albert Simons and Sister Anna Eklund

In 1907 Bishop William Burt appointed Dr. George Albert Simons (1874–1952) to be the new superintendent of the Finland and St. Petersburg Mission Conference and a Presiding Elder (*nadziratel'*) of the Russian District. Simons, an American and son of a Methodist pastor, was trained at Baldwin-Wallace College in Berea, Ohio; New York University; and Drew Theological Seminary.[9] He oversaw the work of the Methodist community in northwestern Russia at its pre-Revolutionary peak.[10] In 1909 the Methodist Church was explicitly

---

4 Dunstan believes Simons questions the reliability of this number. Dunstan, "George A. Simons," 25n25.

5 The religious legislations of 1905, though granting greater religious freedom to the subjects of the Russian Empire, were rather confusing for practical use. The Edict of Toleration of April 1905 legalized conversion from one Christian faith to another under certain conditions and recognized some non-Russian Orthodox faiths. The October 1905 decree that granted "freedom of conscience" was a broader and less clearly defined legislation, which, however, superseded the earlier Edict. Werth, "Arbiters of Free Conscience."

6 Russian State Historical Archive (*RGIA*), f. 821, o. 133, d. 1006, l. 51ob, 52.

7 See reference in *RGIA*, f. 821, o. 5, d. 1040, l. 106.

8 Dunstan, "George A. Simons," 26, 27; S. T. Kimbrough Jr., *Sister Anna Eklund, 1867–1949: A Methodist Saint in Russia. Her Words and Witness, Saint Petersburg, 1908–1931* (New York: GBGM BOOKS, 2001), 11–12.

9 Dunstan, "George A. Simons," 26.

10 Simons, though reluctantly, had to leave Russia in 1918 because the US government recalled him. Dunstan, "George A. Simons," 68. However, even from Riga, Lithuania, his new residence, he continued to oversee the work in Russia until the 1924 General Conference approved establishing the Baltic and Slavic Mission Conference separate from the Russian Mission Conference. Nuelsen, "The Methodist Church," 36.

recognized by the Russian government, and on a typical Sunday, the First Methodist Episcopal Church in St. Petersburg would have a German-speaking service at 10:00 a.m., an English service at 11:30 a.m., Russian at 3:45 p.m., Swedish at 5:00 p.m., and Finnish and Estonian at 6:00 p.m.[11] In 1911, Bishop Burt organized a separate Russian Mission Conference with thirteen preachers, fifteen congregations, eight seminary students, three deaconesses, five hundred members, nine Sunday schools, seven hundred children, four buildings, and a publishing house.[12]

In 1908, Sister Anna Eklund (1867–1949), born in Finland and trained at the Bethany Deaconess Training Centers in Hamburg and Frankfurt, was appointed by Bishop Burt to start deaconess work in St. Petersburg.[13] She opened the "Bethany" (*Vifaniya*) deaconess society the first Sunday of November with four Russian women. During the 1909–1910 appointment year, she reported 87 days of taking care of the sick; 218 visits to sick, poor, and needy; as well as providing free and paid massages to 163 patients. They organized a Christmas party for 125 children and elderly people, whom they fed and provided with gifts and clothes. In one of the villages, 28 family homes, mainly Methodist, burned down in a fire. Three days later Sister Anna and two helpers went there with support "of every kind" to help them.[14]

The Northwest Russian Methodist community directly endured the October Bolshevik Revolution of 1917 and its devastating consequences. "Property and work intact. All well," stated the cablegram that Simons sent to the Methodist Episcopal Church Board of Foreign Mission headquarters in New York City less than a month after the October 25 Bolshevik Revolution.[15]

11 "Evangel'skie Chteniya," *Khristianskii Pobornik: Russkii Organ Metodistskoi Episkopal'noi Tserkvi* 1, no. 1 (January 1909): 8.

12 Malone, "A Methodist Venture," 240.

13 Kimbrough, *Sister Anna*, 9.

14 Sestra Anna [Eklund], "Otchet Obshchiny diakoniss 'Vifania,'" *Khristianskii Pobornik* 1, no. 20 (August 1910): 171–72.

15 Simons, George A. (Rev.), 1912–1948, Missionary Files, 1912–1949, United Methodist Church Archives–CAH, Madison, New Jersey.

At first, the Methodist reaction was still positively colored by the February 1917 Revolution, which had removed the Romanov monarchy and installed the Provisional Government. Simons viewed the new state order as a God-established order. Among other things he was thrilled that "the time of persecution, imprisonment, and exile, for the Word of God, is past in Russia."[16] On May 1, Simons held an open-air Methodist meeting in a park near the First Methodist Episcopal Church, with over one thousand people present and over fifteen Methodist brochures distributed in addition to New Testaments. The Methodists continued this outreach for four years using an orchestra every Sunday at 5:00 p.m. To Simons this openness seemed a fulfillment of Bishop Burt's encouragement that there would emerge a new Russia, probably sooner rather than later, and that the Methodist Church would be there to preach the Word of God to this great nation.[17]

Julius Friedrich Hecker

It was in a similar spirit that Dr. Julius Friedrich Hecker (1881–1938), future Methodist martyr in Russia, returned to his homeland after the Bolshevik Revolution. Born in St. Petersburg of German descent, Hecker immigrated to the United States, where he converted to Methodism in New York and received a call to ministry.[18] He graduated from German Wallace College in Berea, Ohio; Drew Theological Seminary; and Columbia University, where he studied the sociology of religion.[19] Initially joining the East German Conference, he transferred to the New York East Conference and was appointed as assistant pastor at the East Side Parish and the Church of All Nations for

---

16 G.A. Simons, "Voskresenie Rossii," *Khristianskii Pobornik* 9, no. 102 (June 1917): 54.

17 Simons, "Voskresenie Rossii," 55.

18 2573-3-5:03, "Russia: Report by Bishop John Nuelsen, 1922–1923," United Methodist Church Archives–GCAH, Madison, New Jersey, II:7.

19 Julius F. Hecker, "Russian Sociology: A Contribution to the History of Sociological Thought and Theory" (PhD diss., Columbia University, 1915).

work with Russian immigrants.[20] Before returning to Russia, Hecker worked for John R. Mott at prisoner-of-war camps in Austria with the Russian prisoners on behalf of the YMCA.[21] Importantly, in 1916 he developed extension education by correspondence that allowed him to be in contact with the prisoners of war for years, even after he left Austria.[22] He was approved to help with Methodist work in Russia. "Hecker acceptable," stated the cablegram from Simons to the Mission Society headquarters on November 2, 1917.[23]

Hecker required special confirmation from Simons because he was a somewhat "inconvenient" person for the Methodist mission. On the one hand, he was very intelligent and energetic. On the other, Julius Hecker was a Christian Communist or Christian Socialist.[24] Though he did not agree with the methods used by Russian revolutionaries, Hecker believed that the Russian Bolshevik Revolution created a state order preferable to the Tsarist regime.[25] In the past, Hecker's sympathies with the Russian Bolshevik Revolution had caused him problems with the US Department of State.[26] Still, Bishop Nuelsen was confident: "Dr. Hecker is an idealist of the finest type. He does not care for personal gain or comforts, but gives his time and strength unstintedly and without any personal considerations to the cause to which he has committed himself."[27]

---

20 "Russia: Report by Nuelsen," II:7; *Minutes of the Annual Conferences of the Methodist Episcopal Church, Spring Conferences 1912* (New York: The Methodist Book Concern, 1912), 29; *Minutes of the Annual Conferences of the Methodist Episcopal Church, Spring Conferences 1913* (New York: The Methodist Book Concern, 1913), 81–82; *Minutes of the Annual Conferences of the Methodist Episcopal Church, Spring Conferences 1914* (New York: The Methodist Book Concern, 1914), 118–19; *Minutes of the . . . Session of the New York East Annual Conference of the Methodist Episcopal Church*, ed. Harry B. Belcher (New York: The Methodist Book Concern, 1915), 1915, 19, 135; 1916, 28–29, 47; 1917, 18, 126; 1918, 112, 126; 1919, 116.

21 "Russia: Report by Nuelsen," II:7; *Minutes of the . . . Session of the New York East Annual Conference of the Methodist Episcopal Church*, ed. Harry B. Belcher, 1918, 126; 1919, 116.

22 Elizabeth J. Hecker, "Letter to Mr. Bek, Uchtenhagen, June 30, 1922," Hecker, Julius F. (Rev. & Mrs.), 1916–1937, Folder 1: April 1916–Dec. 1923, Missionary Files, 1912–1949, United Methodist Church Archives–GCAH, Madison, New Jersey.

23 George A. Simons (Rev.), 1912–1948, Missionary Files, 1912–1949, United Methodist Church Archives–GCAH, Madison, New Jersey.

24 "Russia: Report by Nuelsen," II:8.

25 "Russia: Report by Nuelsen," II:7.

26 "Russia: Report by Nuelsen," II:7.

27 "Russia: Report by Nuelsen," II:8.

The cause to which Julius Hecker committed himself in Russia consisted of his humanitarian efforts, educational initiative, and engagement with the Russian Orthodox Church. When Hecker, after an absence of many years, returned to Russia in 1921, he returned as a supervisor for the distribution of humanitarian aid and medical supplies that had been collected in the United States.[28] This aid was gathered for Russia, which had been decimated by one of the greatest famines in Europe and had claimed the lives of an estimated six million people.[29] In the course of his visit, Hecker traveled to Samara, Orenburg, and Buzuluk—areas that he stated were some of the worst affected by the famine. He concluded in his general report that the best course of action to help the suffering people of Russia would be to increase the contributions of relief organizations, give financial credit to the Soviet government for purchasing much-needed grain supply, help the Soviet government to reestablish the railroad system, and not be afraid to deal with the Soviet government in general.[30] Another of Hecker's ideas was to appeal to Frank Mason North, the corresponding secretary of the Board of Foreign Missions of the Methodist Episcopal Church, to raise funds in the United States for those children suffering from the famine, both directly as support for individuals and collectively by opening orphanages. This idea had the support and approval of the commissioner of education of Russia, Anatoly Lunacharsky.[31]

In a similar vein, after Hecker had moved to Russia together with his family, he sought to identify and offer to the average Russian person a healthy

---

28 Nadezhda Andreeva, "In the Current of Time: Regarding the Fate of Doctor of Philosophy Julius Hecker and His Family in Russia, America, Europe, and Russia Again ["V potoke vremeni: O sud'be doktora filosofii Yulii Gekkere i ego sem'e v Rossii, Evrope, Amerike i snova v Rossii"], *Inye Berega* 1, no. 5 (2007): 130, accessed February 23, 2018, http://inieberega.ru/files/her15.pdf.

29 For American relief efforts in connection with the Russian Famine of 1921–1922, see, for example, Bertrand M. Patenaude, *The Big Show in Bololand: The American Relief Expedition to Soviet Russia in the Famine of 1921* (Stanford: Stanford University Press, 2002).

30 Julius F. Hecker, "In the Wake of Death and Horror: A Trip Across Starving Russia, December 22–January 10, 1922," Hecker, Julius F. (Rev. & Mrs.), 1916–1937, Folder 1: April 1916–Dec. 1923, Missionary Files, 1912–1949, United Methodist Church Archives–GCAH, Madison, New Jersey.

31 For the copy of the Russian original and its translation, see "R.S.F.S.R., People's Education Commissariat, 12/1–1922, #7261 [R.S.F.S.R., Narodnyi Komissariat po Prosveshcheniyu, 12/1–1922, #7261] in Hecker, Julius F. (Rev. & Mrs.), 1916–1937, Folder 1: April 1916–Dec. 1923, Missionary Files, 1912–1949, United Methodist Church Archives–GCAH, Madison, New Jersey.

and affordable source of nutrition. After conducting some research, he selected oats. The only hindrance that prevented implementation of his idea was the lack of an initial investment. Hecker came into sufficient funds after publishing his book, *Religion under the Soviets*, in the United States in 1927. Consequently, he acquired a factory for processing oats and even came up with a brand name for the product, "Hercules" (*Gerkules*), with the underlying idea being that, by eating oatmeal, one could become as strong as Hercules.[32] Unfortunately, the Soviet New Economic Policy (NEP) that allowed enterprises like this to emerge came to an end with the ascension of Stalin to power in the late 1920s, and Hecker lost his factory in 1929. Nonetheless, the common name of "Hercules" for oatmeal in Russia survived the Soviet period and continues to this day. Indeed, it became one of the iconic descriptors of everyman's life in the Soviet Union.

Hecker's unique educational and cultural background placed him in a position to pursue ambitious projects in this particular historical period. The educational initiative was the most ambitious of them. It was based on Hecker's model of extension education by correspondence that he developed working with the Russian prisoners in Austrian prisoner-of-war camps. Hecker's model, in turn, was based on the Methodist correspondence course of education for their pastors in the United States.[33]

There was an entire generation of young Russian people who grew up in the years of the Russian Revolution and the subsequent Russian Civil War. This generation was entering into adult life with little or no education. The Russian government was concerned about providing them with education, but it did not have the experience, equipment, or funds to build a new educational system. The American system of education by correspondence was of particular interest to the Russian educators, and Julius Hecker was

---

32 Personal communication. Some details of this episode were shared with the author by the members of the Hecker family still living in Klyazma, on his visit together with a retired United Methodist Bishop Ruediger Minor in December 2012. In addition, see Andreeva, "Inye Berega," 132.

33 Elizabeth Hecker, "Letter to Mr. Bek," 1.

the person engaged for the task to bring it to Russia. Lunacharsky and Vladimir Lenin's wife, Nadezhda Krupskaya, supported Hecker's work to the point that in 1922 he was given free use for ten years of a seven-story building in the center of Moscow, in Arbat District,[34] to develop a nation-wide correspondence education particularly for "teachers, foremen, and other qualified workers."[35] The aim was to develop practical education "so that the masses may learn to work and the productivity of the trades and professions be improved."[36] Moreover, Hecker was asked to do this with the help of foreign capital and to put it on a self-supporting basis, if possible.[37] Within a year there were fifteen thousand students enrolled in the teachers' correspondence school. Furthermore, Hecker was asked to lecture on educational sociology and American education at the Moscow Graduate School of Pedagogy. Bishop John Nuelsen, the overseeing bishop in Europe at that time, affirmed that this was work of tremendous significance.[38]

Hecker's primary engagement with the Russian Orthodox Church also was in the area of education. Through the financial aid raised by Bishops Blake and Nuelsen and Dr. Lewis Hartman, the editor of one of the early American Methodist newspapers, *Zion's Herald*, the Russian Orthodox Church was able to reopen the Moscow Theological Academy, which had been closed in 1919 after the Bolshevik Revolution. Once again, as in the case with the Russian State Commissariat of Education, Hecker was invited to take part in teaching at the graduate level. Here he taught in the chair of Christian Ethics and Sociology, educating the future key leadership in the Russian Orthodox Church. Likewise, Hecker was invited to help with its extension correspondence course. The majority of clergy had to be trained

---

34 See multiple mailing address references in Hecker, Julius F. (Rev. & Mrs.), 1916–1937, Folder 1: April 1916–Dec. 1923, Missionary Files, 1912–1949, United Methodist Church Archives–GCAH, Madison, New Jersey.

35 "Dr. Hecker's letter to Bishop Nuelsen" in "Russia: Report by Nuelsen," II:10.

36 "Dr. Hecker's letter to Bishop Nuelsen" in "Russia: Report by Nuelsen," II:9.

37 "Dr. Hecker's letter to Bishop Nuelsen" in "Russia: Report by Nuelsen," II:10.

38 "Russia: Report by Nuelsen," II:10.

through home study courses, particularly in preaching and Bible Study. In 1924, the list of students taking the correspondence course contained about two thousand names.[39]

Hecker also took part in helping the Methodist Episcopal Church to develop a relationship with the Russian Orthodox Church. In conceiving of Christianity fundamentally as the individual and social experience of Christ, along the lines of the Social Gospel movement prominent in the United States in that period, and in contrast to understanding Christianity as an ecclesial tradition, Hecker found himself positioned more closely to the circles of the Russian Orthodox Church that were pursuing reforms in the church than to the traditional Patriarchal Russian Orthodox Church.[40] However, the Methodist Episcopal Church Board of Foreign Missions was careful not to side with any division of the Russian Orthodox Church in the 1920s.[41] In addition, progress along these lines of cooperation was hindered by the fact that the United States did not establish diplomatic relations with the Soviet Union, which was formally founded as a state in 1922, until the end of 1933 during the presidency of Franklin D. Roosevelt.

Through all of these projects, Hecker was led by the basic conviction that communist ideals better corresponded with the ideas of Christ than capitalist ideals did, and he sought to make Christian communism workable both in the life of regular Russians and on the state level in Russia.[42] This is why he

39 J. F. Hecker, "To the New York East Conference of the Methodist Episcopal Church, January 28, 1924," Hecker, Julius F. (Rev. & Mrs.), 1916–1937, Folder 2: Jan. 1924–Feb. 1937, Missionary Files, 1912–1949, United Methodist Church Archives–GCAH, Madison, New Jersey.

40 "Letter to Dr. Frank Mason North, September 24, 1923," Hecker, Julius F. (Rev. & Mrs.), 1916–1937, Folder 1: April 1916–Dec. 1923, Missionary Files, 1912–1949, United Methodist Church Archives–GCAH, Madison, New Jersey.

41 "Russian Orthodox Church, 1922–1924," Missionary Files, 1912–1949, United Methodist Church Archives–GCAH, Madison, New Jersey.

42 There is a growing number of books referring to Dr. Julius F. Hecker and his legacy, in English and Russian, both of academic quality and popular. Their reading of Hecker varies from very sympathetic to very unsympathetic. Among the academic books, see David S. Foglesong, *The American Mission and the "Evil Empire": The Crusade for a "Free Russia" since 1881* (Cambridge and New York: Cambridge University Press, 2007); Dirk Kaesler, *Earle Edward Eubank's Visits with European Sociologists* (New Brunswick and London: Transaction Publishers, 1991); Tim Tzouliadis, *The Forsaken: An American Tragedy in Stalin's Russia* (New York: Penguin Press, 2008); Heather J. Coleman, *Russian Baptists and Spiritual Revolution, 1905–1929* (Bloomington: Indiana University Press, 2005); and Matthew Lee Miller, *The American YMCA and Russian*

went to Russia in the 1920s. He dedicated himself to educating Russians for a better life through the correspondence courses, as well as educating the future Russian Orthodox priests for better parish ministry. He was associated with the renovation groups within the Russian Orthodox Church because he believed that this would better serve the ordinary Russian people. Hecker believed that the Soviet communists were "anti-clerical," but "religious . . . [and] as yet have not developed a definite religious philosophy."[43] "In my talks with the Communists," writes Hecker to North, "I frequently turned the conversation on the subject of religion and found them inevitably deeply interested."[44] He was positive that "much good could be accomplished by anyone who would develop and direct the potential religious forces of the Communist movement."[45]

Hecker's legacy is complicated because in addition to the religious, political, and educational ideals shaping his life's journey, Hecker was in the position of bridging the American and Russian cultures and churches. "As a connecting link between the Russian Church and American Protestantism, Dr. Hecker renders a service of very great importance," pointed out Bishop Nuelsen in his report to the Executive Committee of the Board of Foreign Missions.[46] As part of his position, Hecker, on the one hand, defended Russian communism in the United States and Europe and, on the other, hoped for an opening to influence people religiously in his circle of influence in Russia. The reaction to this prophetic position resulted in the fact that neither of the sides accepted Hecker as their own and eventually promoted accusations of him spying for the opposite side. The United States accused him of being a Red spy, whereas Soviet Russia accused him of being an American spy.

Culture: The Preservation and Expansion of Orthodox Christianity, 1900–1940 (Lanham, MD: Lexington Books, 2013). Among Russian articles, see Nadezhda Andreeva, "In the Current of Time," 128–37.

43 2573-3-5-02, "Report on Conditions in Russia, submitted to Dr. F. M. North by Dr. Julius F. Hecker, February, 1922," 21–22, Missionary Files, 1912–1949, United Methodist Church Archives–GCAH, Madison, New Jersey.

44 2573-3-5-02, 22.

45 2573-3-5-02, 22.

46 "Russia: Report by Nuelsen," II:10.

With Stalin's ascension to power in the late 1920s, Lunacharsky was dismissed as Commissar for Education, and Hecker, like many other Russian leaders associated with the church, was arrested. He spent several months in prison and was released only after the appeal of the Commissar of Foreign Affairs, Georgy Chicherin.[47] In 1934 and 1935 Hecker was allowed to travel to the United States and Europe on lecture tours. In the fall of 1935 the Board of Foreign Missions of the Methodist Episcopal Church entertained the idea of joining up Hecker's lecture tour with the well-known Methodist evangelist E. Stanley Jones, though this did not come to fruition.[48] This was the last time Hecker corresponded with the Board of Foreign Missions. On February 16, 1938, during the Great Purge, Hecker was arrested then executed two months later under the accusation of being an American spy.[49] His good name was rehabilitated by the Soviet Union on April 15, 1957, a few years after the death of Stalin.

American sociologist Earle Edward Eubanks, on meeting with Julius Hecker in 1934, described him as a person making a strange impression of one both younger and older than his real age. His face kept the youthfulness, developed from his idealism and hopes for the future, at the same time having wrinkles caused not only by bitter disappointments but also by deep suffering. His speech was a surprising mix of a deep thinker and impractical dreamer.[50] Interestingly, modern historians often describe Methodism in similar contrasting terms.[51] Pragmatic and naïve, deep thinker and dreamer, idealistic and practical all at the same time, Hecker was formed by the Christian way of life in the Methodist Episcopal Church. It was a distinctive way

---

47 Andreeva, "Inye Berega," 132.

48 "Letter of R. E. Diffenorfer to Dr. Julius F. Hecker, August 2nd, 1935," Julius F. Hecker (Rev. & Mrs.), 1916–1937, Folder 2: Jan. 1924–Feb. 1937, Missionary Files, 1912–1949, United Methodist Church Archives–GCAH, Madison, New Jersey.

49 The record of Julius Hecker's arrest and execution can be accessed in Russian at http://www.ihst.ru /projects/sohist/repress/kom/1938/gekker.htm and http://old.memo.ru/history/arkiv/op1017.htm.

50 Dirk Kaesler, *Earle Edward Eubank's Visit*, 67–75.

51 Nathan O. Hatch and John H. Wigger, introduction to *Methodism and the Shaping of American Culture*, ed. Nathan O Hatch and John H. Wigger (Nashville: Kinsgwood Books, 2001), 11–22.

of being Christian, but this way gave Hecker conviction and strength to return to Russia with five little children, to put his energy, talents, and time to use improving the life of ordinary people in Russia, not to give up even in the face of such a tragic dehumanizing social experiment as Russian Bolshevik communism, but to attempt "by the preaching of the Gospel to elevate, ennoble, Christianize Communism," even at the cost of his own life.[52]

Conclusion

George Simons was recalled by the US government from Russia in 1918. Sister Anna Eklund was then asked to oversee the life of the Methodist community. She had to leave the county in 1931. The 1929–1930 appointment list tells the story of the expansion of this Methodist community from St. Petersburg all the way to Moscow, Ukraine, Belarus, even to Siberia: (1) Detskoe Selo, to be supplied (tbs), (2) Gatchina, John Talonpoika, (3) Kharkov, V. Melnikov, (4) Kiev, tbs, (5) Leningrad, Oskar Poeld, Ivan Tatarinovitch, (6) Luga, Bro. Firsov, (7) Moscow, Oscar Poeld, (8) Minsk, tbs, (9) Novgorod, Boris Pavlov, (10) Oskul, Bro. John Zemtin, (11) Petrozavodsk, John Talonpoika, (12) Pskov, Ivan Tatarinovitch, (13) Sigolovo, Bro. Potap Hoponen, (14) Senyavino, John Talonpoika, (15) Smolensk, tbs, (16) Strugi Krasnyia, Ivan Tatarinovitch, (17) Staraya Russa, Boris Pavlov, (18) Rasskazovo, M. Fomitchov, (19) Handrovo, Bro. Ivan Metso, (20) Tosno, E. Kaufman, (21) Tiflis, tbs, (22) Trotskoie, John Talonpoika, (23) Tchudovo, F.I. Bredis, (24) Tver, tbs, (25) Vitebsk, W. G. Oksotcheskaya, (26) Volossovo, tbs, (27) Vyshnii-Volochek, Boris Gronski, (28) Marinsk, Bro. Carlsson, (29) Novosibirsk, tbs.[53]

Despite the dedicated service of George Simons and Anna Eklund, the martyrdom of Julius Hecker, and sacrifices of several thousand first-generation Methodist Russians who had embraced Methodism as a new lifestyle, Methodist Russians were faced with the aggressive militant atheism promoted by

---

52   Julius F. Hecker (Rev. & Mrs.), 1916–1937, Folder 1: April 1916–Dec. 1923, Missionary Files, 1912–1949, United Methodist Church Archives–GCAH, Madison, New Jersey.

53   "List of Appointments," Leningrad, 31 October 1929, Eklund, Anna (Miss), 1921–1949, Missionary Files, 1912–1949, United Methodist Church Archives–GCAH, Madison, New Jersey.

the Soviet state. When, in 1939, the bishop of northern Europe finally got a visa to enter the Soviet Union after trying for over ten years, he held the annual conference of the Russian Mission, which appeared at that time to be the last. "It lasted all night," recalled Wade in his letter. "I baptized four children and married two couples. No one dared act as Secretary." At the end Wade advised the few remaining Russian Methodists of the Methodist Episcopal Church to join the Baptists or some other evangelical group, thus dissolving the Russian Methodist community in northwest Russia in 1939.[54]

Through the service of Simons, Eklund, Hecker, and other Methodists in Russia between 1889 and 1939, we see fully dedicated Methodist Christians concerned about the faith and lives of ordinary Russians. These Methodists spent their lives in Russia providing humanitarian relief, guiding people to Christ, and seeking to bring the hope and love that the Methodist Church preached to the Russian people. Although their efforts did not result in producing a self-sufficient church that could survive through the Soviet period in Russia, they leave inspiring examples of Christian lives and ideals for the later generations of Russian Methodists.

Epilogue

In the late 1980s Mikhail Gorbachev introduced *perestroika* and *glasnost* to the Soviet Union. This change in policy led to the end of the Cold War, and, ultimately, to the collapse of the Soviet Union. In the early 1990s the deterioration of the post-Soviet economy led to food shortages in Russia. Medical supplies were difficult to obtain. When people were hospitalized, they were often asked to bring their own medicine with them for their treatment.

Russians faced the shortage of food and medicine stoically. It was the collapse of their world as they knew it. They were now thrust into a new reality in which the promises of their education and previous system of belief had been completely torn down. Their jobs, pension, savings, and hopes for the future were no longer secure. Most Russians did not know how to survive

---

54 Mansfield Hurtig, "Russia," in Harmon, "Russia."

in this new context or where to find meaning in life. The United Methodist Church became one of the churches that recognized this situation, helped them to answer life's basic questions, and assisted them to understand and negotiate the new normal.

In 1991 the president of the General Board of Global Ministries, Bishop Woodrow Hearn, and its general secretary, Dr. Randolph Nugent, visited Russia. They gained firsthand experience of the difficult economic situation that Russians faced and began taking measures to provide relief and expertise to Russians. The commitment to support Russian peoples in tangible ways has been a hallmark of Methodism throughout its history.

Independently of these developments, local United Methodist churches started to emerge in Russia. A house church in Kaminitsa, Western Ukraine, with pastor Ivan Vuksta, had endured throughout the Soviet period and became one of the centers of modern Ukrainian and Eurasian Methodism. A young Russian, Vladislav Spektorov, on a visit to Tallinn, Estonia, was converted in a Russian-speaking Methodist church. Upon his return to his hometown of Samara, Russia, Spektorov started a Bible study group that soon became a church and another center of modern Russian Methodism. Another center of recent Russian Methodism emerged in Moscow in the 1990s, where South Korean and American Korean diplomats and businessmen, who lived and worked in Moscow, having engaged in regular Bible study lessons for themselves, opened the meetings to Russian Koreans. Eventually they registered as the Russian–Korean–American Methodist Fellowship, led by Pastor Cho Young Cheul. This Methodist congregation gave birth to three other Methodist local churches in the early 1990s that were founded by the Russian Koreans but consisted predominantly of Russians. Yet another center of Russian Methodism emerged in Yekaterinburg as a result of the exchange of students at Ural State University. An interpreter, Lydia Istomina, became the leader of the new First United Methodist Church of Yekaterinburg, which soon numbered around five hundred worshippers.

Thus, the reemergence of Methodism in Russia in the early 1990s was not the result of any planned mission activity of The United Methodist Church, but rather due to natural social and cultural developments, such as a surviving Methodist house church on the border of the Soviet Union gaining momentum, travel within Soviet borders, international diplomatic and trade contacts, and international academic exchange made possible by the openness of Russian society in that period.

By 1992 there were eleven local United Methodist churches in Russia and Ukraine, with more to come. Supervision became an urgent need. The 1992 General Conference approved organizing the Russia United Methodist Mission Conference. In August of that year, the first meeting since 1939 of the Russia Mission Conference took place. Bishop Ruediger Minor became the episcopal leader of The United Methodist Church in the countries of the former Soviet Union.

The primary challenge that the fledgling Russian churches faced was to raise pastors' salaries and church program support. The "Russia Initiative" was organized by Dr. Bruce Weaver with three major emphases. First was the partner-church program in which American congregations partnered in ministry with local Russian United Methodist churches. Second came the partner-cities program in which local United Methodist churches in the United States partnered with a Russian city to develop cultural cooperation. Those partnerships led to cultural-exchange programs and, often, to the establishment of Russian United Methodist congregations, as in the city of Saratov. The third part of the "Russia Initiative" was the Volunteer-in-Mission program, which provided opportunities for many American Methodists to come to Russia to participate personally in short-term mission projects.

The growing number of local churches underscored the need for trained Russian pastors. In order to meet that need, the Russia United Methodist Theological Seminary was established in Moscow in 1995. On average, fifteen students in the residence program and thirty students in the extension program have been enrolled annually in the seminary to become pastors in Russia. Today, this seminary is a leading institution in the Unified Educational System with branches in Central Asia, the Ukraine, and the Far East of Russia with ninety United Methodist students training for ordained and lay ministry. Moreover, spiritual formation in the form of covenant groups and disciple-making is becoming an important feature of theological education at the seminary.[55] Counseling and social entrepreneurship are identified as future areas of specialization. All aspects are directed toward serving the particular contextual needs of Russian United Methodists.

By 2005 the reemergent Russia United Methodist Church was organized into five annual conferences and twelve districts. It had a theological seminary in Moscow, a retreat center in Voronezh, over one hundred local congregations, over thirty pieces of property, more than one hundred pastors under appointment, and over five thousand church members and a constituency of fifteen thousand.

Today, The United Methodist Church in Eurasia is the largest geographical episcopal area in the United Methodist connection, encompassing eleven time zones. For thirteen years Ruediger Minor was the Episcopal leader of The United Methodist Church in Eurasia. In February 2005 Hans Växby was elected to succeed him. In the fall of 2012 Eduard Khegay was the first Russian citizen elected as bishop. Under his leadership, five priorities were identified in Eurasia Episcopal Area to develop from 2015 forward: quality of ministry; education; mission, evangelism, and growth; self-sufficiency; and social service.[56]

In the 1990s people were very open and willing to look to the church for answers to the life questions that troubled them. Today, Russian people have become more skeptical, even cynical, and often unwilling to trust what the church has to offer them, having been for a full generation under the heavy influence of secularism. Today, to be effective in preaching the good news of Jesus Christ, each pastor and the church are challenged to be effective in evangelism and disciple-making. The Foundation for Evangelism of The United Methodist Church has been a faithful partner in this work.

---

55 More information on the Moscow Theological Seminary of The United Methodist Church can be found at https://www.facebook.com/moscowseminary.umc/.

56 Accessed July 11, 2018, http://old.umc-eurasia.ru/en/mission-evangelism-and-growth-step-1-personal -testimony-faith.

The church has begun to decentralize power. For most of the recent history of United Methodism in Eurasia, the primary power in the church was concentrated in Moscow. The United Methodist Church in Eurasia has decided to divide the power between several centers of Methodism in Eurasia in order to make the church more contextual and capable of fulfilling its mission. Stronger local centers will encourage more effective development of Methodism in those areas, relating specifically to the cultural, historical, and linguistic particularities.

Another sign of change in Russian Methodism is that Russian Methodists changed the name of their episcopal area to Eurasia to emphasize that Ukraine and Central Asia are part of this area. To connect Europe and Central Asia in one church is a source of great challenge and great potential for the future of The United Methodist Church in Eurasia. Though all countries of the former Soviet Union speak Russian, they have different cultures and, often, different understandings of what it means to be a Christian. To shape a Eurasian Methodist identity that includes both European and Central Asian sensibilities is an exciting and challenging task ahead of United Methodism in Eurasia.

The challenges of secularism, multiculturalism in increasingly nationalistic settings, and creating a Protestant identity in primarily Orthodox or Islamic settings are great hurdles. Nonetheless, the Eurasia United Methodist Church is alive with new vigor, relevance, and promise in making disciples of Jesus Christ in Eurasia.

LATIN
AMERICA

Methodism in Argentina (1836–2016)[1]

An Affiliated Autonomous Methodist Church

Daniel Bruno and Pablo R. Andiñach

Introduction

This article consists of two parts. The first part presents the historical development of Methodism in Argentina, which will be addressed in nine stages. The second, briefer part points to the main theological emphases and missionary challenges for the present and future. The criterion for the periodization of the stages is determined by characteristics, objectives, opportunities, and difficulties that accompanied the development of the Methodist mission. As such, we find stages that span thirty years, while another covers just one decade, since each stage tells a story of particular and contextual developments associated with the mission. Because interpreting our history also means being able to consider the future church, we also focus on actions based in those past experiences and theological tendencies that demarcate the place of Methodism within the larger scope of Christian churches that share the mission of proclaiming the gospel.

---

1 This chapter was translated from Castellano by Chivi Capezio, Murray Crookes, and Elaine Robinson.

A Brief History of Methodism in Argentina[2]

Stage 1: Experimental Period — Ethnic Ministry in English (1836–1867)

Methodism arrived in the country toward the end of 1835, but its first message in Spanish was not proclaimed until 1867. During the first thirty-one years, the mission focused on what can be called "ethnic chaplaincy." This was due, on the one hand, to the Argentinian government, influenced by the Catholic Church, that limited worship in the English language to enclosed spaces, and on the other hand, to the authority crisis of the missionary initiative itself. While the Missionary Society of the Methodist Episcopal Church based in New York exercised formal control of the mission, the real and less visible power was effectively in Buenos Aires in the hands of the Society for the Promotion of Christian Worship (SPCW).

There were many factors keeping Buenos Aires isolated from the outside world: distance, difficulty in communications, the financial crisis of the Missionary Society, and isolation provoked by the recurring internal politico-military crisis, which added to the conflict that Governor Rosas had with France (the country that made the Rio de la Plata estuary into a war zone with countless port blockades of Buenos Aires and Montevideo throughout the twelve years from 1838 to 1850). All of this resulted in the weakening of power in the Missionary Society over the mission in Rio de la Plata. Because of these factors, the real power over mission was in the hands of a powerful group of local businessmen who had formed the SPCW in 1843. This group not only controlled the Methodist missionary politics in Rio de la Plata (they preferred a mission centered on the Methodist families that were located in Buenos Aires for commercial reasons), they also abrogated the right to examine the missionaries sent by the Missionary Society about their theological knowledge and pastoral skills until they could prove "their doctrinal soundness and adequate experience."

---

2 For a more complete analysis, see Daniel P. Monti, *Ubicación del Metodismo en el Río de la Plata* (Buenos Aires: La Aurora, 1976). Also helpful is the *Revista Evangélica de Historia*, a publication of the Centro Metodista de Estudios Wesleyanos.

The SPCW became the real owners of the mission. The properties of both the mission in Buenos Aires and in Montevideo had been acquired by the SPCW. Moreover, during the financial crisis of the Missionary Society of New York, the SPCW began to pay the wages of the missionaries.

Around 1856, the Missionary Society of New York started to think about the need to open the mission to the Spanish-speaking population. Up to that point, the strategy was to work with English-speaking Protestants present in the region, increase their numbers, and educate their children in Sunday school to model the true gospel among the many Catholics. This was also the strategy upheld by the SPCW and defended at all costs, even when the Missionary Society of New York started planning a change of course.

In 1857 the Missionary Society appointed Rev. Henry Nicholson as a missionary teacher. Superintendent Goldsmith Carrow, who had recently been appointed to this position, supported this position, and it was strategic for the new course planned by the Society. Nicholson had been working as a teacher in Gibraltar (Spain) and spoke Spanish as his native language. The "Mission House" in London that supported the Wesleyan missions in Spain also agreed to his appointment. This would become a key piece in the movement toward the native population, which the mission had already determined was necessary. However, even though all the facts seemed to favor the new direction for the mission, everything collapsed once again. Due to individual motives and missionary politics, an unsustainable tension existed within the SPCW, and it decided to press for the expulsion from the mission of both Nicholson and Superintendent Carrow.

The expulsion of Carrow and Nicholson, however, actually had a paradoxical effect on the situation. Rev. William Goodfellow, who arrived in the country at the end of 1857, was appointed to replace the removed superintendent. Goodfellow's arrival became the pivot point for the change of destiny of the mission in Rio de la Plata. The new superintendent arrived in the region with clear instructions given by the Missionary Society. These instructions contained three specific steps to accomplish: (1) reorganize the mission on the basis of Quarterly Conferences, (2) dissolve the SPCW, and

(3) utilize all available means to expand the mission and include the native population.

To be clear, the presence of the English speakers in the SPCW, who aimed the mission toward only the foreign Protestants living in the region right up to Goodfellow's arrival, was the source of this delay in beginning the work in Spanish. Now, however, the Board of New York was convinced that the only hope the Methodist mission had of surviving was to open its doors to the Spanish-speaking population. That important step had not yet taken place, but it was among Goodfellow's priorities. In his April 1865 report he affirmed, "We need a service in Spanish in this city (Buenos Aires). Many people would gather to hear the gospel in that language. We pray that persons will be raised up for that task. We have asked in the depths of our hearts what can be done to accomplish this goal. But so far nothing has appeared before our eyes."[3]

Between the years 1862 and 1866, John Thomson studied at the Ohio Wesleyan University. Thomson, who was a Scotsman raised in Argentina, did not lack the qualities that fit Goodfellow's expectations. He was young, energetic, and a good preacher; and above all, he spoke Spanish like a native speaker, having arrived in the country at a very early age. Thomson arrived in Buenos Aires in October 1866, and at that moment Goodfellow's plan began to take shape. In the last months of 1866, there were already three Spanish-language Bible study and prayer groups meeting in homes. The opening as well as the reaction to that initiative had begun.

As long as Methodism was a religion for the foreign English speakers, the Catholic authorities paid little attention to it. But, to the Catholic Church, the advance into the native population was a hostile sign; it was an invasion of their territory where for almost five hundred years no other doctrine had dared to venture. Even in the midst of the conflict, or perhaps thanks to it,

---

3 *Annual Report Mission Society* (New York: J. Collord, 1866), 104.

Methodism prepared to take an active and direct part in the life of the nation and its people.

The Missionary Advocate from November 1867 attests: "The Rev. Thomson preached his first sermon in the Spanish language on June 9 in our church, and it was quite full, about forty people were nationals. From that moment on Thomson continued to be in our church every Sunday afternoon."[4] This event marked the real beginning of Methodism in the Rio de la Plata. At the same time, the need to redesign the mission forced Methodists to perfect the art of controversy and public mission work. The doors were opened. Methodism had finally inserted itself into the national life and would be a part of its history. Even so, the work in the national language did not yet reach into the substantive decisions that were still designed and executed in English.

Stage 2: Opting for Controversy and the Legal Rights of Laity (1867–1893)

Preaching in Spanish opened the door to conflict with the Catholic Church, which had an absolute monopoly over the country's religion prior to that point. For that reason, this stage establishes "controversy" as the axis of the mission and proclamation. The ongoing confrontation with the Catholic Church was clear; controversy was a tool that Methodism adopted to open the way in an adverse terrain, which was marked not so much by doctrinal differences but centered around criticism of the clergy, in general, and the dispute over who was the bearer of the "true gospel" and who promoted "error." This confrontation provided the context for the creation of the publication *El Estandarte Evangélico* in South America, which was to "preach and defend the evangelical truths, never compromise with error, and not allow anyone to deceive humble people by calling themselves Christians."[5]

Another central theme of this stage was the public engagement of Methodism in its alliance with the new liberal governments and Freemasons promoting the separation of church and state. It was in this context that the

---

4 *The Missionary Advocate* (New York: Lane & Tippett, 1867), 67.

5 *El Estandarte Evangélico* 1 (Buenos Aires: Iglesia Metodista en la Argentina, 1883), 1.

church vehemently supported the laws of civil marriage, the right to public cemeteries, the creation of the civil registry office, and—without success— the legality of breaking the bond of marriage. Catholics exerted pressure on legislators so as to make the latter point impossible, though the Methodist Church supported the initiative until the end.

Public education, not religious education, was another focus of the Methodist mission in this stage. Methodism's campaign motto was "Alongside each church, a school," and Methodists viewed education as a key tool for the progress and strengthening of the conscience of the citizenry. This mandate for education led to innumerable parochial schools, including el Americano in Rosario, el Crandon in Montevideo, and el Colegio Ward in Buenos Aires.

Stage 3: Institutional Consolidation and Unification of the Protestant Camp (1893–1932)

On a different note, at this stage, the mission slowly became institutionalized and formed as a conference, rather than merely existing as a provisional missionary enclave. In 1890 it achieved the category of Missionary Conference; in 1893 it became the South American Annual Conference; and toward the end of the nineteenth century, in 1897, it acquired the status of Rio de la Plata Annual Conference.

The beginning of the twentieth century was distinct in that consecutive bishops resided in the country (until this time, the bishops visited the mission sporadically during their episcopal travels). All these steps provided the mission a different position with greater standing in the decisions of the General Conference of the Methodist Episcopal Church. Above all, it resulted in new budgetary considerations related to its financial health, even when the funding was never really significant. By comparison, in this period, the funds sent to South America did not exceed 10 percent of the funds allocated by North American Methodism to its missions in India or China.

This stage would also be marked by the repercussions of the Protestant Congress of Panama and later regional congresses that were held with the objective of contextualizing regionally the general decisions adopted in the

Panama Congress. Although it was an ecumenical congress that gathered the Protestant churches present in South America, including agencies and missionary societies, Methodists from the Rio de la Plata were present with a delegation of four members, including Pastor Francisco Barroetaveña. The impact of this Congress led Barroetaveña, upon his return to Buenos Aires, to undertake one of the most radical actions to occur within the nation's Methodist church.

In essence, between 1917 and 1919, together with a group of pastors and prominent laity, he promoted separating from the mother church in the United States. Policies of the church determined by those in the United States, as well as the shocking salary differences between the missionaries and local pastors, resulted in conflict and protests. This movement in favor of nationalizing the Methodist Church was virtually unknown until quite recently. The postulates that were raised help us visualize more starkly the impact on the present situation. The movement created a National Missionary Society with the objective of raising funds and slowly replacing the power of the Missionary Society based in New York. However, the church's precarious financial structure prevented any solution to these needs by means of local resources. Another side effect of that attempt was the creation, around 1930, of a common fund to support pastors; in this way it was possible to avoid the unjust income disparity between missionaries and local Argentine pastors. Nationalization would have to wait another fifty years, when in 1969, the church declared its autonomy.

Another central theme of this stage is the organization of the *Liga por la Templanza y la Lucha Antialcohólica*, a temperance league. This emphasis became one of the most distinctive traits of Methodism in the region, as preaching about and activities related to temperance increasingly permeated the church, right up until the 1960s. Pastors Ernesto Balloch and Gabino Rodríguez, together with deaconesses Juanita Balloch and Isabel G. B. de Rodríguez, promoted and sustained this work. The third stage came to a close in 1932 with the naming of Pastor Juan Gattinoni as the first indigenous bishop.

Stage 4: The High Point of Mobilization Efforts (1932–1948)

Catholicism, which had been losing ground with secular liberal or representative governments, now recovered some lost ground. The emergence in Europe of inter-war fundamentalist Catholic nationalism was the inspiration and model for local Catholicism, which now seemed supported by a sector of the military that had overthrown the government of the radical Hipolito Yrigoyen in 1930. This resurgence of a more conservative Catholicism provoked among Methodists the revival of its controversial anti-clergy and now anti-fascist practices.

This stage also includes grand evangelization campaigns, outdoor preaching, and the consolidation of a new generation of Methodists, sons and daughters of the first converted immigrants, who were determined to transform Argentine Methodism into a great movement. Indeed, this was the time of large youth organizations, women's organizations, and massive Sunday school gatherings. Methodist congregations had a dynamic role creating and integrating social and cultural spaces that promoted expectations of social advance. This atmosphere reinforced in Methodists a feeling of belonging to the fledgling middle class.

Perhaps the general frame for analyzing and understanding this stage is the emergence of Peronism, although its complexity precludes address here in depth. A large number of Methodists did not accept this political movement and reacted against its political forms and some of its practices. Peronism and reactions against it are important when analyzing the historical difficulties that Methodism has had in creating community and adding members of the lower classes of society.

On the other hand, the great wars, the emergence of the Soviet Bloc, and European totalitarianism were the center of ethical critiques and evangelical affirmations in sermons and public declarations. Methodism at this stage actively involved a large number of its lay members and pastors in the fight for peace, socialism as a means of pacification, and direct critique of capitalism, militarism, and clericalism. These activities consolidated the view of

Methodism as an integral mission in which human beings are subject to the work of Christ in promoting spiritual, as well as personal and social, liberation.

Stage 5: Generational Change and Crisis (1948–1960)

The postwar atmosphere opened space for new theological reflections; Barthian neo-orthodoxy gained ground in the international ecumenical scene. In Argentina a new generation attempted to break with the liberal theology that had dominated Methodist thinking over the previous thirty years. This generation would produce great leaders for Latin American Methodism such as Federico Pagura, José Míguez Bonino, and Roberto Ríos, among others whose influence continues to this day.

On the other hand, compared to the previous stage, the church began to see warning signs of decreasing numbers for various reasons. A strictly formal "cleaning" of the membership rolls around 1948 revealed that the membership statistics did not reflect actual numbers. There were other more serious reasons for decline, such as the progressive gentrification of Methodist congregations. This gentrification led to the formation of mutually supportive and enterprising groups that were closed off to others by means of codes, aesthetic guidelines, and family ties, and made it difficult for "outsiders" to enter the ranks. Also, as was mentioned in the previous stage, the raging anti-Peronism sustained by the Methodists resulted in the loss of many Methodist converts from the suburban areas of Greater Buenos Aires, who believed that one could not sympathize with Peronism and be Methodist. Lastly, toward the end of this stage, the theology of secularization emerged. This impacted a sector of the local leadership and resulted in the loss of interest in or devaluation of religious language, the call to conversion, and the local congregation as the engine of the mission of the church. All these factors taken together explain the beginning and consolidation of the downward trend in membership.

The second indigenous bishop, Sante Uberto Barbieri, was elected in 1949. With his election, he introduced a missionary strategy based on territorial expansion through the construction of churches—an action the missionary agencies of the MEC in the United States promoted. This strategy of building first and growing later became unsustainable when the expected growth did not occur, thereby adding to the financial burden of the general budget and maintenance costs.

Toward the end of this stage and in the face of a new ecumenical scene in which Catholicism ceased to be the enemy to be combatted, a new stage of ecumenical dialogue opened. This approach provoked the discovery for some leaders of liturgical riches that Methodism had rejected in the Catholic form. In this way, a movement of liturgical renewal began in Methodism that included the form of worship, Sunday Eucharist, clergy attire, hymnody, and community singing. Here we must highlight the contributions of Pastor Roberto Ríos in liturgy and Pastor Pablo Sosa in music. The liturgical renewal movement that began in 1959–1960 enriched Methodist worship, but because conservative sectors resisted renewal, it produced one of the most severe conflicts in Argentine Methodist history.

Stage 6: Church, Society, and Autonomy (1960–1975)

The political context of the Cold War, the Cuban Revolution, and the civil unrest in France in May 1968 opened space for new discussion and reflection. Faith likewise found expression in dialogue with new ideologies and doctrines critical of prevailing systems. Social action became central to national and congregational mission work, which led to a dichotomy between those who emphasized the spiritual and those more attentive to the social dimensions of faith.

During the 1970s Methodism dared to take a step forward in this holistic way of understanding social issues and advanced an even bolder conversation. On one side was the stream of secularization, which raised the central question: How can the gospel be relevant to nonreligious people? The central conflict, by definition, was the modern city dominated by anonymity, loneliness, loss of identity, and an inability to understand traditional religious language. As we mentioned in the prior stage, the care for the nonreligious persons constituted the foundation of Methodist congregations.

On the other hand, the dialogue with Marxism helped to generate a holistic understanding of social problems. The content of Marxism was important to this holistic view, yet it tested the faith of Christians who came from very different experiences and languages and, perhaps for the first time, shared truths without positing absolutes. These Christians discovered they held similar objectives to the Marxists, even if pursued by different means.

From 1962 to 1965, the process unfolded following the declarations of the Second Vatican Council that revolutionized ecumenical and theological fields. The only Protestant delegate from Latin America to be included was Pastor José Míguez Bonino from Argentine Methodism. From that experience on, the ecumenical movement moved forward with new vigor and a new Latin American perspective. The Methodist Church took on a remarkable leadership role, heading up ecumenical initiatives that the Council had inspired. Everything indicated that the old controversies and intolerance had been left behind.

The process for autonomy of the Methodist churches in Latin America represents another important development in this stage. Around 1964 the Commission on the Structure of Methodism Overseas (COSMOS) of the Methodist Church was formed as the churched recognized the need for the missions in Latin America to choose whether to remain with or separate from the mother church. The work of COSMOS was the decisive factor in the realization of autonomy. In 1968 COSMOS made a recommendation to the General Conference of the Methodist Church to approve petitions for autonomy from the churches in Chile, Perú, Argentina, and Uruguay (among others). In all, twenty-four of the fifty-four countries with Methodist missions requested autonomous status. Local churches approved the processes for achieving autonomy, thus creating new national Methodist churches: Chile in February 1969; Argentina and Uruguay in October 1969; and Perú in January 1970.

It is important to point out that the process for autonomy of the Methodist churches began in February 1969 at the Council of Methodist Churches of Latin America (*Consejo de las Iglesias Metodistas de América Latina*,

CIEMAL, in Spanish). During its first plenary, it declared: "The time has come when Latin Americans take more responsibility, strengthening the unity of the Latin American Methodism and preventing division through the autonomy of the churches of the continent."[6] In 1969, after a long process of discussions, the Methodist Church in Argentina declared its autonomy from the Methodist Church (which was about to become The United Methodist Church), thus establishing the *Iglesia Evangelica Metodista Argentina* (Protestant Methodist Church of Argentina). This event should be seen, in part, as one more step toward the self-understanding of Argentine Methodism. The autonomy, even if only symbolic (in reality American Methodism, as we saw above, was promoting it), expressed overtly the long-implied criticism of a system that generated centers and peripheries both at the economic level as well as the religious. Above all, autonomy expressed the determination to face the future as a self-determining institution, which could conceptualize the mission from within its own context and according to its own criteria.[7]

The founding General Conference of the *Iglesia Evangelica Metodista Argentina* elected Pastor Carlos T. Gattinoni as its first bishop. These initial years of autonomy were a time of designing a renewed mission. In the new disciplinary understanding, a less vertical episcopal role was established, giving the system a collegial character at all levels and greater power to the laity in decision-making. Above all, it elaborated a master plan that could synthesize the mission of the church in the new and changing times. In this way, the General Conference of 1973 approved a strategy for mission located in open churches, in which a parish would go beyond the walls of the churches and the theoretical ground of an incipient theology of liberation would accompany it.

---

6 Rodolfo Míguez, "Señalando el Reino y haciendo discípulos," CIEMAL 1969–2013, Montevideo, Archivo de la Iglesia Metodista de Uruguay, unpublished (2013), 39.

7 Cf. Elaine Robinson, "El exilio del Metodismo argentino," en *Cuadernos de Teología* 26 (2007): 160–79; reeditado en *Revista Evangélica de Historia* 7 (2012): 145–65. An English versión of this essay is published in *A Living Tradition: Critical Recovery and Reconstruction of Wesleyan Heritage*, ed. Mary Elizabeth Moore (Nashville: Kingswood, 2013).

Stage 7: The Urgency of Mission in the Face of Violence (1975–1990)

But then times changed. The new winds of liberation were brutally ended with one of the bloodiest coup d'états in the history of Argentina. And once again the Methodist Church had to redesign its mission in light of this new and desperate context. The episcopacy of Federico Pagura (1977–1989) covered the most difficult years of the dictatorship and the first years of the democracy that followed.[8]

During this period, the Methodist Church developed a deep commitment to denounce national and international human rights violations committed by the coup, as well as to extend pastoral care to the victims and their families. The bishops, along with many Methodist pastors, were a part of the origins of various organizations for the defense of human rights, like the Permanent Assembly for Human Rights (Asamblea Permanente por los Derechos Humanos, APDH, in Spanish), of which Bishop Aldo Etchegoyen (1989–2001) was one of the cofounders in 1976, and the Ecumenical Movement for Human Rights (Movimiento Ecuménico por los Derechos Humanos, MEDH, in Spanish).

Moreover, the Methodist churches were opened during this period to meetings of the emerging organizations of family members, like mothers and grandmothers, of the victims of this repressive regime. These victims are known as "the disappeared" (*los desaparecidos*). Bishop Gattinoni, already emeritus, formed part of the National Commission on the Disappearance of Persons (Comisión Nacional por la Desaparición de Personas, CONADEP, in Spanish). The president of the Republic, Dr. Ricardo Alfonsín, convened this commission as soon as his government assumed power. This dedicated participation, in addition to being a concrete response to the biblical mandate to "seek the kingdom of God and its justice," can also be interpreted as the Methodist Church making sense of its own mission in light of the nation's

---

8 For additional information and details about this period cf. Pablo R. Andiñach y Daniel Bruno, *Iglesias Evangélicas y Derechos Humanos en la Argentina* (Buenos Aires: La Aurora, 2001).

real situation. Indeed, in this stage, the defense of human rights and the denunciation of their systematic violation was, for the Methodist Church, its missional priority.

The cost of this mission was high. During the dictatorship, Methodist churches suffered bombings, encountered threats intended to intimidate them, and were the subject of defamatory publications, which accused the principal leaders of Argentine Methodism of being "subversives." The church itself experienced the disappearance of twenty-four of its own members, mostly young students but also union members and university professors, like Mauricio López, who was kidnapped two months before starting work as a professor at *Instituto Superior Evangélico de Estudios Teológicos* (ISEDET), the theological school in Buenos Aires. During the period after the dictatorship, Methodism, along with other ecumenical bodies, developed a far-reaching program of pastoral and social care for families of the victims of repression and the reintegration into society of political prisoners who regained their freedom.

Stage 8: "To your tents, Israel" (1990–2000)

The return to democracy in 1983 opened a period of hope and popular mobilization. In this stage, the Methodist Church undertook the continual task of denouncing what happened during the dictatorship and demanding justice and jail for genocides before national and international forums alongside the rest of the human rights organizations. However, by the middle of the decade, the economy began to feel the weight of an enormous external debt left by the military government and the first democratic government of Dr. Raul Alfonsin, and it began to lose stability. During the presidency of Dr. Carlos Menem, this tendency deepened with the privatization of public companies and the implementation of neoliberal economic policies.

Toward the end of the 1980s, a sense of exhaustion arose in the Methodist Church from the demands of this public role. Certain factions used this fatigue to reclaim a more traditional pastoral role centered in the local congregation and less subject to the political tensions of the public space. In parallel, the critical positions expressed in previous stages against structures of external oppression were now spilling over, on a smaller scale, to the internal critique of its own institutional structures. The term *crisis of mission* began to echo in the conferences, and the organizational structure of the church was considered one of the factors in the crisis. The "adjustment" utilized by the neoliberalism of the time to reduce the power of the State also impacted ecclesiastical decisions.

Meanwhile, after many decades in public spaces, Methodism now turned inward with more conservative expressions that sought to reclaim the law of worship and religious equality. At this time, the churches organized several major meetings called *obeliscos* (because they were held around the characteristic monument, the obelisk, in downtown Buenos Aires). The more fundamentalist congregations capitalized on the crowded public meetings, and Methodism's public voice was diluted amid all these denominations.

In 1998 a series of international crises provoked an enormous drain of financial capital from Argentina and an unprecedented recession. Unemployment became widespread, and even wages and pensions lost value in real and nominal ways. All of this ended in 2001 with a crash of the banking system when deposits were frozen and the economy collapsed. In these circumstances, a public discontent exploded that eventually overthrew the government of President De la Rúa. In this context, the Methodist Church seemed unable to find its clear missional path, such that its membership decline and economic crisis were accentuated. The slogans of the General Conferences of that decade are a good demonstration of the church's struggle to find its direction forward: "Come, let's share hope" (1991); "Jesus Christ is our hope" (1993); "Being church today: A community for life" (1995); and "Let us pray with hope, sow with love" (1997).

Stage 9: Questions of Growth and Public Presence (2000–2016)

Even though the economic and ministerial crisis persisted in the church during this stage, a new scene opened with the change of the millennium.

In this stage, Argentine Methodism became the first Latin American church to elect a woman as bishop. Pastor Nelly Ritchie was elected bishop in 2001 and carried out her work until 2009. Thus, the Methodist Church promoted justice, emphasizing the work of witness and service that women had undertaken in the church throughout its history and, in a sense, vindicated the struggle for their rights.

In this phase, Methodism resumed its public presence concerning ethical matters, both personal and political, and managed to recover the voice lost in the previous stage. There was a growing awareness of the need to recover the historical and doctrinal roots that gave rise to the Methodist movement and to strengthen an identity that, for different reasons, had been blurred. The revaluation of the capacity of laity to lead the church resulted in organizing biennial training toward that end.

In terms of institutional organization, the economic and ministerial difficulties forced a reduction in the number of regions that had been created, widening and strengthening the role of circuits and districts, one of the long-standing structures of Methodism in the United States. Toward the end of the episcopacy of Bishop Frank de Nully Brown (2009–2017), a new structural modification was produced, which eliminated the regions altogether, leaving a church composed of seventeen districts.

The search for comprehensive growth of the church numerically, as well in commitment and formation, also marked this stage. After more than two years of preparation, the Comprehensive Strategic Plan was published, and sought to stimulate congregations to develop a mission according to their possibilities and challenges. Beginning in 2007, Methodism resumed its tradition of public pastoral work as the atmosphere of popular participation and expansion of individual and social rights were being realized. The Methodist Church publicly announced that it was in favor of marriage equality and decriminalization of abortion and had been working for several years to overturn laws related to religious worship, fighting for equal treatment under the law for all churches and religions present in the country.

Finally, due to various factors, a process began in this stage in which congregations of independent churches and their pastors expressed desire to join the Methodist Church. This unprecedented phenomenon has opened a new and challenging landscape for Methodism in the years ahead.

Main Challenges in the Years Ahead
The Challenge to Grow

From its beginnings, the Argentine Methodist Church was a small church in the context of the society of the country. It is probable that its influence on the society was greater than the number of its members would suggest. But nowadays the decline in membership leads us to consider the urgent need to evangelize and incorporate new persons into the Methodist Church. This need arises due to the simple fact of seeing its membership dwindle but also from the understanding, generated by this reality, that a church that is not capable of effectively communicating faith and bringing others to the gospel runs the risk of losing one of its essential characteristics. It might even cease "to be church" in order to play another role in society, valuable in and of itself but different than the fundamental one of witnessing to the faith by which it exists. There is awareness in Argentine Methodism that if the membership decline is not reversed, in a few years the number of congregations and places of witness will diminish drastically. It is noteworthy that this perception is not isolated or reduced to a particular group of members, but the church as a whole agrees with this assessment.

In the last few decades there have been several attempts to modify this situation, mostly through local efforts or from leaders who are particularly interested in evangelizing and promoting membership. In general, they have not had the desired success, and their efforts have been abandoned shortly after beginning. The entire church agrees that we must find ways to revise how we communicate the gospel and deliver our preaching to the people, and this widespread consensus is a new phenomenon. An awareness has been brewing that the Methodist Church must recover the neglected but essential task of its founders. The gospel must be communicated effectively today.

Here, two observations are instructive. Some sectors view the growth of the Pentecostal and Charismatic churches with wonder and approval. This leads to a tendency to imitate their methods and techniques with the conviction that the desired growth will be achieved. It can be said that in Argentine Methodism there are some congregations with a charismatic hue, but their theology has not permeated the rest of the church. It is noteworthy that this tendency usually holds conservative positions with respect to certain social topics (family, sexuality, politics, etc.). Such positions are not shared overall in Argentine Methodism, which generally inclines toward progressive positions on such issues. The second consideration is that those with a social and political openness (the majority that represents the historical line in Argentine Methodism) have not yet found a response to the issue of the growth. Their position sustains a theological discourse rooted socially, but they have not been able to join it with an ecclesial practice that contributes to the growth of the church.

Identifying the Demands of the Society

From the beginning, our church has maintained a commitment to the society and its search for justice and equality. The Methodist presence in human rights organizations is recognized and valued. The church has also played and continues to play a prominent role in education on all levels. But this century-old strategy should be reviewed in order to identify and respond to other demands of the twenty-first-century society. A few years ago, the Federation of Methodist Women conducted a country-wide survey where women anonymously answered a questionnaire about different aspects of life and society. Almost one thousand answers were collected, and in response to the question about what is thought to be the most serious problem that women face, the prevailing answer was "loneliness." Some noted that the problem of loneliness was not even mentioned among the problems that the church tackles in its concern for society.

It does not escape the church's notice that this survey was taken in the context of a country that is rich in goods and natural resources and, at the same time, inexplicably mired in endemic economic inequality with 30 percent of its people living below the poverty line. This makes justice and the distribution of wealth of primary importance, a situation that demands that the church continue to speak out. Regularly, the church discovers more challenges related to everyday life and the suffering of people. Millions of persons live in an unequal society where the lack of work is a real threat; however, they do not perceive those issues as their main concern but point to marital conflicts, risk of drug use among their children, domestic violence, the emptiness of a life lived in anonymity, and other problems of a personal and existential nature. Today the Argentine Methodist Church faces the challenge of including issues from that sphere in its comprehensive missional strategy. Up to this moment, problems of a personal and family nature have been treated as the pastor's responsibility when they arise within the pastor's flock. It is expected that the church, as a whole, go out to proclaim the good news of the gospel across the breadth of society where personal and social issues coexist such as unemployment and gender violence, environmental crisis, alcoholism, social injustice, and loneliness.

Theological Education

The Argentine Methodist Church has been a vanguard in theological education in Latin America, establishing, over one hundred years ago, the first theological seminary for the formation of lay and pastoral leadership. That seminary was later transformed into an ecumenical institution that prepared leaders for the whole continent in the highest level of theological formation. However, in the last decade, the institution experienced an internal crisis that turned out to be terminal, leading to its closure in 2015. Today, the Methodist Church faces the challenge of offering, once again, quality theological formation for its leaders and, if possible, for other Methodist churches across the continent.

At this moment, the Methodist Church has asked the university, UCEL (*Universidad del Centro Educativo Latino Americano*), which belongs to the Methodist Church, to create an online degree in theology. This degree would respond to the growing demands of theological formation and reach persons who already have a profession or family and cannot relocate to a university campus for several years. At the same time, the program could be offered to those interested from other Methodist churches in Latin America, including other denominations.

There are three aspects that the church looks to prioritize in shaping the degree so that it responds to the present demands. The first aspect is a missional focus. The curriculum must be oriented to address theologically the challenges that mission presents to pastors and congregations. The issues should not emerge from a preestablished grid determined from within the limited frame of reference of the university, but from the people's experience of confronting the life challenges on our continent.

The second aspect is an ecumenical formation, one not limited to the Wesleyan theological tradition. There are two reasons for this ecumenical approach. On the one hand, because contemporary Christianity is seen as ecumenical, the denominational barriers have been diluted and dialogues have brought them closer together. Where there was rivalry before, there is dialogue today; this is valid for both the dialogue with Catholicism as well as with Pentecostal churches. On the other hand, the Methodist tradition in Latin America, from its inception, has encouraged and inspired ecumenical encounters. Latin American Methodism perceives itself as ecumenical in its essence and, aside from some regional discussions, remains a hallmark that the church is not interested in modifying.

The third aspect is that theological education should offer tools to face the difficult present-day world without moving away from the foundations of the church. It should find a delicate balance between speaking prophetically to denounce incongruities between faith and social practice and hearing the voice of the people of God who gather around the Word and witness to the faith. That double reference—the biblical message and the community of believers—is perhaps the base upon which theological education can be constructed, according to the challenges that Argentine Methodism faces today.

Index

CPSIA information can be obtained
at www.ICGtesting.com
Printed in the USA
LVHW032007100419
613729LV00007B/8